Bc

DC 91 .J7 1938
Joinville, Jean, sire de, 1224?-1317?
The history of St. Louis

THE HISTORY OF
ST. LOUIS

WOODEN STATUE OF SAINT LOUIS FROM
THE RETABLE OF THE SAINTE CHAPELLE
c. 1250
(*Phot. Giraudon*)

THE HISTORY OF ST. LOUIS

By
JEAN SIRE DE JOINVILLE
SENESCHAL OF CHAMPAGNE

*Translated from the French Text
edited by*
NATALIS DE WAILLY
by
JOAN EVANS
D.Litt., D.Lit.
HON. FELLOW OF ST. HUGH'S COLLEGE

OXFORD UNIVERSITY PRESS
LONDON NEW YORK TORONTO
1938

OXFORD UNIVERSITY PRESS
AMEN HOUSE, E.C. 4
London Edinburgh Glasgow New York
Toronto Melbourne Capetown Bombay
Calcutta Madras
HUMPHREY MILFORD
PUBLISHER TO THE UNIVERSITY

PRINTED IN GREAT BRITAIN

TO MY FRIEND
J. M. V.

PREFACE

THE *Histoire de Saint Louis* was the first medieval French book I ever read; and for twenty-five years it has given me pleasure at each re-reading. I had long meant to pay it the tribute of translation, and finally began to do so in 1935 when I was visiting the Crusaders' castles in the Holy Land. The translation has no other claim to attention than that it was done with affection.

I have tried to keep it as literal as may be. The two words with which I have taken most liberties are *et* and *il*: *et* because Joinville uses it, according to the fashion of his time, to begin at least half of his sentences; and *il* because his use of it sometimes presupposes a greater knowledge of the facts than the modern reader is likely to possess. *Et* I have therefore often translated by some other conjunction than *and*, and for *il* I have often substituted the name of the person meant.

My thanks are due to Miss E. A. Francis of St. Hugh's College for help on many linguistic points, to Mademoiselle Jeanne Vielliard of the Archives Nationales for help in identifying some of the persons named; to Professor Henry Balfour for information on horn bows; to Dr. John Naish for correcting the transliteration of Arabic words; to Mrs. Charles Wrinch for permission to reproduce her photograph of Tortosa; and to Mrs. Gerald Lenanton, Mrs. Murdo Mackenzie, Miss K. Lea, and Mr. Loyd Haberly for reading and emending my translation in manuscript.

The translation, without introduction or notes, has already appeared in an *édition de luxe* from the Gregynog Press. My thanks are due to the Misses Davies for allowing me to reprint it here.

J. E.

CONTENTS

INTRODUCTION . . . xiii

PROLOGUE 1

BOOK ONE 5

BOOK TWO 21

NOTES 232

GENEALOGICAL TABLES . . 269

INDEX 273

LIST OF ILLUSTRATIONS

1. Wooden statue of Saint Louis from the retable of the Sainte-Chapelle, *c.* 1250. Musée de Cluny, Paris. Phot. Giraudon . . . . . *Frontispiece*
2. Joinville presenting the *History of Saint Louis* to Louis le Hutin. Bibliothèque Nationale, Paris, MS. français 13658, fol. 1. Phot. Giraudon. . . *facing page* 1
3. St. Theodore as a Crusader. Chartres Cathedral. Phot. Giraudon 64
4. Sidon. The Château de la Mer. Phot. J. E. . . 168
5. Sidon. The Château de Saint Louis. Phot. J. E. . 170
6. The Heights of Ṣubayba. Phot. American Colony, Jerusalem 174
7. Tortosa. The Church of Our Lady. Phot. Mrs. Charles Wrinch 182
8. The Sainte-Chapelle, Paris, built by Saint Louis between 1246 and 1248. Phot. Giraudon . . . 222

INTRODUCTION

IT has lately been my good fortune to read Joinville's *Histoire de Saint Louis* almost in alternate chapters with *The Seven Pillars of Wisdom*. Lawrence has written the epic of what was probably the last great feudal war the world will see; and in that war the same lofty purpose, the same divided aims, the same courage, and the same human frailty are evident as make Joinville's *History* a human and timeless book. Far less divides St. Louis from the Emir Feisal than divides us from those who lived the significant part of their lives before 1918. It is this remoteness, quite as much as his devotion to Malory, that lends to Lawrence's book its character of a medieval epic.

Once history has ceased to be topical it makes little difference whether it is concerned with events that happened twenty or nearly seven hundred years ago; if we can read Lawrence we can probably read Joinville. Like the Arab chieftains, the knights of the French host take shape and character before us; and like the Arab Revolt, the Crusade is unfolded, if to a less triumphant close. In Joinville's narrative we have no deliberate self-dissection; instead of that blaze of illumination it is by flashes of summer lightning that we see what manner of man he was: less wrought upon by thought than Lawrence, more single in his faith, less self-conscious in his relations with other men, less cursed by brilliance, and more blessed with ordinary humanity. Joinville would not have taken Damascus, and never came in triumph to the gates of Jerusalem; but long years of usefulness in his own lands stretched before him when he came back from beyond the seas, and in his courage, which is always simple, and

INTRODUCTION

in his principles, which are always clear, we may find an ensample more lastingly serviceable than that of more heroic endurances.

Jean de Joinville was born at Joinville at an uncertain date in 1224, the second son of Simon, lord of Joinville and Seneschal of Champagne, and of his wife Beatrix, daughter of Stephen Count of Auxonne and of Beatrix, Countess of Chalon-sur-Saône. His family was one held in high honour in Champagne. His great-grandfather, Geoffroy III, had been made Hereditary Seneschal of Champagne in recognition of his bravery in the Crusade of 1148, and the Seneschal of a province was an important personage who presided over its highest Court of Law and over the ceremonial of its lord's household. His grandfather, Geoffroy 'le Jeune', likewise went on Crusade, and died at the siege of Acre; his uncle, Geoffroy 'Trouillard', died in 1203 in the Hospitallers' fortress of the Krak des Chevaliers in Syria; and his father, Simon, had been on Crusade to Acre with Geoffroy 'le Jeune', and had gone east again with Jean de Brienne in 1218, when he had been at the first taking of Damietta. On his return he played an important part in local politics, and did much to save Troyes from the depredations of rival factions in 1230. In the next year he affianced his son Jean—a child of seven—to Alix de Grandpré, sister of Henry VI, Count of Grandpré. Two years later he died. The death of Simon's eldest son in 1239 left Jean de Joinville heir to his titles and possessions. His mother, however, held most of the family wealth inherited from her mother, the Countess of Chalon-sur-Saône. Jean de Joinville's worldly position was now much better than it had been in 1231, when as a second son he had been affianced to a girl who brought him no more than three hundred *livres* a year in land. His mother, therefore, endeavoured to make a better match for him, and to

INTRODUCTION

arrange his marriage with the daughter of the Count of Bar. His suzerain the Count of Champagne would not give his consent, and Jean had formally to renounce the project. A year later his marriage to Alix de Grandpré took place. When he was sixteen Jean went to the Court of his suzerain, Thibault of Champagne, to act as his squire and to learn the code and conduct of courtly life. In a few months he accompanied Thibault to Saumur to a great feast held by Louis IX, King of France, a man about ten years older than himself. Here for the first time he acted as Seneschal. We do not know exactly at what date Joinville was knighted—the usual time was on attaining majority—but it may well have been in 1243, when he took over his father's estates from the guardianship of his mother. In 1248 his first son, Jean, sieur d'Ancerville, was born.

Meanwhile Louis IX had likewise grown to maturity; he had married Margaret of Provence in 1234, and in 1243 his eldest son was born. In 1244 he had been desperately ill, and at the moment of crisis had taken the cross. His example had been followed by his brothers, by many of the chief men of his court, and by such great lords as the Count of Flanders and Joinville's kinsman the Duke of Burgundy. It was natural that one whose ancestors for three generations had gone on Crusade should feel impelled to do likewise; and when it became evident that the King was to go on Crusade in 1248, Jean de Joinville likewise took the cross and started for Marseilles, with three knights banneret and some two hundred men. The story of his adventures is the matter of his book, and needs no retelling. In 1254 Joinville once more set foot on French soil, returned from his pilgrimage a man of thirty years of age, a courtier of experience and reputation, a knight of proved valour, and the accepted friend of his King.

INTRODUCTION

As his father had done before him, he returned to take up his duties and responsibilities in Champagne. He found his Champenois estates the worse for his absence, and seems to have spent much time and energy in pulling them round. The routine of feudal business held him close, but for a few absences to attend the Court of Louis IX at Paris, Corbeil, Rheims, and Orléans. His duties as Seneschal of Champagne were increased by his personal character: in 1255, for example, we find him arbitrating a family quarrel over their father's property among the children of Thibault IV of Champagne, and helping to arrange a marriage between Thibault V and the daughter of his King.

In 1260 both Joinville's mother and his first wife died. In the next year he married Alix de Reynel,[1] the only child of a neighbour. She bore him three sons, and a daughter, who married Henry Earl of Lancaster, grandson of Henry III of England, and established his lineage in England and Wales.

So useful and so ordinary a life provided scope enough even for Joinville's unresting activity; and when in 1267 Louis IX insisted on his coming to Paris and strove to persuade Joinville to join him in taking the cross, he refused. With characteristic common sense he put feudal duty before visionary adventure, and had the courage to declare: 'If I meant to labour according to the will of God in this matter, that I would remain there to help and defend my people; for if I put my body in jeopardy of the pilgrimage of the Cross, wherein I saw full clearly that it would be to the hurt and harm of my people, I should make God wroth thereby, that gave His body to save His people. I held that they all did mortal sin that counselled the King's going, because at the point at which France stood, all the realm was at good peace with

[1] Sometimes spelt Resnel or Risnel.

INTRODUCTION

itself and with all its neighbours; nor ever after he had gone did the state of the realm do aught but worsen.'

So Joinville stayed at his post in Champagne, and Louis went on Crusade and died at Tunis. Nor does Joinville again emerge from his provincial obscurity, until in 1282 the efforts of the son of Louis, King Philip le Bel, secured the consideration and acceptance of Louis IX as a Confessor of the Faith. Joinville had then once more to come to Paris to testify to the virtues of his master. In 1297 the saintly King was canonized; and a year later, a man of seventy-five, Joinville once more returned to Paris to witness the exhumation of the saint who forty-five years before had become his friend. Once more he returned to Champagne, there to pass an old age that was not without its sorrows. His son Jean died in 1303, leaving no children;[1] his second wife was dead; and the old man was alone with his memories.

In 1310, when the *Histoire* had been finished and presented to Louis of Navarre and Champagne, the Seneschal (nearly ninety years old) received an Italian guest, Francesco da Barberino, who left some account of their intercourse.[2] Joinville enjoyed a reputation as an authority on court etiquette, with which as Seneschal of Champagne he had been concerned for some seventy years. 'One day', wrote Barberino, 'being at a place called Poissy on the confines of Normandy, I spake with my lord John of Joinville on this matter, a knight of a great age, the most knowledgeable in these questions now living, whose word carries great weight with the King of France as well as with his court.' Barberino noticed that Joinville was punctilious in maintaining proper

[1] All his sons by his first marriage died childless.
[2] See A. Thomas, *Francesco da Barberino et la littérature provençale en Italie au moyen âge*, 1883; and *Histoire litéraire de la France*, xxxii, 1898, p. 354.

INTRODUCTION

ceremony, and reproved a squire who carved without first washing his hands. But Joinville understood not only etiquette, but also manners. 'I heard my lord John of Joinville tell that a lord would find more honour in letting his squire serve others, than he would convenience in keeping him to serve himself alone. . . . I asked him one day what was the great proof of discrimination in a man who wished to show honour: "It is to honour all men."'

As late as 1311 he served Philippe le Bel at Beaumont as Seneschal of Champagne. In 1319 he died, full of years and honours, and was buried in the chapel of St. Lawrence where he had erected an altar in honour of his friend.

Such a life assured Joinville a place, modest but honourable, in the history of Champagne, but alone it would not have kept his memory green. His castle was rebuilt in the sixteenth century, and destroyed at the Revolution; his tomb was desecrated and destroyed in 1792. No tangible memorial of him remains but his *Histoire de Saint Louis*, and through this all who read it feel that they have known him, and having known, have loved.

The *Histoire de Saint Louis* is remarkable as being the first autobiography written by a gentleman in a modern vernacular. In the Court of Champagne at which Joinville was brought up there was a strong literary tradition alike in prose and poetry; Villehardouin the historian had been educated there fifty years before, and Joinville's own lord was Thibault de Champagne, the song-writer, whose lyrics are those of a true poet. It is uncertain whether Joinville ever tried his hand at poetry: verses written in Acre in 1250 have been ascribed to him,[1] that in their simplicity and directness might well be his. They repeat his plea to the King to stay in the Holy Land to redress the failure of the Egyptian expedition. The first stanza is a prologue; the concluding *envoi* is lost.

[1] *Romania*, xxii, 1893, p. 544.

INTRODUCTION

II. A! gentiz rois, quant Dieus vos fist croisier,
Tote Egipte dotoit vostre renon.
Or perdez tot s'ainsi volez laissier
Jerusalem estre en chaitivoison;
Car quant Dieus fist de vos election
 Et seignor de sa venjance,
Bien deüssiez mostrer vostre poissance
De revengier les morz et les chaitis
Qui por Dieu sont et por vos mort et pris.

III. Rois, vos savez que Dieus a pou d'amis,
Ne onques mais n'en out si grant mestier;
Car por vos est ses peuple mors & pris,
Ne nus, fors vos, ne l'en poroit aidier;
Que povre sont cil autre chevalier
 Si criement la demorance;
Et s'en tel point lor faisiez faillance,
Saint et Martir, apostre et inocent,
Se plaindroient de vos au jugement.

IV. Rois, vos avez tresor d'or et d'argent
Plus que nus rois n'ot onques, ce m'est vis,
Si en devez doner plus largement
Et demorer por garder cest païs;
Car vos avez plus perdu que conquis,
 Si seroit trop grant vitance
De retorner a tot la meschcance;
Mais demorez, si ferez grant vigor,
Tant que France ait recovree s'onor.

V. Rois, s'en tel point vos metez au retor,
France dira, Champaigne, et tote gent,
Que vostre los avez mis en trestor
Et gaaignie avez meins que nient;
Et des prisons qui vivent a torment
 Deüssiez avoir pensance;
Bien deüssiez querre lor delivrance;
Quant por vos sont et por Jesu martir
C'est granz pechiez ses i laissiez morir.

INTRODUCTION

Joinville was a man whose vivid interest in the events of everyday life fitted him better to be a writer of prose than of poetry. When he was at Acre in the winter of 1250–1, recovering from the fatigues of the Egyptian Crusade and with less occupation than usual, he wrote his Credo: 'les articles de notre foi par lettres et par images' including certain edifying anecdotes drawn from his own experience.[1]

In 1272 Joinville's eldest son married Mabile de Villehardouin, and the connexion with the family seems to have brought Villehardouin's Crusading history to his notice. At all events, about that year[2] he began to write a book of his personal experiences beyond the seas, that he probably intended to be a work of history like the Chronicles of Villehardouin or Robert de Clari, but which his own temperament turned into a fresh autobiographical channel. We do not know if he finished these memoirs and circulated them among his friends. By his own account, given in the dedication of the *Histoire de Saint Louis*, Queen Jeanne of Navarre, before her untimely death in 1305, begged him to write a book 'des saintes paroles et des bons faiz nostre roys saint Looys'; and it would seem likely that she made this request at some time before 1297, when the King was canonized, from the desire to have all the possible evidence in favour of a canonization that was to bring peculiar honour to the Royal House. If so, her scheme was vain, for the old man did not finish the *Histoire de Saint Louis* until 1309, four years after

---

[1] He revised it in 1287; see Ambroise Firmin-Didot, *Credo de Joinville*, Paris, 1870.

[2] See Gaston Paris in *Histoire litéraire de la France*, xxxii, p. 429. An important point in the evidence is that in Chapter CVIII Joinville speaks of a Duke of Burgundy 'that is newly dead' called Hugh, who can hardly be other than Hugh IV, who died in 1272. De Wailly, however, is inclined to identify him with a Hugh who died in 1306.

INTRODUCTION

her death and twelve years after the canonization of Louis IX.

Joinville's particular qualification to write about Saint Louis was that as young men they had been friends: it was personal reminiscence that he was qualified to furnish. Therefore he very naturally turned to his own autobiography to provide the major part of his material; and equally naturally did not modify it very much in the process.

Almost every reader of Joinville will be tempted to reconstruct the original memoirs by pruning away the additions that turned it into a work of edification. Most of Book I must go; perhaps the stories of Robert de Sorbon were lifted from the end of the original. The first twenty chapters of Book II have nothing personal in them, though the account of the feudal history of Champagne and of Simon de Joinville's defence of Troyes may have come from some attempted Chronicle by Joinville that did not attain completion. With Chapter XXI we are reading autobiography; and the autobiography continues (with the exception of Chapters XXIV, most of XL, most of XCIII, XCIV, XCV, all of which have the air of being taken from other books, and after all but the first of which Joinville says 'or revenons a nostre matiere') down to Chapter CXXXVI. Here we begin again on the virtues of Saint Louis, without reference to Joinville; CXXXVII seems to be an original composition, but all the other chapters down to the end of CXLIII are taken from the life of Saint Louis written by Geoffroy de Beaulieu or from the analogous passages in the *Grandes Chroniques de Saint Denis*. Chapter CXLIV is pure autobiography; Chapters CXLV and CXLVI are pure plagiarism; and then the book ends with two chapters that did not form part of the original autobiography but are undoubtedly written by Joinville himself.

INTRODUCTION

This shifting of the intention of the book did not succeed in its purpose: it suffices to compare Joinville's *Histoire* with Guillaume de Saint Pathus's *Vie de Saint Louis* to realize that it is no conventional life of a saint, but a personal narrative with two heroes, Saint Louis and Joinville. But the shift of purpose served to turn the book into an example of a recognized *genre*. It is the Latin lives of almost contemporary saints—such as those of the first four abbots of Cluny—which stand as the first medieval essays in biography; and they served to justify this extremely personal life of a saint in the vernacular, and so to establish a tradition of biography and autobiography that is reaching its fullest development only in our own time.

Joinville was not a historian; and except in three or four rather dull and inaccurate chapters[1] does not try to be one. It suffices to compare his account of a battle with that of Villehardouin—a man of his own country, upbringing, and station—to discover it. An even closer comparison may be made between his account of the landing in Egypt and that of Jean Pierre Sarrasin, the King's Chamberlain, given in his *Lettre à Nicolas Arrode*.[2] The same events are far more accurately recorded; there is a better sense of proportion and of the political issues at stake; but there is a total absence of that individual warmth of feeling, that vitality of personal experience, that lends so modern an air to Joinville's story. When we have read Joinville's book we do not know very much of the history of the reign of Louis IX; but we do know both the King and Joinville himself as individuals, and individuals of remarkable character.

Joinville was not a politician, and was too much interested in purely social relations to wish to be. His world was

[1] XVII, XVIII, XIX, XX.
[2] Ed. A. L. Foulet, in series *Classiques français du moyen âge*, 1924.

INTRODUCTION

a limited and feudal one; the fiefs of nearly every knight he mentions are in Champagne, or just outside it; the few exceptions are connexions of his mother's Burgundian relatives. Given a sufficiently large sheet of paper, a genealogical tree could be compiled which would comprise nearly all the characters of his story. Outside the family tree come first a few feudal dependants: priests and burghers and bowmen and cellarers and such like, who emerge for a moment by word or deed out of the undifferentiated host of Crusaders, play a moment's part, and disappear from the scene. Then come the portents: men of importance neither for birth nor vassalship, but for brains or wealth. Each time that Joinville mentions them it is to bring them into mockery or disrepute: Robert de Sorbon, who forgot his peasant ancestry and wore finer cloth than the King, and Artaud de Nogent, who forgot his villeinship and tried to check the generosity of his master.

Joinville's ideal is that untranslatable entity the *prud'-homme*: a word so noble, said Saint Louis, that it fills the mouth of him who utters it. The *prud'homme* is the man who holds the balance between courage and prudence, honour and fanaticism; a man of the world, yet a Christian; a warrior, yet a courtier; a man of judgement, yet a man of complete integrity. But Joinville found it hard to accept the truth that the *prud'homme* was noble by character, but not necessarily by birth; to Robert de Sorbon he ascribes only 'la grant renommée que il avoit d'estre preudome', but to nobles such as the eight who were the counsellors of the King he gives the title without qualification. Joinville unconsciously reveals himself as deserving of the name of *prud'homme*; at moments, indeed, he comes nearer to its essentially balanced ideal than does his sainted master. It is at these moments that a note of criticism creeps into the narrative: a strange note

INTRODUCTION

to find in a book that is entitled the life of a saint. But it is evident that Joinville realized that the good sense which was the fundamental characteristic of the *prud'homme* was in some degree incompatible with the extremes that mark the saint. It is with a conscious joy that he recounts the few occasions when Saint Louis acted rather as *prud'homme* than *dévot*: when he bade them dress handsomely according to their degree, when he refused the demands of the Bishops over secular jurisdiction, and when he warned Thibault II of Navarre against spending too much money on his Dominicans at Provins.

Joinville's standards are often closer to those of the King's brothers than to those of the King. Saint Louis threw their dice overboard when he found them playing at sea; but when they took to playing regularly at Acre Joinville does not criticize their conduct, but lauds their generous thriftlessness with their winnings. 'Li bons chevaliers' appears often in his narrative, but this is said not in praise but in courtesy: an old knight was in virtue of his age and service a good knight. Three hundred and fifty years later Cotgrave's *Dictionary* still gives 'bon' as 'a title commonly bestowed on an old man ... in reverence of their age; whereupon some will merely answer to such as thinke to grace them with that title, "Je ne vas pas encores au baston".'

Joinville is no strategist, but remains feudal in his attitude to war. His ideal is no highly organized army, but one in which every knight banneret could come forward with suggestions, and if he wished could carry them out on his own initiative. Joinville never forgave Lord John of Beaumont (who seems to have acted as a general under the King) for not allowing him to make a foray against the Saracens soon after the taking of Damietta. On the same day my Lord Walter of Autrèche arrayed himself

INTRODUCTION

secretly in armour and mounted his horse within his tent and had his tent-flaps lifted and rode out alone against the Saracens while all his men shouted *Châtillon!* and was killed for his pains. Joinville does not attempt to conceal his admiration, though the King declared that he had no desire to have men such as this in the host, who disobeyed his orders. One of the few bits of scientific fighting that pleased Joinville was the Saracens' use of their foot soldiers like pawns in chess. It is hardly surprising that Joinville was never in a position of command in the Crusade, save over the Champenois squadron he got together in the Holy Land; but he continued (according to his own account) to be forward with suggestions and plans at any moment of crisis, and there is something quick and aggressive about our vision of him that makes us accept his account as true.

His idea of battle is completely feudal; he is the ancestor of the French knights who lost the battle of Poitiers because they would fight according to the code of chivalry. He has not only fear but disapproval of such an instrument of war as Greek fire, and never has a good word for Jocelyn of Cornaut and the King's engineers. But when the King's squadron attacks the Saracens on the Shrove Tuesday of 1250, he bids us note 'that this was a very fair feat of arms; for none shot with the bow or the crossbow, but the strife was all with maces and swords'. So too he finds it natural that Guy Mauvoisin should have been one of the few knights to gain honour at the battle of Mansourah, 'for they told me, they that well knew his pack (*son couvine*), that all his squadron, or all but a few, was of knights of his lineage and of knights who were his liegemen'. Joinville could find time, even at the moment of landing in Egypt, to admire the heraldic displays of the Count of Jaffa; but he had *les qualités de ses défauts*, and it is this same strong feudal sense that makes him refuse

INTRODUCTION

to leave the Holy Land so long as any of his own people are still in prison.

Joinville's attitude to the Church was equally feudal. He chiefly admired its ministers not for clerical but for knightly virtues. His chaplain who discomfited eight Saracens single-handed, and finished saying his Mass in Joinville's arms as he was dying of scurvy and dysentery —'nor did he ever sing Mass again'—made a greater impression on him than any ordinarily successful cleric, for he was as brave as a layman. Otherwise Joinville's test of a cleric was supernatural; he respected the Abbot of Cheminon, because he had heard of the Virgin's being seen to protect him; and believed in the sanctity of Brother Hugh of Digne, because he had heard that many miracles were wrought at his tomb.

Women appear in his book in two roles: as mothers and as audience. It is not his wife that Joinville thinks of as he goes through Champagne on his way beyond the seas, but of her children. As mothers they do not make a brave show. His indictment of Blanche of Castille leaves the reader wondering whether Beatrix of Joinville, Dame de Vaucouleurs, may not also have been a domineering mother. But as audience women provide the motive of the book: first in its ordering by Jeanne of Navarre, and then in the unconscious thought that they will be its hearers, that suddenly finds expression when, at one of the worst moments of the Battle of Mansourah, the old Count of Soissons cries: 'Seneschal, let these curs yelp: for by God's bonnet we shall yet speak of this day, you and I, in ladies' chambers.'

Joinville's admiration of St. Louis did not blind him to the King's unkindness to his wife. It is Joinville who chronicles her sufferings at Damietta, her ill treatment (with no protest from the King) at the hands of his mother, and her dread of his waywardness and difficult

INTRODUCTION

temper. If Joinville had been a lyrical poet he would probably have addressed his songs to Queen Margaret, as Thibault de Champagne addressed his to Queen Blanche. Joinville could write; a charter given by him has an addition that ends: 'Ce fu escrit de ma mein', in no uncertain handwriting. But his book was not written by him, but dictated; and it was intended, as many of its phrases show, for an audience not of readers but of listeners. Consequently few books smell less of the inkpot than does the *Histoire de Saint Louis*; and in few does the author seem in more direct touch with his public. We have none of Lawrence's descriptions that make stay-at-homes see and scent the desert; but sometimes the very bareness of Joinville's narrative drives the imagination to vision. No one who knows his book can go to the Delta and smell the sour marsh smell, or travel up the Syrian coast between mountain and sea, without remembering that Joinville has passed that way before.

The original manuscript of the *Histoire de Saint Louis* is lost; the number of later copies is comparatively small.[1] It had, indeed, no great success; it was finished too late to derive any topical value from the canonization of Saint Louis, and at a time when the chivalry and the Crusades it commemorates were out of fashion. Purely historical narratives such as the Chronicle of Guillaume de Nangis or the *Grandes Chroniques de Saint Denis* were much more popular. It is first cited by Pierre de Baud, who wrote a *Histoire de Bretagne* at the end of the fifteenth century. It was first printed, in an edition by Pierre Antoine de Rieux, at Poitiers in 1547; but the editor found it 'ung peu mal ordonnée et mise en langage assez

---

[1] On these see Natalis de Wailly, *Jean Sire de Joinville, Histoire de Saint Louis*... texte accompagné d'une traduction, Paris, 1874, p. xi, and in *Bibliothèque de l'École des Chartes*, xxxiii, 1872, p. 386; Gaston Paris, in *Histoire litéraire de la France*, xxxii, 1898, p. 370.

INTRODUCTION

rude' and therefore only published it after it had been 'polie et dressée en meilleur ordre qu'elle n'estoit auparavant'. It is not surprising that this edition had no great success. A serious edition on scholarly lines was published by Du Cange in 1668,[1] and was followed by an important one by Capperonnier in 1761. Various editions were produced in the nineteenth century, culminating in the classic version published by Natalis de Wailly in 1874,[2] which is the text that is translated in the ensuing pages.

[1] It was this edition which was followed by the first English translation: *Memoirs of John Lord of Joinville* ... translated by Thomas Johnes Esq., at the Hafod Press, 1807.
[2] This edition (without some of its illustrative matter) is that followed in the cheap student's edition published by Hachette, which was reprinted for the twelfth time in 1931. The ensuing translation follows the numbering of its chapters.

PLATE 2

JOINVILLE PRESENTING *THE HISTORY OF SAINT LOUIS* TO
LOUIS LE HUTIN
Bib. Nat. MS. franç. 13658, fol. 1
(*Phot. Giraudon*)

PROLOGUE

I

TO his good Lord Louis, son of the King of France, by the grace of God King of Navarre, Count Palatine of Champagne and Brie, John Lord of Joinville, his Seneschal of Champagne, giveth greeting and love and honour and his ready service.

Dear my Lord, I would have you know that Madam the Queen your mother (God rest her soul) who loved me well, importuned me with all her might that I would have a book written for her setting forth the holy sayings and good deeds of our King Saint Louis; and so I promised her and by God's help is the book achieved in two parts. The first part telleth how he ruled himself all his days by God and the Church, and to the profit of his realm. The second part of the book speaketh of his knightly emprises and his high feats of arms.

Sir, in that it is written: 'Do first that which pertaineth to God, and he shall instruct thee in all thine other works', have I first had written that which pertaineth to the first three things aforesaid, that is to say what pertaineth to the weal of soul, and of body, and what to the ruling of the people. Other things have I had written that are likewise to the honour of that true saint on earth, so that by these matters told hereafter men shall plainly see that never did layman of our time live in such holy fashion all his days, from the beginning of his reign until his life's end. At the end of his life was I not with him; but Count Peter of Alençon, his son (who loved me well) was there, and bare witness to me of the fair end that he made, as ye shall find written at the ending of this book.

And in this matter it appeareth to me that they that set him not among the number of the martyrs did him not worship enow, having regard to the travails that he endured on the pilgrimage of the Cross, for the space of six years when I was in his company, and especially that he followed Our Lord even to the Cross. For if God died upon the Cross, so likewise did he: for when he died at Tunis he died a Crusader.

The second book will tell you of his knightly emprises and of his deeds of daring, which were such that four times did I see him put his body in peril of death, as ye shall hear tell hereafter, to spare his people from harm.

II

THE first time that he put his body in peril of death was at our coming before Damietta, when all his counsellors, as I have heard, commended his staying in his ship until he should see how his knights that went ashore should fare. The reason wherefor they counselled him thus was that if he had landed, and his folk had been killed and he with them, the venture would have been lost; but if he stayed in his ship he could of himself achieve the winning again of the land of Egypt. Yet would he heed none of them, but leapt into the sea, shield at neck and lance in hand, and was one of the first to land.

The second time that he put his body in peril of death was when he departed from Mansourah to come to Damietta, and his counsellors, as I have been given to understand, advised that he should go to Damietta by galley. These counsels were given him, so they said, because if ill befell his men, he could of himself deliver them from prison. Especially was this counsel given him because of the ill plight of his body by reason of divers

PROLOGUE

maladies, for he had a double tertian fever and a sore flux and the malady of the army in mouth and legs. He would take heed to none of them; but said that never would he abandon his people but would make such an end as they did. And so it befell him, that because of the flux that he had, that at night they had to cut from him the bottom of his breeches, and because of the malady of the host that afflicted him sore he swooned that evening more than once, as ye shall presently hear.

The third time that he put his body in peril of death was when he tarried for four years in the Holy Land, after his brethren had gone home. In great peril of death were we then; since for one man-at-arms that the King had in his company when he stayed in Acre, had the people of Acre full thirty when at last the city was taken. And I know no reason why the Turks did not come and take us in the city save the love that God had for the King, Who put fear into the hearts of our enemies, wherefore they durst not assail us. And of this is it written: 'An thou fearest God, all that see thee shall fear thee.' And this tarrying did he against all his council, as ye shall hear tell hereafter. He put his body in peril to protect the people of that land, who had he not stayed had else been lost thereafter.

The fourth time that he put his body in peril of death was when we came back from beyond the seas and came before the island of Cyprus, where our ship ran aground so hazardously that the land where she struck carried off three fathoms of the keel on which our ship was built. Thereupon the King sent to seek fourteen master mariners, of this ship and of others that were in her company, to counsel him what he should do. All told him, as ye shall hear tell hereafter, that he should go aboard another ship; for they did not see how the ship could endure the blows of the waves, since the nails wherewith the planks of the ship were fastened were all started. And they shewed the King the proof of the peril of the ship in that as we were making the outward voyage across the sea, a ship in like case had been lost; and I saw the woman and child that alone escaped out of that ship in the house of the Count of Joigny.

To this the King made answer: 'Sirs, I see that if I leave this ship, men will have no more to do with her; and I see herein eight hundred souls and more; and since every man loveth his life as much as I do mine, none would dare to stay in this ship, but would all abide in Cyprus. Wherefore, God willing, I will not put so many folk as are herein in peril of death, but will abide here myself to save my people.'

So he stayed; and God, in Whom he put his trust, protected us for ten weeks from the hazards of the sea; and we came to a fair haven as ye shall hear hereafter. Now it so happened that Oliver of Termes, that had borne him well and bravely beyond the seas, left the King and stayed in Cyprus, and we did not see him for a year and a half afterwards. So the King averted harm from eight hundred people who were in the ship.

In the last part of the book I shall speak of his end, of the holy death that he died.

Now I say unto you, my Lord King of Navarre, that I promised to Madam the Queen your mother (on whom God have mercy) that I would have this book written; and to discharge my promise have I done it. And since I see no one that hath as good a right to it as you, that are her heir, to you I send it, so that ye and your brethren and others who shall hear it, may take example from it, and make good use of the example, wherefor shall ye have the favour of God.

BOOK ONE
III

IN THE NAME OF ALMIGHTY GOD I, JOHN, LORD OF JOIN-
VILLE, SENESCHAL OF CHAMPAGNE, HAVE CAUSED THE LIFE
OF OUR SAINTLY KING LOUIS TO BE WRITTEN ACCORDING
AS I SAW AND HEARD FOR THE SPACE OF THE SIX YEARS THAT
I WAS IN HIS COMPANY ON PILGRIMAGE BEYOND THE SEA
AND AFTER WE CAME BACK.

AND ere I tell you of his great deeds and his knightly prowess will I tell you what I saw and heard of his godly sayings and his good precepts, so that they may be found set one after the other to edify those that shall hear them.

This holy man loved God with all his heart and followed His example: as appeareth in that even as God died for the love He bare His people, so put he his body in jeopardy many times for the love he bare his people; and he might well have avoided it an he had wished, as ye shall hear hereafter.

The great love that he had for his people appeareth in his saying to my lord Louis, his eldest son, in a dire illness that he had at Fontainebleau: 'Fair son,' said he, 'I beseech thee to make thyself beloved of the people of thy realm; for in sooth I had liefer have a Scot come from Scotland and govern the people of this realm faithfully and well, than that thou shouldst govern it manifestly ill.'

The saintly King loved truth so well that not even to the Saracens would he lie concerning his covenant with them, as ye shall hear hereafter.

So sober was he of his mouth that on no day of my life did I know him give thought to the ordering of any dish, as many rich men do; but he patiently ate whatsoever his cooks dressed and set before him. In his words was he temperate; for never in my life did I hear him speak ill of another, nor did I ever hear him name the Devil, which name is spilled about the kingdom, which methinks pleaseth God ill. He watered his wine in measure, according as he saw the wine would stand it. He asked me in Cyprus why I did not put water in my wine; and I told him that the physicians were the cause, who said that I had a thick head and a cold stomach, and that therefore I could not get drunk. And he said that they deceived me, for if I did not learn in my youth and then wished to water my wine in mine old age, gout and diseases of the stomach would lay hold of me, so that I should never be in health; and if I drank wine unmixed when I was old, I should be drunken every evening; and it would be over ugly a thing for an old man to be drunken.

He asked me if I wished to be honoured in this world and to have Paradise at my death; and I told him Yea. And he said to me: 'Therefore so keep yourself that knowingly ye neither say nor do aught that if all the world knew it, ye could not avow it: declaring "I did this", or "I said that".' He bade me beware lest I denied or gainsaid any man in aught that he said to my face, unless I should thereby come to sin or hurt or harm; for hard words led to blows of which a thousand men had died.

He said that a man should attire and arm his body in such a fashion that the discreet men of this world should not say he did over much, nor the young men that he did over little. And this matter did I call to mind to the father of the King that now is, concerning the surcoats embroidered with arms that they make nowadays, and told him that never on the way beyond the seas where I had been, had I seen embroidered coats, neither the King's nor any other man's. And he told me that he had such garments embroidered with his arms that had cost him four hundred crowns. I told him he would have used them better to have given them to God and to have ordered for his attire good silk sewn with his arms, as had his sire before him.

IV

ON a time the King called me and said: 'I dare not speak to you myself of the things that concern God, because of the subtlety of your understanding; wherefore have I summoned these two friars, here present, for there is something I would ask you.'
The question was this: 'Seneschal,' said he, 'what thing is God?' And I answered: 'Sir, it is a thing so good that better may not be.'
'Truly,' said he, 'that is well answered; for the answer that ye have given is written in this book that I hold in mine hand. Now I would ask you which ye would rather, that ye should be a leper or that ye should have done mortal sin?'
And I, that never lied to him, answered that I had liefer have committed thirty than be a leper. And when the friars had gone he called me by myself and made me sit at his feet and said: 'How came ye to say this thing to me yesterday?' And I told him that I would say it still. And he said: 'Ye spake like a hasty trifler; for ye must know that there is no leprosy so foul as being in mortal sin, for the soul which is in mortal sin is like unto the Devil, wherefore no leprosy can be as foul. And it is true indeed that when a man dieth, he is cured of the leprosy of the body; but when the man who hath done the deadly sin dieth, he knoweth not nor is assured that he hath felt such penitence in his lifetime that God will have pardoned him; wherefore should he stand in great fear lest this

other kind of leprosy endure so long as God is in Paradise. I beseech you,' said he, 'so far as I can, that ye set your heart to this, for the love of God and of me, that ye should liefer have any ill befall your body, whether leprosy or all other diseases, than that mortal sin should enter your very soul.'

He asked me if I washed the feet of the poor on Maundy Thursday. 'Sir,' said I, 'Heaven forfend! Never will I wash the feet of such peasants.' 'Indeed,' said he, 'that was ill said; for never should ye hold in contempt that which God did as an ensample for us. So I pray you, first for the love of God, and then for the love of me, that ye accustom yourself to wash them.'

V

HE loved so well all manner of men that put their trust and love in God that he gave the Constableship of France to my lord Giles the Black (who was not of the Kingdom of France) because he was of fair repute for trusting and loving God. And truly I believe that he was such a man.

Master Robert of Sorbon, for the great name that he had for discretion, he made to eat at his own table. One day it chanced that he ate beside me and we held converse one with the other. And the King rebuked us and said: 'Speak up, for your companions think that ye speak ill of them. If ye speak at meat of something which should please us, say it aloud; or if not, hold your peace.'

When the King was mirthful, he used to say to me: 'Seneschal, now tell me the reasons why a man of worldly discretion is better than a friar.' Then the disputations between me and Master Robert would begin. When we had argued a great while, the King would give sentence and speak thus: 'Master Robert, well would I like to have the name of a man of worldly discretion, if only I were one, and all the rest should be yours; for a *prud'-homme* is so great and so good a thing that only to name it filleth the mouth.'

Contrariwise he used to say that it was an evil thing to take another's goods, 'for to restore was so hard that only to say *rendre* flayed the throat because of the r's in it, which signified the rakes of the Devil, who ever draggeth back to him them that are of a mind to restore the chattels of another. And the Devil doeth this with subtlety; for he worketh on great usurers and great robbers so that they give to God what they ought to give back to men.' He bade me tell King Thibault from him to beware of the house of Preaching Friars in Provins, which he was building, lest he burden his soul with the great moneys that he was putting into it, 'for wise men, so long as they live, ought to treat their wealth as an executor should do; that is to say that good executors first meet the dead man's obligations and restore other men's chattels; and out of the residue of the dead man's goods make alms.'

VI

THE saintly King was at Corbeil upon a Whitsuntide and eighty knights with him. After meat the King went down into the close below the chapel, and spake in the doorway with the Count of Brittany, father of the Duke that now is, whom may God guard! There did Master Robert of Sorbon come to seek me, and took me by the skirt of my mantle and led me to the King; and all the other knights came after us. Then I asked Master Robert, 'What want ye of me?' And he answered, 'If the King were to seat himself in the close and ye were to seat yourself on the bench above him, I would ask you whether ye would not be greatly to blame?' And I answered, 'Yea.' And he said to me, 'Therefore are ye much to blame in that ye are more nobly clad than the King; for ye are dressed in minever and green cloth, which the King is not wont to be.' And I answered: 'Master Robert, saving your grace, I am not to blame if I dress myself in minever and green; for this robe was left me by my father and mother. But ye are to blame; for ye are the son of a peasant and of a bondswoman, and have given up the dress of your father and mother and are clad in a richer grogram than the King.' Then I took the skirt of his surcoat and of the King's surcoat and said: 'Now see if I speak truth.' And then the King began to defend Master Robert by words with all his might.

After these things, my lord the King summoned my lord Philip, his son, father of the King that now is, and King Thibault, and seated himself at the entrance to his chapel and put his hand to the ground, and said: 'Sit ye here close to me so that no one may hear us.' 'Ah, Sir,' said they, 'we would not venture to sit so close to you.' And he said to me, 'Seneschal, sit ye here.' And so I did, so close that my dress touched his. And he made them be seated after me, and said: 'Manifestly wrong have ye done, when ye who are my sons did not at the first do my bidding; and beware lest it happen again.' And they said that it should not. And then he told me that he had called us there to make avowal to me that he had been wrong to defend Master Robert against me. 'But,' said he, 'I saw him so confounded that I needs must come to his aid. In any case take no heed of what I said to defend Master Robert; for, as said the Seneschal, ye should dress yourselves well and cleanly, that your wives may love you the better and your men esteem you the more. For, as saith the sage, a man should array himself in robes and armour in such wise that the wise men of this world shall not say that he hath done over much, nor the young men of this world that he hath done over little.'

VII

HEREAFTER shall ye hear a precept that he gave me at sea, when we were returning from beyond the seas. It befell that our ship ran aground before the island of Cyprus, by reason of a wind that is called *garbin*, which is not one of the four great winds. And the blow which our ship received struck such despair into the hearts of our sailors that they rent their garments and their beards. The King leapt from his bed barefoot (for it was night) in a coat and no more, and went to lay himself crosswise before the Body of Our Lord, like one that awaited naught but death. The day after this befell, the King summoned me by myself, and said to me: 'Seneschal, now hath God shown us a part of His great power; for one of His little winds, so little that it hath scarce a name, hath all but drowned the King of France, his children, his wife, and his men. Now Saint Anselm saith that these are the threats of our Lord, as if God would say, "Now could I have had you dead, an I had wished." "Lord God," said the Saint, "wherefore dost Thou threaten us? For from the threats Thou makest to us cometh neither honour nor benefit to Thee: for, if Thou shouldst lose us all, Thou wouldst not be the poorer: nor if Thou shouldst win us all, wouldst Thou be any the richer. Therefore the threat Thou makest is not for Thy benefit but for our profit, if we but know how to make use of it."

'We should make use of this threat that God hath made to us in such wise that if we feel that we have in our hearts or in our bodies aught that is displeasing to Him, we should forthwith drive it out; and if there be aught that we deem will please Him, we should strive forthwith to achieve it. And if we do thus, Our Lord will give us greater riches in this world and the next than we can tell. And if we do not do thus, He will do as a good lord should to a bad servant; for after the threat, when the bad servant will not amend his ways, the lord punisheth him with death or other greater misfortunes that are worse than death.'

So let the King that now is take heed, for he hath escaped from as great peril as we did, or worse; let him amend his misdeeds in such wise that God deal not hardly with him or with his belongings.

VIII

THE saintly King strove with all his power by his sayings to make me believe steadfastly in the Christian law which God hath given us, as ye shall hear hereafter. He used to say that we should have such steadfast credence in the articles of faith that neither for death nor for any evil that can befall the body should we be willing to go against them by word or deed. He said further that the Enemy is so subtile that when folk are dying he laboureth with all his might so that they may die in doubt about some point of faith; for he knoweth that the good deeds that a man hath done cannot save him from the Devil; and yet knoweth that the man that dieth in the true faith is lost to the Devil.

Wherefore should a man so keep himself and in such wise guard himself from this ambush that he can say to the Enemy when he sendeth such a temptation: 'Go hence!' 'Go hence!' should he say to the Enemy, 'never shalt thou tempt me that I believe not steadfastly all the articles of the faith; but if thou shouldst have all my limbs cut off, yet would I live and die in this cause.'

BOOK ONE

And whosoever doeth thus, he smiteth the Enemy hip and thigh, wherefor the Enemy would slay him.

He used to say that faith and belief were a matter in which we should have steadfast trust, even though we were only sure of them from hearsay. On this point, he asked me a question: What name did my father bear? And I told him that he was called Simon. And he asked me how I knew it. And I told him that I knew it for sure and believed it for certain, for my mother had testified to it. Then said he to me: 'So should ye believe steadfastly all the articles of the faith, to which the Apostles have borne witness, as ye hear sung on Sunday in the *Credo*.'

IX

HE recounted to me that Bishop William of Paris had told him that a great master in divinity had come to him and had said that he wished to speak with him. And he answered, 'Master, speak your will.' And when the master tried to speak to the bishop, he began to weep exceedingly. And the bishop spake to him saying: 'Master, be not discomforted; for no man can sin so much that God cannot pardon more.'

'But I tell you, my Lord, I cannot choose but weep; for I deem myself faithless, in that I can no longer force my heart so that I believe in the Sacrament of the Altar as Holy Church teacheth it; and well I know it is a temptation of the Enemy.'

'Master,' said the bishop, 'now tell me when the Enemy sendeth you this temptation, if it be pleasing to you?'

And the master said: 'My Lord, it vexeth me as much as can be.'

'Now I ask you,' said the bishop, 'if ye would take gold or silver wherefor ye would utter aught with your

tongue which was against the Sacrament of the Altar, or against the other holy Sacraments of the Church?'
'Nay, my Lord,' said the master, 'know that there is naught in the world that I would take for it; but I would rather that they tore asunder all the limbs of my body than that I should speak against it.'
'Then I will tell you another thing,' said the bishop. 'Ye know that the King of France is making war against the King of England; and ye know that the castle which lieth nearest to the frontiers of both is La Rochelle in Poitou. Now I will ask you one thing: if the King had entrusted La Rochelle to you to defend, which is on the dangerous marches, and he had handed over Montlhéry to me, which is in the heart of France, in a country which is at peace, to whom would the King owe more favour at the end of the war, to you that had defended La Rochelle without loss, or to me that had kept him the castle of Montlhéry without loss?'
'In the name of God, my Lord,' said the master, 'to me that had kept La Rochelle safe.'
'Master,' said the bishop, 'I tell you that my heart is like the castle of Montlhéry, for I have no temptation and no doubt concerning the Sacrament of the Altar. For which reason I say unto you that for any favour God may grant me because I believe in Him surely and in peace, will God grant you four, because ye defend your heart for Him in the war of tribulation, and feel such goodwill towards Him that for no earthly benefit nor for any hurt that may be done to the body, would ye surrender it. Wherefore I tell you to be of good cheer; that your condition is more pleasing to God as it is than is mine.'
When the master heard this, he knelt before the bishop and felt himself well requited.

BOOK ONE

X

THE saintly King told me that many folk of the Albigensians came to the Count of Montfort, who then defended the land of the Albigensians for the King, and bade him come to see the Body of Our Lord which had become flesh and blood in the hands of the priest. And he said to them:
'Go see it yourselves, who do not believe it; for I believe it surely, as holy Church telleth us of the Sacrament of the Altar. And know ye what I shall gain,' said the Count, 'because in this mortal life I believe it as holy Church teacheth us? I shall have a crown in heaven above the angels, who see Him face to face, wherefore perforce they must believe in Him.'

He told me that on a time there was a great disputation between monks and Jews at the Abbey of Cluny. There was a knight present to whom the Abbot gave bread at that place for God's sake; and he asked the Abbot that he should suffer him to speak first; and they granted it with some ado. Then he rose and leant upon his crutch and bade them bring to him the greatest clerk and the greatest master of the Jews; and so they did. And he asked a question which was this: 'Master,' said the knight, 'I ask if ye believe that the Virgin Mary, who bare God in her womb and in her arms, brought forth a Child being a Virgin, and was the Mother of God?' And the Jew answered that he believed none of it. The knight made answer that the Jew had borne himself like a fool, when he neither believed in her nor loved her and yet had come into her abbey and her house. 'And truly,' said the knight, 'ye shall pay for it,' and so he raised his crutch and hit the Jew on the ear and laid him low. And the Jews turned and fled, and took their master with them wounded as he was; and so the disputation ended.

Then came the Abbot to the knight, and told him that he had done a great folly. And the knight said that it was a greater folly to get together for such a disputation; for before the argument had been brought to its end, were there in that place a multitude of good Christians, who would have left it altogether misbelieving, for they would not well have understood the Jews. 'And so I say to you,' said the King, 'that no man, unless he be a very good clerk, should argue with them; but the layman, when he heareth the Christian law reviled, should not defend it but by his sword, wherewith he should pierce the vitals of the reviler as far as it will go.'

XI

THE governance of his land was such that every day he heard his Hours with music, and a Requiem Mass without music, and then the Mass of the day or the holy day, if there fell one, with music. Every day he rested, after meat, on his bed; and when he had slept and rested, the office of the dead was said privately in his chamber between him and one of his chaplains, before he heard vespers. At night he heard compline.

A friar came to him at the Castle of Hyères, where we landed from sea; and to instruct the King, said in his sermon that he had read the Bible and the books which speak of heathen princes; and he said that he had found, among believers and unbelievers alike, that never was a kingdom lost or changed from one lordship to another, but by failure of justice. 'Therefore let the King, who goeth hence to France, have a care,' said he, 'that he do right and speedy justice to his people, wherefore Our Lord will suffer his kingdom to remain in peace all the days of his life.'

They said that this worthy man, who thus taught the King, lieth at Marseilles where Our Lord doth many a fair miracle for him. And he would never tarry with the King, beseech he as he might, but one day.

XII

THE King forgat not this instruction, but governed his land loyally and by the law of God, as ye shall hear hereafter. He had his work so ordered that my lord of Nesle and the good Count of Soissons, and the rest of us who attended him, when we had heard Mass, used to go to hear pleas at the gate, which they now call Petitions.

And when he came out of church, he would send for us, and seat himself at the foot of his bed and make us sit round him, and ask us if there were any suits to be dispatched that could not be dispatched without him; and we would name them to him, and he would send for the suitors, and ask them 'Why do ye not take what our people offer?' And they would answer: 'Sir, because they offer little.' And he would speak to them in this wise: 'Ye would do well to take what they wish.' And so the saintly man used to labour according to his power to set them on the right and reasonable path.

Many times it befell that in summer he would go and sit in the wood of Vincennes after Mass, and lean against a tree, and make us sit round him. All those that had business came there to speak to him, without disturbance of ushers or others. And then he would ask them of his own mouth: 'Is there any here that hath a suit?' And those that had suits would stand up. Then would he say: 'Be silent all, and your cases shall be settled one after the other.' And then he would call my lord Peter of

Fontaines and my lord Geoffrey of Villette and say to one of them: 'Settle this case for me.'

And when he saw something to amend in the sayings of those that spake for him, or in the speech of those that spake for another, he would amend it out of his own mouth.

On a time I saw him in summer, when to do his people's business he came to the garden in Paris, dressed in a coat of camlet, a sleeveless surcoat of linsey-woolsey, a mantle of black silk about his neck, well combed and capless, and a coronal of white peacock's feathers on his head. And he had carpets spread for us to sit on round about him; and all the people who had business to do before him were round him standing. And then he settled their cases, after the manner I have told you of before, as he did in the wood of Vincennes.

XIII

ON another time I saw him again in Paris, where all the prelates of France had sent him word that they wished to speak with him, and the King went to the Palace to hearken to them. And there was Bishop Guy of Auxerre, who was son of my lord William of Mello; and he spake to the King on behalf of all the bishops after this manner:

'Sir, these lords here present, archbishops and bishops, have bade me tell you that Christendom, which should be defended by you, is perishing in your hands.' The King crossed himself when he heard this saying, and answered: 'Now tell me how these things be.'

'Sir,' said he, 'it is because in these days men hold excommunication so lightly that they allow themselves to die excommunicate without absolution and have no mind to make restitution to the Church. We would

earnestly require you, Sir, for God's sake and your duty's, to command your judges and magistrates that all those that lie under excommunication for a year and a day should be constrained to seek absolution by the confiscation of their goods.'
To this the King answered that he would order it willingly for all those whom they could prove to him had done wrong. And the bishops said that they would on no account act thus, for so they would owe him jurisdiction over their suits. Then the King said he would not do otherwise; for it would be against God and against reason if he forced men to seek absolution when the clergy had done them wrong. 'And of this,' said the King, 'will I give you an ensample in the Count of Brittany, who for seven years, although excommunicate, was at law with the bishops of Brittany, and so laboured that the Apostolic See condemned them all. So that, had I constrained the Count of Brittany after the first year to seek absolution from them, I should have done wrong towards God and to him.' And then the prelates forbore; nor ever after did I hear of their asking for the aforesaid things.

XIV

THE peace which he made with the King of England did he make against the will of his council, who said to him: 'Sir, it appeareth to us that ye cast away the land that ye give to the King of England, since he hath no right to it; for his father lost it by decree.' Whereto the King answered that he well knew that the King of England had no right to it; but there was a reason wherefor he did well to give it him. 'For we twain have two sisters to wife, and our children are cousins german; wherefore is it fitting that there should be peace.

I have come to much honour in the peace that I make with the King of England, since now he is my liegeman, the which he was not heretofore.'

The uprightness of the King may be seen by the tale of my lord Renaud of Trie, who brought the saint a charter, declaring that the King had given the county of Dammartin in Gouelle to the heirs of the Countess of Boulogne, that was lately dead. The seal of the charter was broken, so that naught remained but the half of the legs of the figure on the King's seal, and the stool on which the King set his feet. And he showed it to all of us who were in his council that we might help him to give judgement.

Forthwith we said with one accord that he was in no wise holden to put the charter into deed. Then he told John Sarrasin, his chamberlain, to give him the charter that he had asked for. When he had this charter, he said unto us, 'My lords, see here the seal that I was wont to use before I went beyond the seas, and a man may see clearly by this that the impression of the broken seal is like unto the whole seal; wherefore I would not dare to keep that county with a clear conscience.' Then he summoned my lord Renaud of Trie and said to him: 'I give you the county back.'

BOOK TWO

XV

IN THE NAME OF ALMIGHTY GOD HAVE WE ERE THIS WRITTEN A PART OF THE FAIR SAYINGS AND GOOD PRECEPTS OF OUR SAINTLY KING LOUIS THAT THOSE THAT HEAR THEM MAY FIND THEM SET ONE BESIDE THE OTHER, WHEREFOR THEY MAY HAVE GREATER PROFIT FROM THEM THAN AS IF THEY HAD BEEN WRITTEN AMONG HIS DEEDS. AND HEREAFTER WE ENTER UPON HIS DEEDS, IN THE NAME OF GOD AND IN HIS OWN NAME.

AS I have heard say, he was born on St. Mark's Day after Easter. That day they bear crosses in procession in many parts, and in France they call them the black crosses; so that this was as it were a prophecy of the great plenty of the people that were to die in these two Crusades, that is to say in that of Egypt, and in that other on which he died at Carthage; wherefor was there much heavy grief in this world, and much great joy is there in Paradise for those who died on these two pilgrimages bearing the true cross. *25 April 1214*

He was crowned on the first Sunday of Advent. On this Sunday the Mass beginneth *Ad te levavi animam meam,* and what followeth sayeth thus: 'Fair Lord God, I will lift up my soul unto Thee and in Thee is my trust.' In God did he put his trust from his childhood to his death; for as he lay dying, in his last words he called upon God and the saints and especially my lord Saint James and my lady Saint Genevieve. *29 November 1226*

XVI

GOD, in Whom he put his trust, guarded him always from his childhood until the end; and especially did He defend him when he was a child and there was great need of it, as ye shall hear tell hereafter. As to his soul, God kept it through the good precepts of his mother, who taught him to have faith in God and to love Him, and drew round him all manner of religious. And she made him, child as he was, say all his Hours, and go to hear sermons on feast days. He recalled that his mother had many a time given him to understand that she had liefer that he were dead than that he had done mortal sin.

Much had he need of the help of God in his youth; for his mother, that came from Spain, had neither kinsmen nor friends in all the realm of France. And since the barons of France saw the King a child, and the Queen his mother a foreign woman, they made the Count of Boulogne, the uncle of the King, their chief, and held him likewise to be their lord. After the King was crowned, there were barons among them who demanded of the Queen that she should give them great fiefs; and since she would do none of this, all the barons assembled *1227* at Corbeil.

The saintly King told me that neither he nor his mother that were at Montlhéry dared return to Paris until folk came armed from Paris to fetch them. And he told me that from Montlhéry onwards the roads were full of men, armed and unarmed, as far as Paris, and that all cried upon Our Lord to give him long life and good, and to defend and keep him from his enemies. And so God did, as ye shall hear.

At this parley that the barons held at Corbeil, so they say, those that were there arranged that the good old knight Count Peter of Brittany should show himself against the King; and they agreed further that they should go in person to answer the summons that the King would make against the Count, and that each should have but two knights with him. And this they did to see if the Count of Brittany could overcome the Queen, who was a foreign woman as ye have heard; and many men said that the Count would have overcome the King and the Queen had not God, Who never failed him, aided the King in this need.

The help that God gave him was that Count Thibault of Champagne, who afterwards was King of Navarre, came to attend on the King with three hundred knights and by the aid that the Count lent the King the Count of Brittany was driven to the mercy of the King; so he left to the King, in making peace, the County of Anjou, as they say, and the County of Perche.

XVII

SINCE it is fitting to call to mind certain things that ye shall hear hereafter, it is well that I should leave my subject for a space. Therefore we will tell here how the good Count Henry Greatheart had by the Countess Mary, who was sister to the King of France and sister to King Richard of England, two sons, of whom the elder was named Henry and the other Thibault. This Henry, the elder, took the Cross and went on pilgrimage to the Holy Land, when King Philip and King Richard laid siege to Acre and took it.

So soon as Acre was taken, King Philip came back to France, for which he was much blamed; and King Richard tarried in the Holy Land and did such great deeds that the Saracens so feared him that, as it is written in the

July 1191

book of the Holy Land, when the children of the Saracens made an uproar, the women cried out on them and said: 'Hold your tongue, here is King Richard!' to make them hold their peace. And when the horses of the Saracens and the Bedouins were frightened at a bush, they used to say to their horses, 'Thinkest thou that it be King Richard?'

This King Richard achieved so much that he gave to Count Henry of Champagne, who had stayed by him, the Queen of Jerusalem, that was the heiress of the kingdom in the direct line. By the said queen had Count Henry two daughters, of whom the first was Queen of Cyprus, and the other wedded my lord Everard of Brienne, from whom is descended a great lineage, as appeareth both in France and in Champagne. Of the wife of my lord Everard of Brienne will I now say no more, but will tell you of the Queen of Cyprus, for she concerneth my matter; so will I tell.

XVIII

AFTER the King had overcome Count Peter of Brittany, all the barons of France were in such a turmoil against Count Thibault of Champagne that they were of a mind to send to fetch the Queen of Cyprus, who was daughter of the eldest son of Champagne, to disinherit Count Thibault, who was the son of the second son of Champagne. Some of them set about making peace between Count Peter and the said Count Thibault, and the matter was so arranged that Count Thibault promised that he would take to wife the daughter of Count Peter of Brittany. The day was fixed when the Count of Champagne was to wed the damsel, and they were to bring her for the wedding to an abbey of Premonstratensians which lieth near Châtel-Thierry and

BOOK TWO

is, as I understand, called Val-Secret. The barons of France, that were nearly all kinsmen of Count Peter, undertook to do this, and brought the damsel to Val-Secret for the wedding, and sent for Count Thibault that was in Châtel-Thierry.

And as the Count of Champagne was going to the wedding, my lord Geoffrey of La Chapelle came to him from the King, with a letter of credence, and spake thus: 'My lord Count of Champagne, the King hath heard that ye have made an agreement with Count Peter of Brittany to take his daughter in marriage. The King sendeth to tell you that if ye would not lose whatsoever ye have in the realm of France, ye go not through with it; for ye know that the Count of Brittany hath done worse to the King than any man alive.' The Count of Champagne, by the advice of those that were with him, went back to Châtel-Thierry.

When Count Peter and the barons of France, who were waiting at Val-Secret, heard this, they were as it were beside themselves at the despite that he had done them, and forthwith sent for the Queen of Cyprus. So soon as she had come, they agreed by one consent that they were to send all that they had of men-at-arms to invade Brie and Champagne from the side of France; and the Duke of Burgundy, that was wedded to the daughter of Count Robert of Dreux, was on his side to enter the county of Champagne from Burgundy. And they fixed a day when they were to meet together before the city of Troyes, to take the city of Troyes an they could.

The Duke summoned as many men as he could and the barons likewise all that they had. The barons came, burning and harrying on the one side, and the Duke of Burgundy on the other; and the King of France on yet another, to give them battle. The plight of the Count of Champagne was such that he himself was driven to burn his own towns before the coming of the barons, lest they find them victualled. Among the other towns that the Count of Champagne burnt were Épernay and Vertus and Sézanne.

XIX

1230 THE citizens of Troyes, when they saw that they had lost the help of their lord, sent word to Simon Lord of Joinville, father of the Lord of Joinville that now is, to ask him to come to their succour. And he, who had summoned all his men-at-arms, left Joinville at nightfall so soon as the news reached him, and came to Troyes before it was day. Wherefore the barons failed in the intent that they had to take the said city and for this reason the barons passed before Troyes without more ado, and went to lie in the meadow ground of Isle, where the Duke of Burgundy was.

The King of France, who knew that they were there, made straight towards them to give them battle, and the barons sent word to him and besought him to betake his own person into the rear, and they would give battle to the Count of Champagne and the Duke of Lorraine and the rest of his people, with three hundred knights less than the Count or the Duke. And the King sent word that never should they give battle to his people unless he were with them in person. They sent answer to him and told him that if it pleased him they would gladly incline the Queen to peace. And the King answered them that he would come to no peace, nor suffer the Count of Champagne to come thereto, until they had left the County of Champagne.

They left it in such fashion that from Isle, where they were, they went to lie below Jully; and the King lay at Isle whence he had driven them. When they knew that

BOOK TWO

the King had gone there, they went to lie at Chaource; and durst not wait for the King, but went on and encamped at Laignes, which belonged to the Count of Nevers, who was of their faction. And the King accorded the Count of Champagne and the Queen of Cyprus, and peace was made in such wise that the said Count of Champagne gave the Queen of Cyprus about a thousand crowns a year in land, and twenty thousand crowns that the King paid for the Count of Champagne.

1234

And the Count of Champagne sold the King for the twenty thousand crowns the fiefs named hereafter: which is to say the fief of the County of Blois, the fief of the County of Chartres, the fief of the County of Sancerre, and the fief of the Viscounty of Châteaudun. Some men said that the King held these fiefs aforesaid only in pawn; but it is not true, for I asked our sainted King Louis when we were beyond the seas.

The land which Count Thibault gave to the Queen of Cyprus is held by the Count of Brienne that now is and by the Count of Joigny, for the grandmother of the Count of Brienne was daughter of the Queen of Cyprus and wife of the great Count Walter of Brienne.

XX

SO that ye may know whence came the fiefs that the Lord of Champagne sold to the King, will I tell you that the great Count Thibault, who lieth at Lagny, had three sons: the first was named Henry, the second was called Thibault, and the third was Stephen. This Henry aforesaid was Count of Champagne and Brie, and was called Count Henry Greatheart, and well was he so named for he was great of heart to God and to the world: great-hearted to God, as appeareth in the church of St. Stephen at Troyes and in the other fair churches which he founded in Champagne; and greathearted to the world as appeareth in the story of Artaud of Nogent, and in many other points that I would tell you but that I feared to hinder my tale.

Artaud of Nogent was the burgher in whom the Count trusted most in the world, and he was so rich that he built the castle of Nogent l'Artaud with his own money. Now it befell that Count Henry came down from his hall of Troyes to hear Mass in Saint Stephen's on a Whitsunday. At the foot of the stairs there came before him a poor knight, who knelt before him, and spake thus: 'Sir, I beg you for the love of God that ye will give me of your substance marriage portions for my two daughters, whom here ye see.' Artaud, who came behind him, said to the poor knight, 'Sir knight, ye do discourteously thus to ask of my lord; for he hath given so much that he hath naught to give.' Count Greatheart turned to Artaud and said, 'Sir peasant, ye speak not truth when ye say that I have naught to give: aye, I have you. Take him, Sir knight, for I give him to you, and will pass him by warranty.' The knight was not abashed, but took him by the hood, and told him he would not let him go until he had done with him. And before he got away, Artaud had concluded with him for two hundred and fifty crowns.

The second brother of Count Henry was named Thibault, and was Count of Blois; and the third brother was named Stephen, and was Count of Sancerre. And these two brothers held all their heritage and their two counties and their appurtenances from Count Henry, and afterwards they held them from his heirs that held Champagne, until that time when King Thibault sold them to the King of France as I have said ere now.

BOOK TWO

XXI

NOW come we back to our matter, and tell how *1241* after these things the King held a great court at Saumur in Anjou; and I myself was there, and testify to you that it was the best ordered that ever I saw. For there ate beside the King at his table the Count of Poitiers that he had newly knighted at the feast of Saint John; and after the Count of Poitiers ate Count John of Dreux, that he had likewise newly knighted; after the Count of Dreux, ate the Count of La Marche; after the Count of La Marche, the good old Count Peter of Brittany. And before the King's table, in front of the Count of Dreux, ate my lord the King of Navarre, in coat and mantle of satin, well arrayed with baldric and clasp and coronal of gold; and I carved before him.

Behind the King, the Count of Artois his brother served meat, and the good old Count John of Soissons carved before him. To keep the King's table were there my lord Imbert of Beaujeu who afterwards was Constable of France, and my lord Enguerrand of Coucy and my lord Archambaud of Bourbon. Behind these three lords were there full thirty of their knights in coats of silken stuff, to wait upon them; and behind these knights was there great plenty of servants, wearing the arms of the Count of Poitiers sewn upon taffetas. The King was dressed in a coat of blue satin, with surcoat and mantle of vermilion satin furred with ermine, and a cotton cap on his head, which ill became him, for he was then a young man.

The King held his feast in the halls of Saumur; and they said that the great King Henry of England had built them to hold his great feasts therein. And the halls are built like the cloisters of the white monks; but I think that there are no others by any means so great. And I will tell you why it seemeth so to me: for by the wall of the cloister where the King ate, being surrounded by knights and men-at-arms that took much room, there also ate at one table twenty bishops and archbishops; and again besides the bishops and archbishops did there eat at this table the Queen Blanche his Mother, at the end of the cloister on the side where the King was not. And to serve the Queen there were the Count of Boulogne that was later King of Portugal, and the good old Count Hugh of Saint Pol, and a German of the age of eighteen years, said to be the son of Saint Elizabeth of Thuringia: wherefore they said that Queen Blanche kissed him upon the forehead for devotion's sake, for she knew that his mother must oft-times have kissed him there.

At the end of the cloister on the other side were the kitchens, the butteries, pantries, and larders; from this end did they serve meat, wine, and bread for the King and the Queen. And in the other walks of the cloister and in the garth in the middle did there eat such foison of knights that I know not how to tell the number of them. And many men said that they had never seen so many surcoats and other robes of cloth of silk and gold at a feast as there; and they said that there were present full three thousand knights.

XXII

1242

AFTER this feast the King took the Count of Poitiers to Poitiers to resume possession of his fiefs. And when the King was come to Poitiers, he would liefer have been back in Paris; for he found that the Count of La Marche, that had eaten at his table on St. John's Day, had assembled as many men-at-arms as he might at Lusignan near Poitiers. There did the King

BOOK TWO

tarry for nearly a fortnight, for he durst not leave until he had made an agreement with the Count of La Marche, I know not how. More than once did I see the Count of La Marche come to Poitiers from Lusignan to have speech of the King; and ever did he bring with him the Queen of England, his wife, that was mother of the King of England. And many men said that the King and the Count of Poitiers had made a bad peace with the Count of La Marche.

After the King had come back from Poitiers, it was not long before the King of England came into Gascony to make war against the King of France. Our saintly King, with such a host as he could gather together, rode forth against him. Thither came the King of England and the Count of La Marche to fight before a castle called Taillebourg, which is set on an evil river called the Charente, which no man may pass but by a very narrow bridge of stone.

So soon as the King came to Taillebourg and the armies beheld each other, our folk, that had the castle on their side, strove with much ado and crossed perilously by boats and bridges and fell upon the English; and then did the battle begin, stubborn and mighty. When the King saw this, he went into danger with the rest: because for every man the King had when he had crossed to the English side, the English had full twenty. None the less it befell, by God's will, that when the English saw the King cross, they were discomfited and withdrew to the city of Saintes; and several of our men entered the city among them and were taken prisoner.

Those of our men that were taken prisoner at Saintes told that they heard a great quarrel arise between the King of England and the Count of La Marche; and the King said that the Count of La Marche had sent for him because the Count said that he would find great succour in France. That very night the King of England left Saintes and went away into Gascony.

XXIII

THE Count of La Marche, even as a man that could not help himself, went to the King's prison, and thereto brought his wife and children; wherefore the King in making peace did strike off a great piece from the Count's land; yet I know not how much, for I was not at this occasion, for I had never yet worn coat of mail. But I have heard say that with the land that the King took, the Count of La Marche gave over to him five thousand crowns that he had in his coffers, and every year as much.

When we were at Poitiers, I saw a knight that was called my lord Geoffrey of Rancon, who for a great wrong that the Count of La Marche had done him, so men said, had sworn on relics that he would never be shorn like a knight, but would wear his hair parted as women do, until he had avenged himself on the Count of La Marche, in his own person or by another. And when my lord Geoffrey saw the Count of La Marche, his wife, and his children on their knees before the King, and begging his mercy, he had a trestle brought and brushed back his parting and had his hair cut forthwith in the presence of the King, the Count of La Marche, and all that were there. And in this expedition against the King of England and the barons, the King gave great gifts, as I have heard from them that came thence. Yet not for gifts, nor for payment that was made to that host, or to any other this side the sea or beyond it, did the King demand or take levy from his barons or from his knights or from his men or from his good towns, of which complaint was made. Nor was this marvel, for he did it by the counsel

BOOK TWO

of his good mother who was with him, and whose counsel he took, and by the counsel of the men of worth that remained with him from the time of his father and grandsire.

XXIV

AFTER these things aforesaid it befell, as God willed, *1244* that a great sickness laid hold on the King in Paris, whereby he was in such evil case that, as they tell, one of the ladies who tended him wished to draw the sheet over his face, and said that he was dead. And another lady, that was the other side the bed, would not suffer it; but said that the soul was still in his body. And as he heard the contention of these two ladies, Our Lord worked upon him and straightway gave him health; for before he had been dumb and could not speak. And so soon as he was able to speak, he asked that they should give him the Cross, which they did. When the Queen his mother heard tell that speech had come back to him she was in such great joy as might be. And when she knew that he had taken the Cross, as he himself used to tell, she grieved as much as if she saw him dead.

After he had taken the Cross, so too did Robert Count of Artois, Alfonse Count of Poitiers, Charles Count of Anjou, who was after King of Sicily, all three brothers of the King; and Hugh Duke of Burgundy took the Cross, William Count of Flanders, brother of Count Guy of Flanders now lately dead, the good old Hugh Count of Saint Pol, my lord Walter his nephew, who bore himself passing well oversea, and would have been of much avail had he lived. And there took the Cross likewise the Count of La Marche and my lord Hugh the Black his son, the Count of Sarrebruck, my lord Gobert of Apremont his brother, in whose company I, John,

Lord of Joinville, crossed the sea in a ship that we hired, for we were cousins; and we crossed all told twenty knights, of whom he had command over nine and I over nine.

XXV

1248 — At Easter, in the year of grace in which our age stood at a thousand two hundred and forty-eight, did I summon my men and my vassals to Joinville; and on the eve of that Easter, when all the folk that I had summoned had come, was born my son John, Lord of Ancerville, by my first wife, who was sister to the Count of Grandpré. All that week did we dance and make holiday, for my brother, the Lord of Vaucouleurs, and all the other rich men who were present, gave feasts one after the other on the Monday, the Tuesday, the Wednesday, and the Thursday.

On the Friday I said to them: 'My lords, I am going away beyond the seas, and I know not if I shall return. Come forward; and if I have done you wrong in aught, I will right it, one by one, as my custom is to any that has aught to ask of me or of my folk.' So I made matters right with each, according to the opinion of all the common people of my land; and so that I should have no weight with them, I went from the council and accepted whatsoever they rehearsed without debate.

Since I was not of a mind to take away any money to which I had no right, I went to Metz in Lorraine to leave great part of my lands in pawn. And I would have you know that on the day that I left our country to go to the Holy Land I did not hold five hundred crowns a year in land, for Madam my mother yet lived; and so went I forth at the head of nine knights and with two others that were knights banneret. These things do I recount

BOOK TWO

to you, because if God had not succoured me, Who never failed me, I should scarcely have had enough for so long as the space of six years that I tarried in the Holy Land.
At the time I was making ready to go, John, Lord of Apremont, and Count of Sarrebruck in right of his wife, sent to me and told me that he had all his affairs set in order to go oversea, at the head of nine knights; and asked me if I were willing that we should hire a ship between us; and I consented thereto; and his folk and mine hired a ship at Marseilles.

XXVI

THE King summoned all his barons to Paris and made them take an oath that they would do fealty and give loyalty to his children, if aught befell him on the way. He asked it of me likewise; but I would take no oath for I was not his liegeman.
As I went thither, I found three men that a clerk had slain, dead on a wagon; and they told me that they were taking them to the King. When I heard this, I sent a squire of mine after them to know what had befallen. And my squire whom I sent said that the King, when he came out of chapel, went into the foreporch to see the dead men, and asked the Provost of Paris how it had chanced.
And the Provost told him that the dead were three of his sergeants of the Châtelet, and that they used to go through the streets outside the walls to steal from folk. And he said to the King that 'they found this clerk that ye see here, and took from him all his habit. The clerk went in naught but his shirt into his house, and took his crossbow, and had a child bring him his falchion. When he saw the sergeants he cried out to them and told them that they were to die there. The clerk bent his bow and drew

it, and struck one of them through the heart; and the two took to flight; and the clerk took the falchion that the child held, and gave them chase by the light of the moon that was clear and full.

'One thought to pass behind a hedge in a garden, and the clerk struck him with the falchion,' said the Provost, 'and cut off all his leg in such wise that it held only by the boot, as ye see. The clerk took up the chase of the other, who thought to get into a strange house, where the folk were not yet abed; and the clerk struck him with the falchion on the head, so that he split it to the teeth, as ye may see,' said the Provost to the King. 'Sir,' said he, 'the clerk displayed his deed to the neighbours in the street, and then he went to put himself in your prison; and, Sir, I have brought him to you, that ye may do your will with him; and here he is.'

'Sir Clerk,' said the King, 'ye have lost your priesthood by your prowess; and for your prowess I will keep you in my pay, and ye shall come with me oversea. And I would have you know that I do this unto you because I wish that my people should see that I will not uphold them in their evildoings.' When the people that were assembled there heard this, they cried upon Our Lord and prayed that God should give him good life and long, and bring him back in joy and health.

XXVII

AFTER these things I came back into our country and we arranged, the Count of Sarrebruck and I, that we should send our baggage in wagons to Auxonne, to be put on the Saône, to go to Arles from the Saône to the Rhône.

The day that I left Joinville, I sent for the Abbot of Cheminon, that was reputed the most worthy in the

Order of White Monks. I had heard testimony borne to him at Clairvaux on a Lady Day, when the saintly King was there, by a monk that pointed him out to me and asked me if I knew him. And I questioned him wherefore he asked me. And he answered: 'Because I believe that he is the most worthy that there is in all the White Order. And know ye furthermore,' said he, 'what I have heard tell from a worthy man who lay in the dorter where the Abbot of Cheminon was sleeping; and the Abbot had uncovered his breast for the great heat that there was; and this man who lay in the dorter where the Abbot of Cheminon slept, saw the Mother of God who went to the Abbot's bed, and drew his robe over his breast so that the wind should not do him hurt.'

This Abbot of Cheminon gave me my scrip and staff; and then I set forth from Joinville, not to enter the castle again until my return, on foot, unshod and in my shirt; and so I went to Blécourt and Saint Urbain, and to visit other relics that are thereabouts. And as I went to Blécourt and to St. Urbain, never would I turn mine eyes towards Joinville, lest my heart melt for the fair castle that I was leaving and my two children.

I and my company ate at La Fontaine l'Archevêque before Donjeux; and there Abbot Adam of Saint Urbain (God rest his soul) gave great plenty of fair jewels to me and to the nine knights I had with me. Thence we went to Auxonne, and went with our baggage, that we had caused to be loaded into boats, from Auxonne to Lyons down the Saône; and they led the great war horses beside the boats. At Lyons we came into the Rhône to go to Arles the White; and on the Rhône we found a castle that is called Roche de Glun, that the King had had ruined because Roger, the lord of the castle, was accused of robbing pilgrims and merchants.

XXVIII

August 1248

IN the month of August we boarded our ship at the Rock of Marseilles. On the day that we boarded her they had the outer door of the ship opened and put all our horses therein that we were to take oversea; and then they shut the door and made it fast, as when a barrel is to be sunk, because when the ship is in the open sea all the door is under water.

When the horses were inside, our master mariner called to his sailors, who were in the prow of the ship, and said: 'Is your work made ready?' And they answered: 'Aye, Sir; let the clerks and the priests come forward.' So soon as they were come, he cried to them, 'Sing, in the name of God!' And they sang with one voice *Veni Creator Spiritus*. And he cried to his mariners, 'Set sail, in the name of God!' And so they did. And in a little while the wind took the sail, and carried us away from sight of land, so that we saw naught but sky and water; and each day the wind carried us farther away from the country where we had been born. And these things do I tell you that ye may see that he is a rash fool that dareth to put himself in such peril having another man's goods in his possession or being in mortal sin; for at night a man goeth to sleep and knoweth not if he will be at the bottom of the sea by morning.

At sea a great marvel befell us, for we sighted a mountain that is quite round, that is before Barbary. We sighted it near the hour of vespers, and sailed all night and thought to have made more than fifty leagues; and the next day we found ourselves still before this same mountain; and so it befell twice or thrice. When the mariners saw it they were amazed, and told us that our ships were in great jeopardy, for we were off the country of the Saracens of Barbary. Then a worthy priest, that was called the Dean of Maurupt, told us that never had there been affliction in his parish, whether by default of water, or by over-much rain, or other affliction, but that so soon as they had made three processions on three Saturdays, God and His Mother had delivered them. Saturday it was; we made the first procession round the two masts of the ship. I had myself carried in men's arms, for I was grievously sick. Never again did we see the mountain, and we came to Cyprus on the third Saturday.

XXIX

WHEN we came to Cyprus, the King was already in Cyprus, and we found great plenty of the King's provisions: that is to say the King's store of wine and money and the granaries. The store of wine was such that his people had made in the fields by the sea-shore great stacks of barrels of wine, which they had bought for two years before the King came; and they had laid them one upon the other, so that when a man saw them from before they seemed like barns. The wheat and barley had they laid in heaps in the fields, and when a man saw them it seemed as if they were hills; for the rain which had long fallen upon the corn had made it sprout on the outside, so that naught showed but green grass. Now it befell that when they wished to take it to Egypt, they brake down the outer crust with the green, and they found the wheat and the barley as fresh as though it had been newly threshed.

The King would lief have gone forward to Egypt without tarrying, as I heard tell in Syria, had it not been for his barons that counselled him to wait for his people that were not yet all come.

At this time when the King was sojourning in Cyprus, the great King of Tartary sent an embassy to him with many fair and courteous words. Among other matters, he sent word that he was ready to help him to conquer the Holy Land and to deliver Jerusalem from the Saracens. The King received his envoys very graciously, and sent his own in return, who tarried two years before they came back to him. And by the envoys did the King send to the King of Tartary a pavilion made after the fashion of a chapel, which cost him dear, for it was all made of fine scarlet cloth. The King, to see if he could draw them to our faith, caused to be worked in the said chapel, in figures, the Annunciation of Our Lady and all the other points of the faith. These things he sent them by two Friars Preachers that knew the Saracen tongue, to show and teach them what they ought to believe.

The two friars came back to the King at the moment that the King's brothers were going back to France; and they found the King, who had left Acre, where his brothers had quitted him, and had come to Caesarea which he was fortifying, nor was there then truce nor peace with the Saracens. How the envoys of the King of France were received will I tell you, and how they themselves recounted it to the King; and in their report to the King might ye hear many marvels, which I will not tell now, for it would make me break off the tale that I have begun, which is this.

I, that had not five hundred crowns a year in land, charged myself when I went oversea with nine knights and two knights banneret under me, and so it befell that when I reached Cyprus, I was left with no more than twelve score florins, when I had paid my ship; wherefore some of my knights apprised me that if I did not provide myself with money they would leave me. And God, who never failed me, provided me in this wise, that the King who was at Nicosia sent for me and took me into his service and put four hundred crowns in my coffers; and then had I more money than I needed.

XXX

AT this time that we sojourned in Cyprus, the Empress of Constantinople sent me word that she had come ashore at Paphos, a city of Cyprus, and that I should go to fetch her, I and my lord Everard of Brienne. When we got there, we found that a great wind had broken the ropes of the anchors of her ship, and had borne the ship towards Acre; and there remained of all her baggage naught but the mantle she had on, and a surcoat for meals. We brought her to Limassol, where the King and the Queen and all the barons of France and of the host received her most honourably.

The next day I sent her cloth to make her a robe, and fur of ermine therewith; and I sent her linsey-woolsey and silk to line the dress. My lord Philip of Nanteuil, the good old knight, who was in attendance on the King, met my squire who was on his way to the Empress. When the worthy knight saw this, he went to the King and told him that I had done great shame to him and to his other lords, by reason of these robes that I had sent her, when they had not taken thought to it before.

The Empress came to seek help of the King for her lord, that tarried in Constantinople, and importuned so well that she took away an hundred letters in duplicate, and more, both from me and from other friends that were there; in which letters we were bound by our oath that if the King or the Legate wished to send three hundred knights to Constantinople, after the King had gone back from oversea, we should hold ourselves bound to go by our bond. And I, to discharge my oath, petitioned the King, at our leaving, before the Count of Eu whose letters I have, that if he were willing to send three hundred knights, I would go in discharge of my oath. And the King answered me that he had not the means and that he had no such treasury that he had not now drained it to the dregs. After we had come to Egypt, the Empress went to France, and took with her my lord John of Acre her brother, whom she married to the Countess of Montfort.

XXXI

AT the time when we were come to Cyprus, the Sultan of Iconium was the richest king in all heathendom. And he had wrought a wonder: for he had caused great part of his gold to be melted into earthen pots such as they put wine in oversea, which hold three great measures of wine or four; and he had the pots broken; and the ingots of gold were left in the open in the midst of a castle of his, so that each man that entered the castle could see and touch them; and there were full six or seven of them.

His great riches appeared in a pavilion that the King of Armenia sent to the King of France, that was worth two hundred and fifty crowns at the least, and the King of Armenia sent word that a *farrāsh* of the Sultan of Iconium had given it to him. A *farrāsh* is the man that hath charge of the Sultan's tents and keepeth his houses clean.

The King of Armenia, to discharge himself from his vassalage to the Sultan of Iconium, went over to the King of Tartary, and entered his vassalage to have his aid; and brought back such plenty of men-at-arms that he was able to give battle to the Sultan of Iconium. The battle lasted a long time, and the Tartars killed so many of the Sultan's men that never after was there news of him. The fame of this battle that was toward reached us, and therefore did some of our foot-soldiers cross over to Armenia to profit and to be in the battle; but never a one of them came back.

The Sultan of Cairo, that awaited the King's coming to Egypt in the spring, bethought himself that he would go and overcome the Sultan of Hama, who was his mortal enemy; and went to besiege him in the city of Hama. The Sultan of Hama knew not how to rid himself of the Sultan of Cairo, for he saw well that if the Sultan lived long he would in time overcome him. And so he bargained with the *farrāsh* of the Sultan of Cairo, that the *farrāsh* should poison him. The manner of poisoning was this: the *farrāsh* was aware that the Sultan came every day in the afternoon to play chess on the mats which were at the foot of his bed; and that on which he knew that the Sultan sate every day, he poisoned. So it befell that the Sultan, who was barefoot, leaned over on a sore that he had on his leg. Forthwith the poison struck to the quick, and took from him the power of half his body on the side where it had entered; and each time that the poison pricked at his heart, it was a good two days before he could drink, or eat, or speak. So they left the Sultan of Hama in peace and his folk took the Sultan of Cairo back to Egypt.

XXXII

BY the King's command, now that March was beginning, the King, the barons, and the other pilgrims gave orders that their ships should be reladen with wine and victuals, to set sail when the King should command. Wherefore it befell that when the King saw the matter set in order, the King and the Queen boarded their ship the Friday before Whitsun; and the King bade his barons come after him in their ships 1249

1249

21 May 1249

straight to Egypt. On Saturday the King set sail, and all the other ships with him, which was a very fair thing to see: for it seemed as if all the sea, so far as the eye could reach, was covered with napery, from the sails of the ships, which were numbered at eighteen hundred both great and small.

The King cast anchor at the foot of a hillock which is called the point of Limassol, and all the other ships round about. The King went ashore on Whitsunday. When we had heard Mass, a grievous and strong wind, that came from over against Egypt, arose in such wise that of two thousand eight hundred knights that the King was leading to Egypt, there remained to him but seven hundred that the wind had not parted from the King's company; and the rest were driven to Acre and other foreign parts, of whom great part came not back unto the King until long afterward.

The day after Pentecost the wind had fallen; the King and those of us who had stayed with him, by God's will, set sail forthwith, and met the Prince of the Morea and the Duke of Burgundy, who had tarried in the Morea. On the Thursday after Pentecost, the King came to land off Damietta, and we found there all the forces of the Sultan on the sea-shore, folk very fair to look upon; for the Sultan beareth arms *or*, and where the sun struck the gold it made the arms to glitter. The noise that they made with drums and Saracen horns was horrible to hear.

The King summoned his barons to have counsel of them what he should do. Many advised him to wait until his folk were come together again, for there remained with him but a third of his men; but he would in no wise take heed to them. The reason therefor, he said, was that it would put heart into his enemies; and especially that in the sea off Damietta there was no harbour where he could await his people, and that a strong wind might take them and drive them to other lands, as on Whitsunday the others had been driven.

XXXIII

IT was agreed that the King should go ashore on the Friday before Trinity Sunday, and should give battle to the Saracens if any of them remained. The King ordered my lord John of Beaumont to hand over a galley to my lord Everard of Brienne and to me, to take us and our knights ashore, for the great ships were not able to get to the land. By the will of God, when I came back to my ship, I found a little ship that my lady of Beyrout, that was cousin german to the Count of Montbéliard and to us, had given me, in which were eight of my horses. When it came to the Friday, I and my lord Everard, armed at all points, went to the King to ask for the galley; and to this my lord John of Beaumont made answer that we should not have it.

When our people saw that we should not have a galley, they let themselves drop from the great ship into the ship's boat, as many as they could and how they could, until the ship's boat was near foundering. When the sailors saw that the ship's boat was sinking little by little, they escaped back on to the great ship and left my knights in the boat. I asked the captain how many too many there were therein; and he told me twenty men-at-arms; and I asked him whether it would take our people safely to land, were I to lighten it by so many folk; and he answered 'Aye'. And I lightened it in such fashion that thrice did it take them to the ship wherein my horses were.

As I directed these men, a knight that was under my lord Everard of Brienne, that was called Plonquet, thought to get from the great ship into the ship's boat; and the boat moved off and he fell into the sea and was drowned.

When I came back to my ship, I put in my little boat a squire whom I had knighted, who was called my lord Hugh of Vaucouleurs, and two most valiant squires, of whom one was named my lord Villain of Versey, and the other my lord William of Dammartin, who were grievously angered one against the other. Nor could any make peace between them, for they had taken each other by the hair in the Morea; and I made them forgive their ill will and kiss one another, for I swore to them on relics that we would not go ashore in company with their ill will.

Then set we out to go ashore, and went alongside the ship's boat of the King's great ship, wherein was the King. And for that we went faster than they, his people began to cry out after me to land with the banner of Saint Denis that was going in another boat before the King. But I gave no heed to them; but had us land before a great host of Turks, wherein there were full six thousand mounted men. So soon as they saw that we had reached the land, they set spur to their horses and came at us. When we saw them coming we fixed the points of our shields in the sand and the staves of our lances in the sand with the points towards them. When they saw these thus ready to strike them in the belly, they turned and fled.

XXXIV

MY lord Baldwin of Rheims, a right good man who had come ashore, sent word to me by his squire that I should wait for him; and I answered that gladly would I, for a man of such worth should be waited for in such a pass; wherefore all his life was he grateful to me. With him there came to us a thousand knights; and know ye that when I landed, I had neither squire nor knight nor man-at-arms that I had brought with me from mine own country; and yet God never left me without succour.

On our left hand landed the Count of Jaffa, that was cousin german of the Count of Montbéliard and of the lineage of Joinville. He it was that landed in the most noble fashion; for his galley came to shore all painted, within and without, with shields of his arms, which arms are *or* a cross patée *gules*. He had full three hundred rowers in his galley, and each rower had a targe of his arms, and each targe had a pennon of his arms sewn in gold. While he was coming to land it seemed that the galley flew, by reason of the rowers that laboured at the oars; and it seemed that thunder fell from heaven, by the noise that the pennons made, and the nakirs and the drums and the Saracen horns that were in his galley. So soon as the galley had touched the sand as far forward as they could beach her, he and his knights leapt from the galley well armed and well arrayed, and came and ranked themselves beside us.

I have forgotten to tell that when the Count of Jaffa had landed, he straightway had his tents and pavilions pitched; and so soon as the Saracens saw them pitched, they came together before us and came at us again, spurring their horses, as if to ride us down; and when they saw that we did not give way, forthwith they rode back again.

On our right hand, a long cross-bow shot away, there came to shore the galley in which was the banner of Saint Denis. And there was a Saracen, when they were landed, that came charging among them either because he could not hold his horse or because he thought the rest would follow him; but he was cut to pieces.

XXXV

WHEN the King heard tell that the banner of Saint Denis had got to land, he strode across his galley, nor heeded the Legate that was with him and that would have hindered him, and leapt into the sea, and was in the water up to his armpits. And he went forward, shield at neck and helmet on head and lance in hand, to his people that were on the sea-shore. When he got to land and perceived the Saracens, he asked what folk they were; and they told him that they were Saracens; and he couched his lance under his arm and set his shield before him, and would have set upon the Saracens had the trusty men that were with him suffered it.

The Saracens sent word thrice to the Sultan by carrier-pigeons that the King had landed, but had no word from him, for he was stricken with his sickness; and when they saw this, they thought that the Sultan was dead, and left Damietta. The King sent to find out concerning this by a knight envoy. The knight came back to the King and said that he had been within the Sultan's house and that it was true. Thereupon the King sent for the Legate and all the bishops of the host, and they sang aloud *Te Deum Laudamus*. Then the King and all of us took horse and went to encamp before Damietta.

Manifestly ill did the Turks leave Damietta in so far as they did not cut the bridge of boats, which would have done us great hindrance; but great mischief did they do at their leaving, in that they set fire to the market where all the merchandise was and all goods sold by weight. Such harm ensued from this as if a man should tomorrow set fire (which Heaven forbid) to the Petit Pont at Paris.

Now let us tell what great favour Almighty God showed us, when he defended us from death and danger at our landing, when we came ashore on foot and set upon our enemies who were on horseback. Very gracious was Our Lord to us at Damietta when He gave it into our hands, that we ought not to have taken but by starving it out; and this we may clearly see, for it was by famine that King John took it in our fathers' time.

XXXVI

OUR Lord might have said of us as he spake of the Children of Israel, when he said: *Et pro nichilo habuerunt terram desiderabilem.* And what saith it further? It saith that they forgat God who had delivered them. And how we forgat him will I tell you hereafter. I will bring you first to the King, who summoned his barons, clerks, and laymen, and bade them help him with their counsel how they should divide the spoil they had taken in the town. The Patriarch was the first that spake, and said thus: 'Sir, meseemeth that it would be well that ye should keep the wheat and the barley and the rice, and all that on which men may live, to victual the town; and let them cry through the host that all other movables should be brought to the Legate's lodging, under pain of excommunication.' All the other barons were of one mind in this counsel. Now it so happened that all the goods that they brought to the Legate's lodging were not worth more than three thousand crowns. When this was done, the King and the barons sent for my lord John of Valery, a good man and true, and spake to him thus: 'My lord of Valery,' said the King, 'we are agreed that the Legate should hand over to you the three thousand crowns, to divide them as ye shall think best.' 'Sir,' said the worthy man, 'of your goodness ye do me great honour; but this honour and this offer will I not accept, please God; for I should thereby set at naught the good customs of the Holy Land, which are these: that when they take the cities of the enemy, of the goods that they find therein the King should have a third, and the pilgrims two-thirds. And this custom was maintained by King John when he took Damietta; and as old men say, the Kings of Jerusalem that were before King John held by this custom. And if it please you that ye should hand over to me the two parts of wheat and barley, of rice, and other victuals, readily will I undertake to divide them among the pilgrims.' The King was not of a mind to do this, and so the matter rested; wherefore many men thought themselves ill used because the King set aside the good old custom.

The King's folk, that should courteously have restrained them, hired men stalls instead whereat to sell their wares as dearly, so men said, as they could; and the fame thereof was bruited into foreign parts, wherefor many merchants forbore to come to the host. The barons, that should have kept their goods to use them well in fit time and place, took to giving great feasts and food beyond measure. The common people took to frequenting wanton women; whence it befell that the King dismissed great number of his people when we came out of captivity. And I asked wherefore he had done this; and he told me that he had found for certain that those whom he had discharged had their brothels a small stone's-throw from his pavilion, and that at the time of the greatest misery that ever the host was in.

XXXVII

NOW we come back to our matter and tell that a little after we had taken Damietta, there came before the camp all the horsemen of the Sultan, and beleaguered the camp on the land side. The King and all his knights armed themselves. I went in full armour to speak to the King, and found him armed, sitting on a bench, and the noble knights who were of his squadron with him, all in harness. I asked him that he should allow me and my people to go forth outside the camp, so that the Saracens should not make an onslaught into our lodging. When my lord John of Beaumont heard my request, he cried out with a loud voice, and commanded me on the King's behalf that I should not leave my lodging until the King so ordered.

Of the trusty knights that were with the King have I spoken, for there were with him eight, all good knights, that had borne arms this side the sea and the other; and such knights are men wont to call good knights. The names of those who were knights attending on the King are these: my lord Geoffrey of Sargines, my lord Matthew of Marly, my lord Philip of Nanteuil, my lord Imbert of Beaujeu, Constable of France, who was not then there but was outside the camp, he and the master of the cross-bowmen, with most of the King's sergeants-at-arms, to guard the camp lest the Turks should do it harm.

Now it befell that my lord Walter of Autrèche had himself armed in his tent at all points, and when he had mounted his horse, shield at neck, and helmet on head, he had the flaps of his pavilion raised, and spurred on to go against the Turks; and as he set out from his pavilion all alone, all his household cried with a loud voice 'Châtillon!' Then it befell that before ever he came to the Turks, he had a fall, and his horse bounded over his body, and the horse sped on, covered with his arms, to our enemies, for most of the Saracens were mounted on mares, and therefore the horse drew towards the Saracens.

And those told us who saw it that four Turks came to my Lord Walter, who was lying on the ground; and as they went by before him, they struck great blows with their maces on him as he lay. Thence did the Constable of France and many of the King's sergeants-at-arms rescue him, and brought him back in their arms to his pavilion. When he was come there, he could not speak. Many of the surgeons and physicians of the host went to him; and since it seemed to them that he was in no danger of death, they bled him in both arms.

That night very late my lord Aubert of Narcy said to me that we should go to visit him, for we had not yet seen him and he was a man of a great name and great valour. We came into his pavilion, and his chamberlain came to meet us to bid us go softly and not to wake his master. We discovered him lying on a counterpane of miniver, and we went towards him very softly, and found him dead. When they told the King, he answered that he desired not to have a thousand such, should they disobey his orders as this man had done.

XXXVIII

THE Saracens came on foot every night into the host, and slew men as they found them asleep; whence it befell that they slew the watchman of the Lord of Courtenay, and left him lying on a table, and cut off his head and bare it away. And this they did because the Sultan gave for every head of a Christian a besant of gold. And this affliction befell us because the squadrons kept watch over the camp, one each night, on horseback; and when the Saracens were of a mind to get into the camp, they waited until the noise of the horses and the squadrons had passed; and then gat them into the host behind the backs of the horses, and were out again ere dawn. Wherefore the King commanded that the squadrons that were wont to keep watch on horseback should watch on foot; so that all the host was made safe by our people that kept watch, since they were spread out in such wise that one man touched the next.

After this was done, the King was of a mind not to leave Damietta until his brother the Count of Poitiers should be come, who was bringing the yeomen of France. And lest the Saracens should rush suddenly into the camp on horseback, the King caused all the camp to be enclosed with great ditches; and over the ditches the crossbowmen kept watch, every night, and foot soldiers with them, and at the gates of the camp likewise.

When Saint Remi's Day was past, and there was no news of the Count of Poitiers (whereby the King and all the host were sore troubled, for they feared that some mischief had befallen him), then I recounted to the Legate how the Dean of Maurupt had caused us to have three processions at sea, on three Saturdays, and before the third Saturday we were come to Cyprus. The Legate took heed to me, and had the three processions on three Saturdays cried through the host. The first procession began at the Legate's lodging and went to the church of Our Lady in the town: which church was made in the mosque of the Saracens and the Legate had dedicated it in the honour of the Mother of God. The Legate preached there for two Saturdays. The King was there and the rich men of the host, to whom the Legate gave the great absolution.

1 October 1249

By the third Saturday the Count of Poitiers had come, and it would not have availed had he come before; for between the three Saturdays was there such a tempest at sea off Damietta that there were at least twelve score vessels, great and small, broken to pieces and lost, with all the men that were therein lost and drowned. Wherefore had the Count of Poitiers come before, he and his men would all have been confounded.

When the Count of Poitiers was come, the King

summoned all the barons of the host, to know which road he should take, whether to Alexandria or to Cairo. Wherein it befell that the good old Count Peter of Brittany and most of the barons of the host were agreed that the King should go to lay siege to Alexandria, since before that town was a fair haven, whither ships might come to victual the host. The Count of Artois was contrary to this, and said that he would never agree to their going except to Cairo, for it was the chief city of all the realm of Egypt; and he said too that he who would kill a snake should first crush its head. The King set aside all the other counsels of his barons, and held with the opinion of his brother.

XXXIX

November 1249 AT the beginning of Advent, the King set out and the host with him to go towards Cairo, as the Count of Artois had counselled. Hard by Damietta we found a stream that came out of the great river, and therefore it was agreed that the host should tarry a day to stop up the arm of the stream, so that they might cross. The thing was done easily enough; for they dammed the channel close to the great stream, in such wise that the water was turned without much toil into the great stream. To this crossing-place of the stream the Sultan sent five hundred of his knights, the best mounted that he could find in all his army, to harry the King's host to delay our starting.

6 December 1249 On Saint Nicholas' Day the King gave orders that they should make ready to ride forth, and forbade that any should be so bold as to assail the Saracens that were there. Now it befell that when the host set forth to ride out, and the Turks saw that no assault was made upon them, and knew by their spies that the King had for-

BOOK TWO

bidden it, they waxed bold and gathered against the Templars, that had the first squadron; and one of the Turks bare a Knight of the Temple to the ground, under the feet of the horse of Brother Renaud of Vichiers, that was then Marshal of the Temple.

When he saw this, he cried to his brethren: 'Now at them, in the name of God! For I can bear it no longer.' He set spur to his horse, and all the host likewise; our horses were fresh, and the horses of the Turks were already wearied, wherefore have I heard tell that none of them escaped, but that all were slain; and many gat them into the stream and were drowned.

XL

IT is fitting that we should first speak of the river that cometh through Egypt and from the earthly Paradise; and these things will I tell you to give you understanding of certain matters that pertain to my tale. This river is unlike all other rivers; for the farther the other rivers flow downstream, the more of little rivers and small brooks flow into them; and into this river there fall none; but it so haps that it cometh all in one channel as far as Egypt, and then floweth into seven branches that spread throughout the land of Egypt.

And when the season cometh after the feast of St. Remi, the seven rivers spread through the land and cover the flat ground; and when they go down, the husbandmen go each man to plough his land with a plough without wheels, wherewith they turn over in the soil the wheat, barley, cumin, and rice; and they spring up so well as no man could better it. Nor doth any know whence this flood cometh, but by the will of God; and if it were not, no good would come of the land, by reason of the great heat of the sun which would burn up everything, since it never raineth in that land. The stream is ever muddy; wherefore the country folk who would drink of it, take it towards evening, and crush therein four almonds or four beans; and in the morning it is as good to drink as may be.

Before the river cometh into Egypt, the folk who are accustomed so to do cast their nets loose into the stream in the evening; and when morning is come, they find in their nets such goods as are sold by weight as they bring from that country, that is ginger, rhubarb, *lignum aloes*, and cinnamon. And men say that these things come from the earthly Paradise; for the wind bloweth down the trees that are in Paradise, as the wind bloweth down dry wood in the forests of our land, and what dry wood falleth into the stream do the merchants in this land sell us. The water of the river is of such a kind that when we hanged it up to the ropes of our tents in pots of white earth that they make in that country, the water by the heat of the day became as cold as spring water.

They used to say in the land that the Sultan of Cairo had oftentimes striven to find whence the stream cometh; and he sent men who took with them a kind of bread that is called biscuit, for it is twice baked; and on this bread did they live until they came back to the Sultan. And they brought tidings to him that they had searched the stream and had come to a great cliff of sheer rock, where no man could climb. From this rock flowed the river; it seemed to them that there was abundance of trees at the top of the mountain; and they said that they had found marvels of all manner of wild beasts and of divers sorts, lions, serpents, and elephants, that came to look at them from above the river as they went upstream.

Now come we back to our first matter, and say that when the stream reacheth Egypt it throweth out seven branches, as I have said before. One branch goeth to Damietta,

BOOK TWO

another to Alexandria, a third to Tanis, and a fourth to Daraksa. And to this branch which goeth to Daraksa came the King of France with his host, and encamped between the stream of Damietta and that of Daraksa; and all the force of the Sultan encamped on the stream of Daraksa on the other side, before the host, to defend the crossing from us; which thing was easy for them to do, for no man could cross that water before them unless we passed over swimming.

XLI

THE King was of opinion that he should have a causeway made over the river to cross over to the Saracens. To guard those who laboured at the causeway, the King had two towers called *Chatschâtels* made; for there were two turrets or *châtels* before the *chats* or covered ways and two shelters behind the turrets, to give cover to those that kept watch from the stones of the engines of the Saracens, who had sixteen engines trained upon them. When we were come thither, the King caused eight engines of war to be made, of which Jocelyn of Cornaut was the master engineer. Our engines shot at theirs and theirs at ours, but I never heard that ours achieved great things. The King's brethren kept watch by day, and we, the other knights, guarded the covered ways by night. So we came to the week before Christmas.

When the covered ways were finished, they began to make the causeway, for the King did not desire that the Saracens who used to shoot at us, aiming across the river, should wound those that were bearing earth. In making this causeway were the King and all the host as men blinded; but since they had stopped one of the branches of the river, as I have told you before (which they did easily because it lent itself to being dammed where it left the great stream) so likewise did they think to stop the Daraksa stream, which had left the great river a good half-league upstream. To hinder the causeway which the King was making, the Saracens made pits in the earth before their camp; and so soon as the river reached the holes, the water beat down the holes and made a great channel anew. Thus it befell that all that we had done in three weeks did they undo in a day, since for all that we dammed the river before us, they widened it behind by the pits that they had digged.

In place of the Sultan that was dead, of the sickness that he caught before the city of Hama, they had made their chieftain a Saracen that was called Fa<u>kh</u>ru-d-dīn, son of the sheik. Men said that the Emperor Frederick had knighted him. This man sent word to a part of his army that they should go assail our host on the side of Damietta, and this they did; for they crossed at a town which is on the Daraksa stream, called <u>Sh</u>armisa.

25 December 1249 On Christmas Day I and my knights did eat with my lord Peter of Avallon; while we ate they came, setting spur to their horses, as far as our camp and slew many poor folk that had gone into the fields on foot. We went to don our armour. We could not get back soon enough to find my lord Peter, our host, who was outside the camp, whither he had gone after the Saracens. We spurred after him and rescued him from the Saracens, who had borne him to the ground; and him and his brother, the lord of Le Val, did we bring back into the camp. The Templars, who had come up at the clamour, kept the rearguard bravely and well. The Turks came harrying us even into the camp; wherefore the King ordered that the camp should be enclosed on the side of Damietta, from the Damietta stream to the Daraksa stream.

BOOK TWO

XLII

FAKHRU-D-DĪN, whereof I have told you ere this, the chieftain of the Turks, was the man most esteemed of all the paynim. On his banner be bare the arms of the Emperor that had knighted him. His banner was impaled; on one pale were the arms of the Emperor that had knighted him; on the next were the arms of the Sultan of Aleppo, and in the last pale were those of the Sultan of Cairo.

His name was Fakhru-d-dīn, son of the sheikh; which is as much as to say 'the old man son of the old man'. This name do they hold a very great thing in paynim lands; for they are the people in the world who most honour old folk, if it so be that God hath kept them from base reproach even to old age. Fakhru-d-dīn, this valiant Turk, as the King's spies brought word, boasted that he would eat on the feast of St. Sebastian in the pavilions of the King.

The King, who knew these things, arrayed his host in such wise that the Count of Artois, his brother, should guard the covered ways and the engines of war; the King and the Count of Anjou, that was afterwards King of Sicily, were set to guard the camp on the side of Cairo; and the Count of Poitiers and we of Champagne were to guard the camp on the side of Damietta. Now it befell that the Prince of the Turks before named made his people cross to the island that lieth between the stream of Damietta and the stream of Daraksa, where our army lay; and he arrayed his squadrons from one stream across to the other.

Against these came the company of the King of Sicily and discomfited them. Many were drowned in one stream or the other; nevertheless there was left of them the main body against whom none dared gather, for the engines of the Saracens were throwing across the two streams. In the attack that the King of Sicily made on the Turks, Count Guy of Forez pierced through the army of the Turks on horseback, and he and his knights attacked a body of Saracen foot-soldiers who bare him to the earth; and he brake his leg, and two of his knights brought him back in their arms. With great ado did they draw the King of Sicily out of the peril in which he was, and much was he esteemed for that day's work.

The Turks came against the Count of Poitiers and us, and we rode out against them and drove them a long way; and of their folk were some killed, and we came back without loss.

XLIII

ONE evening it happened as we were keeping the night watch over the turrets of the covered ways that they brought up against us an engine that is called a Fowler, which they had not yet done, and put Greek fire into the sling of the engine. When my lord Walter of Écurey, the good old knight that was with me, saw this, he spake to us thus:

'Lords, we are in the greatest danger that ever we have been in; for if they burn our turrets and we abide, we are lost and burned; and if we leave our defences which have been given to us to guard, we are dishonoured; wherefore no man can save us from this peril but God. So I advise and counsel that so often as they throw fire against us, that we get to our elbows and knees and pray to Our Lord to save us from this peril.'

So soon as they threw the first cast at us, we gat ourselves to our elbows and knees as he had instructed us. The first casts that they threw came between our two turrets, and fell in that part before us which the host had made to stop up the river. Our slakers were ready to quench the fire; and since the Saracens could not aim at them because of the two wings of the shelters that the King had caused to be made, they aimed straight at the sky, so that the darts fell straight down upon them.

The fashion of Greek fire was such that it came out as big as a barrel of verjuice, and the tail of the fire that came from it was as big as a great lance. It made so great a noise as it came that it seemed that it was thunder from heaven; it seemed as a dragon that flew through the air. So great a light did it cast that we saw as clear over the camps as if it had been day, for the abundance of fire that cast such light. Thrice did they hurl Greek fire against us that night, and four times did they shoot it from the swivel crossbow.

Each time that our saintly King heard that they cast Greek fire at us, he arose in his bed and stretched out his hands to Our Lord and said weeping: 'Fair Lord God, guard me my folk!' And truly do I believe that his prayers succoured us in our need. At night, each time that the fire fell, he sent one of his chamberlains to us to know in what case we were, and whether the fire had done us any hurt.

Once that they cast at us, it fell beside the turret that the people of my lord of Courtenay guarded and struck the bank of the river. Then behold a knight that was called him of Albi: 'Sir,' said he to me, 'unless ye help us, we burn; for the Saracens have shot so many fiery bolts that there is as it were a hedge that cometh burning towards our turret.' We leapt forth and went thither and found he spake true. We quenched the fire and ere we had put it out the Saracens assailed us with darts that they shot from across the stream.

XLIV

THE King's brothers kept watch over the guard towers by day, and climbed into the top of the turrets to shoot bolts on the Saracens from crossbows, to fall into the Saracens' camp. Now the King had so ordered it that when the King of Sicily kept watch in the towers by day, we should watch them by night. This day the King of Sicily had the day watch and we were to have the night watch; and we were in great trouble of mind for the Saracens had broken in our towers. The Saracens brought up the engine in full daylight, which ere this they had never done but by night, and hurled Greek fire at our towers.

Their engine had they brought so close to the causeway which the army had made to stop up the stream, that no man dared go to the towers, because of the engine that hurled great stones that fell in the path. Whence it befell that our two towers were burned; wherefore the King of Sicily was so far beside himself that he wished to go in person to strike at the fire to quench it; and, though he was angered, I and my knights gave thanks to God, for had we been on guard that night we should all have been burned.

When the King saw this, he sent to fetch all the barons of the host and besought that each should give him of the boards of his ships to make a covered way to stop up the river; and he showed them so that they saw well that there was no wood whereof it could be made, unless it were of the boards of the ships that brought our gear upstream. They gave each as much as he would; and when the covered ways were made, the timber was appraised at five thousand crowns and more.

The King decided likewise that they should not push the covered way forward on to the causeway until the day came that it was the turn of the King of Sicily to keep watch, to make good the misadventure that had befallen the other towers that were burned during his watch. As it had been ordered, so was it done; for so soon as the King of Sicily was come on watch, he had the covered way pushed forward as far as the place where the other two towers had been burned.

When the Saracens saw this, they arranged that all their sixteen engines of war should cast upon the causeway, where the covered way now was. And when they saw that our men feared to go into the covered way, because of the stones from the engines which fell upon the causeway on which the covered way had been taken, they brought up the Fowler and cast Greek fire at the way and burned it all. This great courtesy did God show to me and to my knights; for we should that night have kept watch in great jeopardy, as we should have done on that other watch, as I have told you ere now.

XLV

WHEN the King saw this, he summoned all his barons to hold council. Then they agreed together that they were not able to make a causeway by which they could pass over towards the Saracens, since our men could not dam up the stream as much on their side as the others could widen it on theirs.

Then the Constable, my lord Imbert of Beaujeu, told the King that a Bedouin had come, who had told him that he would show them a good ford, but on condition that they give him five hundred besants. The King said that he would agree that they should give them, but that the Bedouin must prove the truth of what he promised. The Constable spake of this with the Bedouin, and he said that never would he show the ford save after they had given him the besants. It was agreed that they should hand them over, and given they were.

The King arranged that the Duke of Burgundy and the rich men from oversea that were in the host should keep watch over the camp, so that no man should do it harm; and that the King and his three brethren should cross by the ford that the Bedouin was to show them. This thing was undertaken and planned for the Shrove Tuesday, on which day we came to the Bedouin's ford. So soon as the dawn appeared, we drew together from every side and when we were arrayed, we went to the stream and set our horses to swim. When we were come into the midst of the stream, we found land on which our horses took their footing; and on the river bank we found full three hundred Saracens all mounted on horseback.

8 February 1250

Then said I to my people: 'My lords, look only to the left hand and in no wise to the right, so that each may tend thither, for the banks are wet, and the horses are falling upon men and are drowning them.' And true is it that there were men drowned at the crossing, and among others was drowned my lord John of Orleans, that bore a banner *vivrie*. We arrayed ourselves in such wise that we turned upstream against the water, and found the way clear; and crossed in such wise, by the mercy of God, that none of us ever fell; and so soon as we had crossed, the Turks took to flight.

Orders had been given that the Templars should have the vanguard and that the Count of Artois should lead the second squadron after the Templars. Now it befell that so soon as the Count of Artois had crossed the stream, he and all his people assailed the Turks that fled before them. The Templars sent word that he treated them very scurvily, when he was to have gone after them and not before; and they begged him to let them go first, as had been agreed by the King. Now it so befell that the Count

PLATE 3

ST. THEODORE AS A CRUSADER
CHARTRES CATHEDRAL
(*Phot. Giraudon*)

of Artois did not dare answer them, because of my lord Foucauld of Le Merle, that held his bridle; and this Foucauld of Le Merle, who was a very good old knight, heard naught that the Templars said to the Count, for he was deaf; and cried 'At them! Now at them!'
When the Templars saw this, they bethought themselves that they would be dishonoured if they let the Count of Artois go before them; so they set spur to their horses, every man with all his might, and gave chase to the Turks who fled before them right through the city of Mansourah and into the fields beyond towards Cairo. When they thought to turn back, the Turks cast beams and boards into the streets, which were strait. There did the Count of Artois meet his death, and the Lord of Couci that was called Raoul, and as many other knights as was reckoned at three hundred. The Templars, as the Master has told me since, lost there fourteen score armed men, and all mounted.

XLVI

I AND my knights agreed that we should go and set upon several Turks that were bearing their gear to the left hand in their camp, and we set upon them. And as we chased them through the camp, my eye lighted upon a Saracen that was mounting his horse, and one of his knights held the bridle.
Even as he laid his two hands upon the saddle to mount, I struck him with my lance below the armpit and laid him dead; and when his knight saw this, he left his lord and his horse, and stayed me as I passed with his blade between my shoulders, and couched me down on the neck of my horse and held me so squeezed that I could not draw the sword which I had at my girdle. So I had to draw the sword that was at my saddle-bow; and

when he saw that I had my sword drawn, he withdrew his lance and left me.

When I and my knights came out of the Saracens' camp, we found full six thousand Turks, at a guess, who had left their lodgings and taken to the fields. When they saw us, they made at us, and slew my lord Hugh of Trichâtel, Lord of Conflans, who was banneret with me. I and my knights set spur to our horses and went to the rescue of my lord Raoul of Wanou, who was with me, whom they had borne to the ground.

While I was coming back thence, the Turks bare down upon me with their lances; my horse was brought to its knees by the weight, and I went over the horse's ears. And I got up as quickly as I might, shield at neck and sword in hand; and my lord Everard of Siverey (whom God assoil) who was with me, came to me and said that we should betake ourselves nigh to a ruined house, and there await the coming of the King. And as we went, a great rout of Turks on foot and on horseback came to strike at us, and bare me to the ground and went over me and tore off the shield from my neck.

And when they had passed on, my lord Everard of Siverey came back to me, and led me away and we went as far as the walls of the ruined house; and thither there came back to us my lord Hugh of Écot, my lord Frederick of Loupey, and my lord Renaud of Menoncourt. Here the Turks assailed us from every side; a party of them went into the ruined house, and pricked us with their lances from above. Then my knights told me to take their bridles; and so I did, that the horses should not run away. And they defended themselves vigorously from the Turks: wherefore they were praised by all the men of worth in the host, both by those that saw the deed and by those that heard tell of it.

There was my lord Hugh of Écot wounded by three

lances in the face, and my lord Raoul, and my lord Frederick of Loupey by a lance between the shoulders; and the wound was so great that the blood gushed from his body as from the stopple of a cask. My lord Everard of Siverey was struck by a sword across his face, so that his nose fell over upon his lip. And then my Lord Saint James came to my mind, to whom I prayed: 'Fair Lord Saint James, help me and succour me in this need.'

So soon as I had made my prayer, my lord Everard of Siverey said to me, 'Sir, if ye think that neither I nor my heirs will be held to blame, I will go to seek aid for you from the Count of Anjou, whom I see yonder in the fields.' And I said to him: 'My lord Everard, meseemeth that ye will do yourself great honour if ye go to seek us aid to save our lives, for your own is likewise in jeopardy.' And indeed I spake truth; for he died of that wound. He asked counsel of all our knights that were there, and all advised him as I had advised; and when he heard this, he asked me to let go his horse, that I held by the bridle with the others; and so I did.

To the Count of Anjou came he, and asked him to come succour me and my knights. A rich man, that was with him, would have dissuaded him, but the Count of Anjou told him that he would do as my knight asked; he reined about to come to our aid and many of his sergeants set spur to their horses. When the Saracens saw them, they left us. Before these sergeants rode my lord Peter of Auberive, sword in hand; and when he saw that the Saracens had left us, he charged straight at the Saracens that held my lord Raoul of Wanou, and brought him off sorely wounded.

XLVII

WHERE I was on foot, and my knights, as sorely wounded as is before told, thither came the King with all his squadron with a great stir and a great noise of trumpets and drums; and came to a halt on a raised causeway. Never did I see so goodly an armed knight; for he appeared above all his men from the shoulders up, a gilded helmet on his head, and a sword of Allemaine in his hand.

When he had halted there, his trusty knights that he had in his squadron, whom I have named to you ere now, charged against the Turks, and many of the valiant knights that were in the King's squadron with them. And know ye that this was a very fair feat of arms: for none shot with the bow or the crossbow, but the strife was all with maces and swords between the Turks and our folk, who were all melled together. One of my squires who had escaped with my banner and had come back to me, gave me a Flemish charger of mine on which I mounted, and betook me toward the King, side by side.

As we stood thus, my lord John of Valery, the noble knight, came to the King, and told him that his counsel was that he should bear to the right hand above the stream to have the aid of the Duke of Burgundy and the others who were guarding the camp that we had left, and so that his foot-soldiers should have drink, for the heat was already great.

The King commanded his sergeants to go fetch his good knights, that he had round him in his council; and named them all by their names. The sergeants went to seek them in the battle, where great was the contention betwixt them and the Turks. They came to the King, and he asked their advice; and they told him that my lord John of Valery gave him good counsel; and then the King bade the standard of Saint Denis and his banners to bear towards the right over by the stream. At the moving forward of the King's host was there again great noise of trumpets, drums, and Saracen horns.

Hardly had he set out ere several messengers came from the Count of Poitiers his brother, the Count of Flanders, and several other great men who there had their squadrons, that all besought him not to move; for they were so hard pressed by the Turks that they could not follow. The King called back all the noble knights of his council, and all advised him to wait; and a little after my lord John of Valery came back, who blamed the King and his council that they tarried. After this all his counsellors advised that he should bear off towards the river as my lord John of Valery had counselled him.

At this instant the Constable my lord Imbert of Beaujeu came to him, and told him that the Count of Artois his brother was defending himself in a house in Mansourah, and that he should go to his succour. And the King said to him, 'Constable, go ye first and I will follow you.' And I told the Constable that I would be his knight, and he thanked me much. We set ourselves on the road to go to Mansourah.

Then there came to the Constable a sergeant of the mace, all afeared, and told him that the King was stayed, and the Turks had set themselves betwixt him and us. We turned, and saw that there were a full thousand of them and more between him and us; and we were but six. Then said I to the Constable, 'Sir, we are not able to get to the King through these men; but let us go upstream, and set this ditch which ye see before you between us and them, that so may we get back to the King.' And as I advised, so did the Constable. And know ye that if the enemy had heeded us, they could have had us all dead; but their thought was only of the King and the other great squadrons; whereby they believed that we were of their folk.

XLVIII

AS we made our way back downstream above the river, between the brook and the stream, we saw that the King was come to the river, and that the Turks were driving the other squadrons of the King thither, striking and fighting with swords and maces, and were pressing all the other squadrons and the King's squadron upon the river. Then was the discomfiture so great that many of our people thought to cross back by swimming towards the Duke of Burgundy; the which they could not do, for the horses were weary and the day hot, so that we saw as we came downstream the river covered with lances and shields, and horses and men that drowned and perished.

We came to a little bridge which was over the brook, and I told the Constable that we should stay to guard this bridge; 'For if we leave it, they will charge upon the King from hence, and if our people be assailed from both sides, they may well be defeated.' And so we did. And they said that we should all have been lost that day, had not the King been there in person. For the lord of Courtenay and my lord John of Saillenay recounted to me that six Turks reached the King's bridle and were taking him away captive, and that he freed himself by the great blows that he gave them with his sword. And when his men saw that the King was defending himself, they took heart, and many of them gave up the crossing of the river and turned towards the King to bear him aid. Straight to us who were guarding the bridge came Count Peter of Brittany, who was riding directly from Mansourah and was wounded by a sword-cut in the face, so that the blood ran into his mouth. He sat on a sturdy horse; he had thrown the reins on the saddle-bow and held it with his two hands, so that his people who were behind him and pressed close upon him, should not thrust him from the path. It appeared that he esteemed them little, for when he had spat the blood out of his mouth, he said several times, 'Look! By God's head, have ye ever seen such scoundrels?' At the tail of his host came the Count of Soissons and my lord Peter of Neuville who was called Caier, who had suffered blows enough that day.

When they had crossed and the Turks saw that we were guarding the bridge, and had turned our faces towards them, they let them go. I went to the Count of Soissons, whose cousin german I had married, and said to him, 'Sir, I think ye would do well if ye were to stay to guard this bridge; for if we leave the bridge, those Turks that ye see there before you, will forthwith make their way over it, and so will the King be attacked both before and behind.' And he asked, if I would stay if he stayed; and I answered, 'Certes aye,' and when he heard this, he told me not to quit that place until he came back, and he would go seek us aid.

XLIX

THERE stayed I on my charger, and the Count of Soissons kept with me to the right, and my lord Peter of Neuville on the left. Soon, behold a Turk that came from the direction of the King's squadron, which was behind us; and he struck my lord Peter of Neuville from behind with his mace, and beat him down on to the neck of his horse with the blow that he gave him, and then made over the bridge and dashed into the midst of his own people. When the Turks saw that we would not leave the bridge, they crossed the brook and set themselves between the brook and the river, as we had done coming downstream; and we bore off towards them in such wise that we were all ready to charge, whether they wished to pass towards the King or to cross the bridge.

Before us there were two of the King's sergeants, of whom one was called William of Boon and the other John of Gamaches, at whom the Turks who were come between the river and the brook sent any number of peasants on foot, that cast clods of earth at them, but could never force them back on us. At last they brought up a peasant on foot who thrice cast Greek fire at them. Once William of Boon took the pot of Greek fire on his targe; for if aught upon him had caught alight, he must have been burned to death.

We were all covered with the bolts that missed the sergeants. Now it chanced that I found a long quilted footsoldier's coat belonging to a Saracen, lined with tow; I turned the slit towards me, and made a shield of the coat, which did me good service; for I was only wounded by their bolts in five places, and my charger in fifteen. Now it befell also that a burgher of mine from Joinville brought me a banner of mine arms with a lance-head, and each time that we saw that they pressed upon the sergeants, we made at them and they fled.

The good old Count of Soissons, in this plight in which we were, jested with me and said; 'Seneschal, let us let these curs yelp; for by God's bonnet (for so he was wont to swear) we shall yet speak of this day, you and I, in ladies' chambers.'

BOOK TWO

L

THAT night at sunset the Constable brought to us the King's dismounted crossbowmen, and they arrayed themselves before us; and when the Saracens saw them set their feet in the footholds of the crossbows, they took to flight and left us. Then said the Constable to me, 'Seneschal, that was well done; now get ye to the King, and leave him not this day until he be back again in his pavilion.' So soon as I was come to the King, my lord John of Valery came to him and said, 'Sir, my lord of Châtillon beseeches you to give him the rearguard.' And the King did so right willingly, and then set out upon his road. As we went thence, I made him doff his helmet and gave him my iron cap to have the air.

And then came to him brother Henry of Ronnay, Provost of the Hospitallers, that had come across the river, and kissed his mailed hand. And the King asked him if he had any news of the Count of Artois his brother, and he told him that he had news for sure, for it was certain that his brother the Count of Artois was in Paradise: 'Aye, Sir,' said the Provost, 'ye may take comfort thereat; for such great honour came never before to a King of France as hath come to you. For to give battle to your enemies have ye crossed a river by swimming, and have discomfited them and driven them from the camp, and taken their engines of war and their lodging where ye shall lie this night.' And the King answered that God be praised for all that He had given him; and then great tears dropped from his eyes.

When we were come to the camp, we found that Saracens on foot were pulling at the cords of a tent that they had let down, on one side, and our people of the meaner sort were pulling on the other. We charged at them, the Master of the Temple and I, and they took to flight and the tent remained with our folk.

In this battle there were many people, men of great pretensions, that took to flight most shamefully, making their escape over the little bridge of which I have told you, and flying in affright; and never a one could we keep to stay by us; of whom could I name many, but forbear, for they be dead. But concerning my lord Guy Mauvoisin will I not forbear, for he came out from Mansourah with honour. And all the way that I and the Constable went upstream, he came downstream. And as the Turks pressed upon the Count of Brittany and his host, so did they press also upon my lord Guy Mauvoisin and his host, who earned much praise, he and his folk, this day. And it was no marvel if he and his men approved themselves well this day; for they told me, they that well knew his pack, that all his squadron, or all but a few, was of knights of his lineage and of knights who were his liegemen.

When we had discomfited the Turks and driven them from their lodgings, and none of our folk were left in the camp, the Bedouins attacked the tents of the Saracens, that were great folk. Naught in the world did they leave in the Saracens' camp, but took everything that the Saracens had left; nor did I ever hear that the Bedouins, who are subject to the Saracens, were less considered for anything that they had taken or robbed, because such is their custom and wont, that they ever assail the weakest.

LI

SINCE it pertaineth to my tale, I will tell you what folk are the Bedouins. The Bedouins do not believe in Mahomet, but believe in the law of Ali, that was uncle to Mahomet; and likewise the Old Men of the

Mountain believe therein, that sustain the Assassins. And they hold that when a man dieth for his lord or in any good intent, his soul goeth into a better body and of better estate than before; and therefore the Assassins do not trouble overmuch should they be slain when fulfilling the orders of the Old Man of the Mountain. Concerning the Old Man of the Mountain will we now hold our peace, and speak of the Bedouins.

The Bedouins dwell neither in towns nor in cities nor in castles, but sleep always in the fields; and their households, their wives and their children are established at evening for the night, or for the day when the weather is foul, in a kind of shelter which they make of barrel hoops bound to poles, like ladies' litters; and over these hoops they throw sheepskins which are called Damascus hides, cured with alum; the Bedouins themselves wear great pelisses of them which cover all their bodies, their legs and feet.

When it raineth at night and the weather is foul, they enfold themselves in their pelisses, and take off the bridles of their horses and let them feed near by. When morning cometh they spread out their pelisses in the sun and rub them and beat them; and thereafter is there naught to show that they have been wet in the night. Their faith is this, that no man can die but on the appointed day, wherefore they will not wear armour; and when they curse their children, they say to them, 'Mayst thou be cursed, like the Frank who wears armour for fear of death!' In battle they bear naught but sword and lance.

Nearly all are dressed in surplices, like priests; their heads are wound about with cloths, which go under their chins; wherefore are they ugly folk and hideous to look upon, for the hair of their heads and of their beards is quite black. They live on the milk of their beasts, and buy pasturage in the plain-lands of rich men, whereon their beasts feed. The number of them no man can tell; for they are found in the Kingdom of Jerusalem and in all the other lands of the Saracens and of the misbelievers, to whom they pay great tolls each year.

I have seen in this country, after I came back from oversea, certain unfaithful Christians who kept the Bedouin law, and said that no man could die before his time; and their faith is so disloyal that it is as much as to say that God hath no power to help us. For they would be fools that were to serve God, did we not believe that He had power to lengthen our lives and keep us from evil and mischance; and in Him should we believe, for He hath power to do all things.

LII

9 February 1250

NOW will we tell how at nightfall we came back from the perilous battle before told, we and the King, and we lodged in the place whence we had driven our enemies. My people who had stayed in the host whence we had gone, brought me a tent that the Templars had given me and pitched it for me in front of the engines which we had taken from the Saracens; and the King set a guard of foot-soldiers over the engines. When I had gone to my bed, wherein I had great need to rest for the wounds that I had received the day before, it did not so befall, for ere it was fully day, they cried in our camp 'To arms! To arms!' I waked my chamberlain that lay at the foot of my bed, and bade him go see what it was. And he came back altogether dismayed, and told me: 'Up, Sir, up! For here are the Saracens come on foot and on horseback and have discomfited the King's soldiers that were guarding the engines, and driven them among our tent-ropes.'

I arose and threw a quilted coat on my back and a steel cap

BOOK TWO

on my head and cried to our soldiers: 'By St. Nicholas! They shall not stay here.' My knights came to me, sore wounded as they were, and we beat off the Saracen foot-men from the engines as far as a great squadron of mounted Turks, that were level with the engines that we had taken. I sent word to the King that he should aid us, for I and my knights were not able to don coats of mail by reason of the wounds we had received; and the King sent us my lord Walter of Châtillon who set himself between us and the Turks that were before us.

When the Lord of Châtillon had driven back the Saracen foot-soldiers, they retreated towards a great squadron of Turks on horseback, that were arrayed before our camp to keep watch lest we surprised the Saracen host which was encamped behind them. From this squadron of Turks had dismounted eight of their chieftains, in fine armour, who had made a shelter of worked stone, so that our crossbowmen should not hit them; these eight Saracens shot at a venture into our camp, and wounded several of our men and horses.

I and my knights put our heads together and agreed that when night had fallen, we would carry off the stones behind which they sheltered. A priest of mine, that was called Sir John of Voisey, was at this council, but did not tarry so long; but went from our camp all alone, and made towards the Saracens, armed in his gambeson, his steel cap on his head, and his lance, point to the ground, trailing under his armpit so that the Saracens should not notice it.

When he came close to the Saracens, who took no heed of him because they saw that he was alone, he drew his lance from under his arm and charged at them. Not a man of the eight put up a defence, but all turned and took to flight. When the horsemen saw that their lords were fleeing, they set spurs to their horses to rescue them and as many as fifty foot-soldiers sallied out of our camp; and the horsemen came spurring on and durst not assault our foot-men, but swerved away from them.

When they had done this twice or thrice, one of our foot-soldiers took his spear by the midst and hurled it at one of the Turks on horseback, and it struck him between the ribs; and he that was struck by the spear bare it away, trailing, with the blade between his ribs. When the Turks saw this, they durst not attack and retreat more, and our foot-soldiers bare off the stones. Henceforth was the priest well known in the host, and men pointed him out one to the other and said, 'Look, there goeth the priest of my lord of Joinville, who discomfited the eight Saracens.'

LIII

9 February 1250 — THESE things befell on the first day of Lent. That very day a valiant Saracen, whom our enemies had made chieftain in the stead of Fakhru-d-Dīn, Son of the Sheikh, whom they had lost in the battle on Shrove Tuesday, took the coat of the Count of Artois that was slain in the battle, and showed it to all the people of the Saracens, and said it was the coat of arms of the King, who was dead.

'These things I show you because a body without a head is in no wise to be feared, nor a people without a King. Wherefore if it please you, we will make an assault upon them on Friday; and ye should agree to this, as I think; for we cannot fail but take them all, since they have lost their chieftain.' And all were of one mind that they should come and assail us on the Friday.

11 February 1250 — The King's spies that were in the host of the Saracens came to bring word of these tidings to the King. Then the King ordered all the chiefs of squadrons that they should have their men armed by midnight, and should lead them outside the pavilions as far as the stockade, which was made of long stakes so that the Saracens should not sally into the camp; and the stakes were driven into the ground in such wise that a man could pass betwixt them on foot. And as the King commanded so was it done.

At the moment of sunrise the Saracen aforesaid, whom they had made their chieftain, led against us full four thousand Turks on horseback and had them arrayed all round our camp, and about himself, from the stream that flowed from Cairo to the stream which went from our camp and flowed towards a town that is called Daraksa. When they had done this, he brought against us such great plenty of Saracens on foot as surrounded all our camp, as had the horsemen before. After these two hosts that I have told, they arrayed all the forces of the Sultan of Cairo, to lend them aid if need be.

When they had done this, the chieftain came by himself on a little stallion to see the array of our host; and as he saw that our squadrons were thicker in one place than in another, he went back to send for more of his people and strengthened his squadrons against ours. After this, he caused the Bedouins, of whom there were at least three thousand, to cross towards the camp that the Duke of Burgundy guarded, which was betwixt the two rivers. And this he did because he believed that the King would send some of his men to the Duke to lend him aid against the Bedouins whereby the King's host would have been that much the weaker.

LIV

IT took him till midday to arrange all these matters; and then he caused the drums that are called *nakirs* to be sounded and then they charged upon us, horse and foot. First of all I will tell you of the King of Sicily (then Count of Anjou), for he was the first on the side towards Cairo. They came at him in the fashion of men playing chess; for they charged him first with footmen (like pawns) so that the men on foot could cast Greek fire at him. And they pressed so hard upon him, horse and foot, that they discomfited the King of Sicily that was among his knights on foot.

And men came to the King and told him of the plight in which his brother was. When he heard this, he spurred through his brother's squadrons, sword in hand, and struck so far forward among the Turks that they set the crupper of his horse alight with Greek fire. And by this sally that the King made, he succoured the King of Sicily and his men, and drove away the Turks from their squadron.

After the host of the King of Sicily came the squadron of the barons from oversea, of whom my lord Guy of Ibelin and my lord Baldwin, his brother, were chieftains. After their squadron came the host of my lord Walter of Châtillon, full of men of worth and fine chivalry. These two squadrons defended themselves with such vigour that never could the Turks break them or drive them back.

After my lord Walter's squadron came Brother William of Sonnac, Master of the Temple, with such few of his brethren as remained to him after the Tuesday's battle. He had caused a fence to be reared in front of the Saracen's engines that we had taken. When the Saracens attacked, they cast Greek fire against the hoarding that they had set up; and the fire took quickly, for the Templars had put great quantity of deal boards therein. And know ye that the Turks did not wait for the fire to be burnt out, but charged the Templars through the burning flame.

And in this battle Brother William, the Master of the Temple, lost an eye; and the other had he lost on Shrove Tuesday; and the said lord (whom God assoil) died thereof. And know ye that there was a furlong of land behind the Templars which was so charged with bolts that the Saracens had shot at them, that the earth was not to be seen for the foison of bolts.

After the host of the Temple came the squadron of my lord Guy Mauvoisin, which squadron the Turks could never vanquish; and yet it befell that the Turks so covered my lord Guy Mauvoisin with Greek fire that his men were hard put to quench it.

LV

FROM the squadron of my lord Guy Mauvoisin the stockade which enclosed our camp went down towards the river a good stone's-throw. Thence the stockade curved in front of the host of Count William of Flanders, and stretched as far as the stream running down to the sea. By the stockade that came from the side of my lord Guy Mauvoisin was our squadron; and since the squadron of Count William of Flanders was face to face with them, the enemy durst not come at us; wherein God showed us great courtesy; for I and my knights had neither coats of mail nor shields, since we had all been wounded in the battle of Shrove Tuesday.

They charged the Count of Flanders eagerly and vigorously with horse and foot. When I saw this, I bade our crossbowmen shoot at those on horseback. When the horsemen saw that they were being hit from our side,

THE HISTORY OF ST. LOUIS

they came near to flight; and when the Count's men saw this, they left the camp and thrust themselves over the stockade, and charged down on the Saracens on foot and discomfited them. There were many dead and many of their targes taken. There did Walter of La Horgne approve himself sturdily, that bare the banner of my lord of Apremont.

After the squadron of the Count of Flanders came the host of the Count of Poitiers, the King's brother; which host of the Count of Poitiers was on foot, and he alone was mounted; the which host the Turks discomfited altogether and took the Count of Poitiers prisoner. When the butchers and the other camp-followers and the women that sold food heard this, they raised the alarm in the camp and with the help of God they rescued the Count and drove the Turks out of the camp.

After the host of the Count of Poitiers came the squadron of my lord Josserand of Brancion, who had come with the Count to Egypt, one of the best knights that were in the host. He had so arrayed his men that all the knights were on foot; and he was on horseback, and his son my lord Henry, and the son of my lord Josserand of Nanton with him, and these he kept mounted because they were lads. Several times did the Turks get the better of his men. Each time that he saw his folk discomfited, he set spurs to his horse and attacked the Turks in the rear; wherefore time and again did the Turks leave his people in order to ride against him. Natheless this would not have availed much to keep the Turks from killing them on the field, if it had not been for my lord Henry of Cosne, who was in the host of the Duke of Burgundy, a wise knight, both brave and wary; and each time that he saw the Turks assailing my lord of Brancion, he had the King's crossbowmen shoot at the Turks across the stream. And so the lord of Brancion escaped from that day's evil pass, when of twenty knights that he had round him he lost twelve, without taking account of other men-at-arms; and he himself was so ill handled that never again did he stand on his feet, and died of this wound received in God's service.

I will tell you of the lord of Brancion. He had been, when he died, in thirty-six battles and hand-to-hand conflicts whence he had carried off the prize of arms. I saw him on a time in the host of the Count of Chalon, whose cousin he was; and he came up to me and my brother and said to us on a Good Friday: 'Nephews, come lend me your aid, ye and your men; for the Germans are breaking into the church.' We went with him and rode against them with swords drawn; and with great labour and great brawling drove them from the church. When this was done, the noble knight knelt before the altar, and gave thanks aloud to Our Lord and said: 'Lord, I pray Thee to take pity upon me, and keep me from these battles between Christians, in which I have spent great part of my life; and vouchsafe that I may die in Thy service, whereby I may come to Thy Kingdom in Paradise.' And these things have I recounted to you, because I believe that God vouchsafed it, as ye may have seen heretofore.

After the battle of the first Friday in Lent, the King sent for all his barons to come before him, and said to them: 'Great thanks do we owe to Our Lord for that he hath twice granted us glory in this week: that on Tuesday, the day of Shrovetide, we drove them from their camp where we are now lodged; and this last Friday, which is past, we defended ourselves against them, when we were on foot and they were mounted.' And many other fair sayings did he make to them to give them comfort.

LVI

SINCE it behoveth us to get on with our tale, we must interlace it somewhat to tell how the Sultans maintain their folk in order and array. And true is it that most of their horsemen used they to form from strangers, whom merchants took captive in strange lands to sell them; and they used to buy them gladly and dear. And these folk that they brought into Egypt they were wont to take in the East, because when one of the Kings of the East had discomfited another, he would take captive the poor folk whom he had conquered, and sell them to the merchants, and the merchants brought them to sell again in Egypt.

The matter was so ordered that the children, until their beards grew, were nurtured in the Sultan's house; in such wise that the Sultan had bows made befitting them according to their strength, and so soon as they were stronger, he threw back their weak bows into his arsenal, and the master bowyer gave them bows as strong as they could bend.

The Sultan's arms were *or*, and such arms as the Sultan bore were borne by these young folk; and they were called *baḥriyya* or men from oversea. When their beards were grown, the Sultan knighted them. And they used to bear the Sultan's arms, but with a difference: that is to say red charges, bends or roses *gules*, or birds, or other charges which they set upon the field *or* as it pleased them. And these folk that I tell you of were called the men of the Ḥalqa or guard, for the *baḥriyya* lay in the Sultan's tents. When the Sultan was encamped, the men of the Ḥalqa were lodged round the Sultan's lodging and appointed to guard the Sultan's person. At the door of the Sultan's lodging were housed the Sultan's porters in a little tent, and his minstrels, who had Saracen horns and drums and nakirs. And they made such a din at daybreak and nightfall that those that were near them could not make themselves heard; and they were clearly audible through all the host.

Nor would the minstrels have been bold enough to sound their instruments by day, unless it were by order of the Master of the *Ḥalqa*; wherefore it was that when the Sultan wished to make an assault, he would send for the Master of the *Ḥalqa* and give him his orders. And then the Master would have the Sultan's instruments sounded, and then all the host would gather together to hear the Sultan's commands; and the Master of the *Ḥalqa* would speak them aloud, and all the host would fulfil them.

When the Sultan went to war, he would make emirs of such of the knights of the *Ḥalqa* as approved themselves well in the battle, and hand over for their company two hundred knights or three hundred; and according as they excelled so did the Sultan give them more.

The prize of their chivalry is this: that, when they are doughty and rich beyond question, and the Sultan is afraid lest they kill or dispossess him, he hath them hanged and dead in his prison, and taketh from their widows all that they have. And these things did the Sultan do to them that took prisoner the Count of Montfort and the Count of Bar, and so did Baybars to them that vanquished the King of Armenia; for because they thought to have reward, they dismounted and came to salute him where he was hunting wild beasts. And he said to them: 'I salute you not', for they had disturbed him in the chase. And he had their heads cut off.

LVII

NOW let us come back to our tale and tell how that the Sultan that was dead had a son of twenty-five years of age, wise and notable and crafty; and since he feared that this son would dispossess him, he gave him a kingdom that he had in the East. As soon as the Sultan was dead, the Emirs sent for him; and so soon as he was come to Egypt, he deprived and took from his father's seneschal and constable and chamberlain their golden wands of office, and gave them to those that had come with him from Damascus. When they saw this, great was their despite thereat, and all the others that had been in the father's council, for the dishonour that he had done them. And since they feared that he would do to them as his father had done to those that had taken the Count of Bar and the Count of Montfort, as hath been told ere now, they so wrought on the men of the Ḥalqa before named (who should guard the King's person) that they convenanted with them that whensoever they asked they would slay them the Sultan.

LVIII

AFTER the two battles that I have told of, great ills came to the host; for at the end of nine days, the bodies of our men whom they had killed came to the surface of the water; and they said it was because the gall in them had rotted. They came floating as far as the bridge that was between our two camps and could not pass it, for the bridge touched the water. Such plenty of them was there that all the stream was full of dead men from one bank to the other, and lengthwise as far as a man might throw a small stone.

The King caused to be hired an hundred base fellows,

that were at it for eight days. The bodies of the Saracens, that were circumcised, they cast on the other side of the water and let them go downstream; and the Christians they laid in great pits, one with another. I saw there the chamberlains of the Count of Artois, and many others that sought their friends among the dead; but I heard of never a one that was found there.

We ate no fish in the camp all Lent but eels, and the eels used to feed upon the dead men, for they are gluttonous fish. And for this ill-hap, and for the unwholesomeness of the country wherein there never falleth a drop of rain, the sickness of the host came upon us, which was such that the flesh of our legs altogether dried up, and the skin of our legs became blotched with black and earth-colour, like to an old boot; and on us that had this sickness there grew rotten flesh upon our gums; nor did any man recover from this sickness, but he must come near to dying thereof. The sign of death was this, that when his nose bled, then a man must die.

A fortnight after, the Turks, to starve us out (whereat many men marvelled), took several of their galleys above the camp and had them dragged overland and put into the stream that cometh from Damietta, a good league below our camp. And these galleys brought us famine; for no man dare come to us upstream from Damietta to victual us because of the galleys. We had no news of these things until a little ship of the Count of Flanders escaped from them by the currents of the stream, and brought us word and told that the galleys of the Sultan had taken eighty of our galleys which had come from the side of Damietta, and had killed the men that were therein. Hence came such dearth in the camp that by the time Easter had come an ox was worth forty crowns *27 March* in the camp, and a sheep fifteen and a pig fifteen, and an *1250* egg twelve pence, and a measure of wine five crowns.

LIX

WHEN the King and the barons saw this, they agreed that the King should have his army pass towards Cairo into the camp of the Duke of Burgundy, which was on the stream that went to Damietta. To gather in his people more safely, the King had a barbican made before the bridge which was between our two camps, in such wise that a man could enter in at the barbican on either side on horseback.

When the barbican was ready, all the King's squadron took arms, and there was a great assault by the Turks upon the King's camp. Natheless the King would not give way, nor his men, until all the baggage had been carried over; and then the King crossed and his squadron after him, and all the other barons after but my lord Walter of Chatillon who kept the rearguard. And at the entry to the barbican, my lord Everard of Valery rescued my lord John his brother, whom the Turks were bearing away captive.

When all the host had come within, those that stayed in the barbican were in grievous plight, for the barbican was not high, so that the Turks shot at them level from their horses, and the Saracens on foot threw clods of earth in their faces. All was lost but for the Count of Anjou (who after was King of Sicily) that came to their rescue and led them away safely. In this day's work did my lord Geoffrey of Mussanbourc bear away the prize, the prize of all those that were in the barbican.

On the Eve of Shrove Tuesday I saw a marvel that I would tell you of; for that very day was my lord Hugh of Landricourt, that was banneret with me, laid to earth. There where he lay upon his bier in my chapel, were six of my knights resting upon sacks full of barley; and since they spake aloud in my chapel and annoyed the priest, I went to them and bade them hold their peace, and told them it was a churlish thing for knights and gentlemen to talk while mass was being sung. And they began to laugh at me, and told me laughing that they were finding another husband for his wife. And I upbraided them and told them that such speeches were neither good nor seemly and that they had soon forgotten their comrade. And God did such vengeance on them that the next day was the battle of Shrove Tuesday, wherein they were killed or wounded unto death; wherefore fresh husbands had to be found for their wives, all six of them.

LX

FROM the wounds that I received on Shrove Tuesday the sickness of the host laid hold on me, in the mouth and the legs, and a double tertian fever, and so great a rheum in my head that the rheum flowed out of my head by the nostrils; and for these said maladies I took to my bed sick at Mid-Lent, so that it befell that my priest sang Mass for me before my bed in my pavilion; and he had the sickness that I had. *6 March 1250*

Now it befell that at the Sacring he swooned. When I saw that he would fall, I who had on my coat leapt from my bed barefoot and took him in my arms and told him that he should do his sacring fair and softly, for I would not let go of him until he had done it all. He came to himself and did his sacring, and sang through his Mass to the end; nor did he ever sing again.

After these things the King's council and the council of the Sultan set a day to come to an agreement. The clauses of the treaty were that they should give back Damietta to the Sultan, and the Sultan should give up to the King the Kingdom of Jerusalem, and the Sultan should keep the sick folk that were at Damietta and the salted meats (for they were not wont to eat pork) and the King's engines of war until such time as the King could send back to fetch them.

They asked the King's council what surety they would give that they should have Damietta again. The King's council proffered that they should hold one of the King's brethren until they had Damietta back, either the Count of Anjou or the Count of Poitiers. The Saracens said that they would do naught unless the King in person was left them as hostage; whereat my lord Geoffrey of Sargines, the good old knight, said that he had liefer that the Saracens held them all dead or captive than that the reproach should be brought against them that they had left the King in pledge.

The sickness began to wax so grievous in the host that so much dead flesh swelled upon the gums of our men that the barbers had to cut it away before the men could chew their meat and swallow it. Pitiful was it to hear the men crying out through the camp from whom they were cutting the dead flesh; for they cried out like women labouring of child.

LXI

5 April 1250

WHEN the King saw that it lay not in his power to stay there unless it were for death, both for him and his men, he gave orders and arranged that he should shift camp on the Tuesday after the octave of Easter in the evening at nightfall, and go back to Damietta. He caused the shipmen that had the galleys to be told in what manner they should get together all the sick folk and take them to Damietta. The King commanded Jocelyn of Cornaut and his brethren and the other engineers that they were to cut the ropes which held the bridge between us and the Saracens; and none of it did they do.

We went aboard on the Tuesday after the midday meal, two of my knights that I had remaining, and my household. When night began to fall, I bade my sailors weigh anchor and take us downstream, and they said that they durst not because the galleys of the Sultan, that lay between us and Damietta, would destroy us. The sailors had made great flares to get the sick aboard the galleys, and the sick folk had crawled down to the bank of the river. As I besought the mariners to get us gone, the Saracens made their way into the camp; and I saw by the light of the flare that they were killing the sick men on the bank.

As they raised the anchor, the sailors that were to bring the sick, cut the ropes of their ships and came swiftly alongside our little vessel, and shut us in on one side and on the other, so that they all but sent us down to the bottom. When we were escaped from this peril and were going downstream, the King, who had the sickness of the host and a sore flux, might have been saved harmless on the galleys an he had been willing; but he said that if God willed he would never leave his people. That night he swooned more than once; and because of the sore flux that vexed him, they had to cut off the bottom of his breeches, each time that he went down to go to the privy.

They cried out to us who were out in the stream that we should await the King; and when we would not wait for him, they shot bolts at us; wherefore we had to wait until they gave us leave to float downstream.

LXII

NOW I will leave you here, and tell you as he himself told it to me, how the King was taken captive. He told me that he had left his own squadron and had put himself, him and my lord Geoffrey of Sargines, in the squadron of my lord Walter of Châtillon, that kept the rearguard.

And the King recounted to me that he was mounted on a little stallion, harnessed with a housing of silk; and he said that behind him there remained of all the knights and all the men-at-arms but my lord Geoffrey of Sargines, who brought the King to the village where he was taken; in such fashion that the King told me that my lord Geoffrey of Sargines defended him from the Saracens as a good servitor defendeth his master's goblet from the flies; for each time that the Saracens came near, he took his hunting-spear that he had fixed between himself and his saddle-bow, and set it under his arm, and charged at them and drove them from before the King.

And so he brought the King to the village; and they got him down into a house, and laid him in the lap of a burgher woman of Paris, like one dead, and thought that he would never live to see the night. Thither came my lord Philip of Montfort, and told the King that he had seen the Emir with whom he had treated concerning the truce; and that if he willed he would go to him to make truce again on the Saracens' terms. The King begged him to go and said that he was willing. He went to the Saracen; and the Saracen had taken off the turban from his head and the ring from his finger in pledge that he would keep the truce.

Meanwhile a great mischance befell our people; for a traitor man-at-arms, that was called Marcel, began to cry to our men, 'Sir knights, give yourselves up, for so the

King biddeth; and cause not the King to be slain!' All thought that the King so bade them, and gave up their swords to the Saracens. The Emir saw that the Saracens were bringing in our men captive. The Emir told my lord Philip that it did not beseem him to give a truce to our men, for he saw clearly that they were taken.

Now it thus befell my lord Philip that all our men were taken prisoner and that he was not, because he was an envoy. But there is another evil custom in the country of the paynim, that when a King sendeth envoys to the Sultan or the Sultan to a King, and the King dieth or the Sultan before the envoys return, then are the envoys prisoners and slaves, on whichever side they be, whether Christian or Saracen.

LXIII

WHEN this mischance befell our people, that they were taken prisoners on land, it likewise befell that we were taken captive on the water, as ye shall hear hereafter; for the wind came to us from towards Damietta, which deprived us of the current of the stream; and the knights whom the King had set in his smaller vessels to defend the sick, took to flight. Our shipmen lost the channel of the river and got into a creek, whence we had to turn back towards the Saracens.

We who were going by water got a little before day brake to the strait where the Sultan's galleys were, which had cut us off from victuals coming from Damietta. There were we well harried, for they shot at us and at our men who were on the river bank on horseback such foison of bolts tipped with Greek fire as made it seem that the stars were falling out of heaven.

When our sailors had brought us back out of the creek

wherein they had driven us, we found the King's boats, which the King had given us to defend our sick folk, making their way in flight towards Damietta. Then arose a wind from the side of Damietta, so strong that it took away the force of the current. On the one bank of the river and the other was there great plenty of small vessels of our people's which could not get downstream, which the Saracens had stopped and taken; and they slew the men and threw them into the water and dragged off the chests and baggage from the ships that they had taken from our folk. The Saracens that were on horseback on the bank shot bolts at us, so that we should not go to attack them. My men had arrayed me in a tourneying coat of mail, so that the bolts which fell in our vessel should not do me hurt.

At this moment my men that were on the prow of the vessel downstream, cried out to me, 'Sir, Sir, your sailors, because the Saracens threaten them, wish to take you to land.' I had myself lifted up in their arms, weak as I was, and drew my sword against them, and said that I would kill them if they took me to land. And they answered that I might have my choice: either they would take me to the land, or they would anchor me in midstream until such time as the wind fell. And I told them that I had liefer have them anchor me in midstream than that they should take me to land where I saw our slaughter plain; and they anchored.

It was not long ere we saw four of the Sultan's galleys coming, in which there were fully a thousand men. Then I called my knights and my men, and asked them what they would have us do, whether to give ourselves up to the Sultan's galleys or give ourselves up to those that were on land. We all agreed that we would liefer yield to the Sultan's galleys, because they would hold us prisoner all together, than that we should give ourselves up to those that were on land, because they would scatter us and sell us to the Bedouins.

Then spake a cellarer of mine, that was born at Doulevant, 'Sir, I do not agree to this counsel.' I asked him to what he agreed, and he said: 'I am of opinion that we should let ourselves all be killed, for then we should all go hence to Paradise.' But we took no heed of him.

LXIV

WHEN I saw that it must be that we should be taken prisoner, I took my casket and my jewels and cast them into the stream, and my relics likewise. Then one of the sailors said to me, 'Sir, unless ye give me leave to say that ye be a cousin of the King, they will kill you and us with you.' And I said that I was willing for him to say what he would. When the men in the first galley, which came towards us to strike our vessel amidships, heard this, they cast anchor near to our ship.

Then God sent me a Saracen that was of the Emperor's country, dressed in breeches of unbleached linen; and he came swimming through the stream to our vessel, and embraced me round the waist and said to me: 'Sir, ye are lost, unless ye take heed to yourself; for ye should leap from your vessel on to the beak which is at the end of this galley: and, if ye jump, they will take no heed to you; for their intent is on plundering your ship.' They threw me a rope from the galley and I jumped on to the point, as was the will of God. And know ye that I tottered so much that had he not leapt after me to hold me up I should have fallen into the water.

They got me into the galley where there were full fourteen score men of their folk, and he held me always in his arms. And then they bare me to the ground and leapt upon my body to cut my throat, for the man that would have killed me thought to be honoured. And this Saracen held me always in his arms and cried 'Cousin of the King!' In such fashion they bare me twice to earth, and once to my knees; and then I felt the knife at my throat. In this pass God saved me by the aid of the Saracen, who bare me towards the castle of the ship, where were the Saracen knights.

When I came among them, they took off my coat of mail; and for the pity that they had for me, cast over me a coverlet of mine of scarlet furred with minever, that Madam my mother had given me; and another brought me a white belt, and I girt myself over the coverlet, wherein I had made a slit, and had put it on; and the others brought me a hood that I put upon my head. And then by reason of my fear I began to tremble very much, and because of my sickness also. And then I asked for drink, and they brought me water in a pot; and so soon as I put it to my mouth to swallow it, it gushed out of my nostrils. When I saw this, I sent for my men and told them that I was dying, for that I had an inward swelling in the throat; and they asked me how I knew it; and I showed them, and when they saw the water pouring out from my throat and my nostrils, they took to weeping. When the Saracen knights who were there saw my people weeping, they asked the Saracen who had saved us why they wept; and he answered that he understood that I had the swelling in the throat from which I could not be saved. And then one of the Saracen knights said to him that had saved us, that he would give us solace; for he would give me such a thing to drink that within two days I should thereby be healed; and so he did.

My lord Raoul of Wanou, who was in my company, had been hamstrung in the great battle on Shrove Tuesday and could not stand; and know ye that an old Saracen knight that was in the galley used to carry him to the privy on his back.

LXV

THE Grand Admiral of the galleys sent for me and asked me if I were cousin to the King; and I told him nay, and recounted to him how and why the sailor had said that I was the King's cousin. And he said that I had done wisely, or else we had all been dead. And he asked me if I belonged in any wise to the lineage of the Emperor Frederick of Germany, that then lived; and I answered him that I understood that Madam my mother was his cousin german; and he told me that he loved me that much the better for it. As we ate he had a burgher of Paris come before us. When the burgher was come, he said to me, 'Sir, what do ye?' 'What do I?' said I. 'In God's name,' said he, 'ye are eating flesh on a Friday!' When I heard this, I pushed away my bowl. *8 April 1250* And the Admiral asked my Saracen why I had done this, and he told him; and the Admiral answered that God would not remember it against me, for I had done it unwittingly. And know that this same answer was made me by the Legate when we were out of captivity; yet therefore I did not cease from fasting every Friday of Lent thereafter, on bread and water; whereby the Legate was angered with me because there remained with the King no other man of substance but myself.

The Sunday after, the Admiral caused me and all the other prisoners that had been taken on the water to land on the bank of the river. As they brought Sir John, my good priest, out of the hold of the galley, he swooned; and they slew him and cast him into the river. His clerk, that swooned also from the sickness of the host that was on him, had a mortar thrown at his head; and he died and was cast into the river. *10 April 1250*

As they brought the other sick folk out of the galleys where they had been imprisoned, there were Saracen men ready, with naked swords, who slew them that fell and cast them all into the stream. I had them told, by my Saracen, that meseemed it was not well done; for it was against the precepts of Saladin, who said that a man should not slay another after he had given him of his bread and salt to eat. And he answered that these were men of no account, for they could not help themselves because of the sickness that was on them.

He had my sailors brought before me, and told me that they were all renegade; and I told him never to trust them; for as quickly as they had left us would they leave him, if they saw their time and place. And the Admiral made answer to me that he was of my mind, for Saladin was wont to say that no man ever saw a bad Christian make a good Saracen, or a bad Saracen a good Christian.

And after these things he had me mount a palfrey, and took me beside him. And we crossed a bridge of boats and came to Mansourah, where the King and his men had been taken; and we came to the entry of a great pavilion where the scribes of the Sultan were sitting; and they had my name inscribed. Then my Saracen told me: 'Sir, I shall not follow you farther, for I may not; but I pray you, Sir, that ye keep fast by the hand this child that ye have with you, that the Saracens take him not from you.' And this child was named Bartholomew and was a bastard son of the Lord of Montfaucon.

When my name had been written down, the Admiral led me into the pavilion where the barons were and more than ten thousand persons with them. When I came therein, the barons so rejoiced that we could not hear each other speak, as they gave thanks to Our Lord and said that they had thought to have lost me.

BOOK TWO

LXVI

WE had not long stayed there when they made one of the men of most substance there stand up, and led us into another pavilion. Many knights and other folk did the Saracens hold captive in a court that was shut in with walls of mud. From this close where they had put them, they brought them out one after another and asked them: 'Wilt thou disavow thy faith?' Those who would not forswear it, they set on one side and cut off their heads; and those who forswore it they set on another.

At this instant the Sultan sent his council to speak with us; and they asked to whom should they speak the message the Sultan sent us. And we told them they should speak it to the good old Count Peter of Brittany. There were men present that knew the Saracen tongue and French, whom men call dragomans, who turned the Saracen speech into French for Count Peter. And the message was this: 'Sir, the Sultan sendeth us to you to know if ye would be set free.' The Count answered: 'Aye.' 'And what will ye give to the Sultan for your deliverance?' 'What we can do and bear in reason,' said the Count. 'And will ye give,' said they, 'for your deliverance any of the castles of the barons oversea?' The count answered that he had no power therein, for they were held from the Emperor of Germany that then lived. They asked if we would give up any of the castles of the Templars or the Hospitallers for our deliverance. And the Count answered that this could not be; that when they set castellans therein, they made them swear on relics that for the delivery of man's body would they never give up their castles. And they answered that it appeared to them that we had no desire to be set free, and that they would go thence and send men to us who would fence with us with their swords as they had done to the others. And they went away.

So soon as they were gone, there broke into our pavilion a horde of young Saracens, their swords girt on, and brought with them a man of great age, white-haired, who had us questioned whether it were true that we believed in a God who had been taken for us, wounded and slain for us, and had risen on the third day. And we answered, 'Aye.' And then he told us that we should not be discomforted if we had borne these persecutions for Him, 'for not yet', said he, 'have ye died for Him, as He died for you; and if He was able to rise up again, be certain that He will deliver you when it shall please Him'. Then he went away and all the other young men after him; whereat I rejoiced, for I believed for a certainty that they had come to cut off our heads. And it was not long before the Sultan's folk came, who told us that the King had purchased our freedom.

After the old man that had given us solace had gone away, the council of the Sultan came back to us, and told us that the King had purchased our deliverance, and that we were to send four of our people to him to hear what he had done. We sent thither my lord John of Valery, the noble knight, my lord Philip of Montfort, my lord Baldwin of Ibelin, Seneschal of Cyprus, and my lord Guy of Ibelin, Constable of Cyprus, one of the best-nurtured knights that ever I saw, and that best loved the folk of this land. These four reported to us the manner in which the King had bought our deliverance; and so was it done.

LXVII

THE council of the Sultan tried the King in the fashion whereby they had tried us, to see if the King would promise to hand over any of the castles of the Temple or of the Hospital, or any of the castles of the barons of the land; and as God willed, the King answered them after the manner that we had answered. And they threatened him and said that since he would not do it, they would put him in the *bernicles*.

The *bernicles* are the most grievous torture that a man can suffer; and they are two folding beams of wood, indented at the top, and the one fits into the other, and they are bound together by strong thongs of ox-hide at the head. And when they would put men therein, they make them lie on their sides and set their legs between the pegs, and then make a man sit on the beams; whence it haps that there remaineth not half a foot of bone unbroken, but they are all smashed. And to do the worst that they can, at the end of three days when the legs are swollen they put the swollen legs back into the *bernicles* and break them all over again. To these menaces the King answered that he was their prisoner, and that they could do with him as they would.

When they saw that they could not vanquish the noble King by threats, they came back to him and asked him how much he would give the Sultan in money, and therewith give him back Damietta. And the King answered them that if the Sultan were willing to take a reasonable sum of money from him, he would send word to the Queen that she should pay for their deliverance. And they said: 'How is it that ye will not say to us that ye will do these things?' And the King answered that he knew not whether the Queen would wish to do it, for she was his lady. And then the council went back again to have speech of the Sultan and brought word to the King that if the Queen would pay a million besants of gold, which were worth two hundred and fifty thousand crowns, he would set the King free.

And the King asked them on their oath if the Sultan would deliver them for so much, if the Queen were of a mind to do it. And they went back to talk with the Sultan and on their return took oath to the King that they would thus deliver him. And so soon as they had sworn, the King spake and promised the Emirs that he would freely pay the two hundred and fifty thousand crowns for the deliverance of his men, and Damietta for the deliverance of his own person, because he was not of such a sort that he should be bought back with gold. When the Sultan heard this, he said: 'By my faith! Generous is the Frank not to have bargained over so great a sum of money. Now go tell him,' said the Sultan, 'that I give him fifty thousand crowns towards the payment of the ransom.'

LXVIII

THEN the Sultan had the men of substance get aboard four galleys, to take them down to Damietta. In the galley wherein I was put, was the good old Count Peter of Brittany, Count William of Flanders, the good old Count John of Soissons, my lord Imbert of Beaujeu, Constable of France; and the good knight my lord Baldwin of Ibelin and my lord Guy, his brother, were put there likewise.

Those that steered us in the galley brought us to land before a lodging that the Sultan had caused to be pitched on the bank in such fashion as ye shall hear. Before this lodging there was a tower of pine-poles, closed in with dyed cloth; and it was the door of the lodging. And within this door was a pavilion pitched, where the Emirs, when they went to have speech of the Sultan, left their swords and their armour. After this pavilion there was another door like the first, and by this door did men go into a great pavilion that was the hall of the Sultan. After the hall there was a tower as before, whereby one entered the Sultan's chamber.

After the Sultan's chamber there was a court, and in the midst of the court a tower higher than all the others, whither the Sultan used to go to see all the country and all the camp. From the court an alley went down to the river where the Sultan had had a pavilion pitched over the river to bathe there. All these lodgings were shut in with wooden trellis and the trellis was covered outside with blue cloth, so that those who were without could not see within; and all four towers were covered with cloth. We came to this place, where these lodgings were pitched, *28 April* on the Thursday before Ascension Day. The four *1250* galleys in which we were in captivity together cast anchor before the Sultan's abode. In a pavilion which was near the Sultan's lodgings, they landed the King. The Sultan had thus arranged it: that on the Saturday before Ascension Day they should give him Damietta, and he would release the King.

LXIX

THE Emirs that the Sultan had removed from his council, to put in their place his own people that he had brought from foreign lands, took counsel together, and a wise Saracen spake thus: 'Lords, ye see the shame and dishonour that the Sultan doeth us, when he depriveth us of the honourable place wherein his father had set us. For which thing we should be sure that if he findeth himself within the fortress of Damietta, he will have us captive and dead in his prison, as did his father to the Emirs that took the Count of Bar and the Count of Montfort. And therefore meseemeth it is better that we should slay him before he escapeth out of our hands.' They went to the men of the Ḥalqa, and made request to them that they would slay the Sultan, so soon as the Emirs had eaten with the Sultan, who had invited them. Now it befell that after they had eaten, and the Sultan was going away into his chamber and had taken leave of the Emirs, one of the knights of the Ḥalqa that bare the Sultan's sword, struck the Sultan with his own sword through the hand, between the four fingers, and split the hand as far as the arm.

Then the Sultan turned to his Emirs who had caused this to be done to him, and said to them, 'Lords, I make accusation to you of the men of the Ḥalqa, that have intent to kill me, as ye may see.' Then the knights of the Ḥalqa answered with one voice to the Sultan, and spake thus: 'Since thou sayest that we wish to kill thee, it were better for us to kill thee than that thou shouldst kill us.'

Then they had the drums sounded and all the host came to ask the Sultan's will. And they answered that Damietta was taken and that the Sultan was going to Damietta and bade them go thither after him. All armed and galloped off towards Damietta. And when we saw that they were going away to Damietta, our hearts were very heavy for we thought that Damietta was lost. The Sultan, that was young and fleet of foot, fled into the tower that he had caused to be made, with three of his imams who had been eating with him; and the tower was behind his chamber, as ye have heard ere now.

The men of the Ḥalqa, that were five hundred horsemen, brake down the Sultan's pavilions and beleaguered him round and about the tower that he had had made, with the three of his imams that had been eating with him, and they cried out to them that they were to come down.

BOOK TWO

And he said that he would do so, but that they must warrant his safety. And they said that they would make him come down by force, and that he was not in Damietta. They cast Greek fire against him, which set light to the tower, that was made of planks of deal and cotton cloth. The tower caught fire swiftly, so that never did I see so fair a flame nor so straight. When the Sultan saw this, he came down with all speed and fled towards the river all along the alley, of which I have told you before.

The men of the Ḥalqa had broken down the laths of the alley with their swords, and, at the passing of the Sultan to go towards the river, one of them struck him with a lance in the side, and the Sultan fled to the river dragging the lance after him. And they went down there until they were swimming, and slew him in the river nigh our galley in which we were. One of the knights, that was named Fārisu-d-din 'Uqṭayy, clove him with his sword and snatched the heart from his belly; and then he came to the King, his hand all bloody, and said: 'What wilt thou give me? For I have slain thine enemy, who would have had thee dead had he lived.' And the King answered him never a word.

LXX

FULL thirty of them came into our galley with bare swords in their hands, and at their necks Danish axes. I asked my lord Baldwin of Ibelin, that well knew the Saracen tongue, what these men were saying, and he answered that they said they had come to cut off our heads. There was any number of men that confessed their sins to a brother of the Trinity, that was called John and was with Count William of Flanders. But as for me, I could not remember a sin that I had committed; but bethought me that the more I defended myself and the more I strove to escape, the worse my plight would be. And thereupon I crossed myself and knelt at the feet of one of them, that held a carpenter's axe, and said: 'Thus died Saint Agnes.' My lord Guy of Ibelin, Constable of Cyprus, knelt beside me and confessed himself to me; and I said to him, 'I absolve you by such power as God hath given me.' But when I arose, never could I remember aught that he had told or recounted to me.

They made us rise from where we were, and put us in prison in the hold of the galley; and many of our people thought that they had done this because they did not wish to attack us all together, but to kill us one after the other. Therein were we in such ill plight, at evening and all night, that we lay so close together that my feet touched the good Count Peter of Brittany and his were by my face.

3 May 1250 The next day the Emirs had us brought out of the prison where we were, and their messengers told us that we were to go to have speech of the Emirs, to renew the covenants which the Sultan had made with us; and they told us that we could be sure that if the Sultan had lived, he would have cut off the head of the King and of all of us likewise. Those who could go there, went; the Count of Brittany and the Constable and I, who were grievously sick, stayed where we were. The Count of Flanders, Count John of Soissons, the two brothers of Ibelin, and the others who were in fit state to go, went thither.

They made an agreement with the Emirs in such wise, that so soon as Damietta had been handed over to them, the King and the other great folk who were there should be set free; for the Sultan had already sent the lesser folk towards Cairo, save them that he had caused to be killed. And this had he done contrary to the covenants that he had with the King; wherefore it seemeth truly that he would have had us killed likewise so soon as he had possession of Damietta.

And the King had to swear to them to gratify them with an hundred thousand crowns before he left the river and with an hundred thousand crowns in Acre. The Saracens, by the covenants which they had made with the King, were to keep the sick men that were in Damietta, the crossbows, armour, salt meat, and engines of war until such time as the King should send to fetch them.

LXXI

THE oaths which the Emirs were to take to the King were drawn up and were these: that if they did not keep their covenants with the King, they should be as much dishonoured as the man who for his sins goeth on pilgrimage to Mahomet to Mecca with his head uncovered; and as those that leave their wives and take them again thereafter. For according to the law of Mahomet, a man may leave his wife only on condition that he never take her again, unless he hath seen another man lie with her: then may he have her again. The third oath was this: that if they did not keep their covenants with the King, they should be as much dishonoured as a Saracen that eateth the flesh of pigs. The King accepted the oaths aforesaid from the Emirs favourably, for my lord Nicholas of Acre, that knew the Saracen tongue, said that they could not take stronger according to their law.

When the Emirs had sworn, they had the oath that they wished to receive from the King put in writing, by the counsel of the priests that had gone over to their side; and the document said this: that if the King held not his covenants with the Emirs, then might he be as much dishonoured as the Christian who denieth God and His

Mother, and be deprived of the fellowship of his twelve apostles and of all the saints both men and women. To this the King gave full agreement. The last clause of the oath was this, that if he held not his covenants with the Emirs, might he be dishonoured as the Christian who forsweareth God and His law, and who in God's despite spitteth upon the cross and treadeth it underfoot.

When the King heard this, he said that, God willing, such an oath would he never take. The Emirs sent Master Nicholas, that knew the Saracen tongue, to the King, who spake to the King these words: 'Sir, the Emirs are greatly vexed that they have sworn all that you desired, and that ye will not swear what they ask of you; and be ye assured that if ye swear it not, they will have you beheaded and all your people.' The King made answer that they could do as they would; for he would liefer die a good Christian than live under the wrath of God and His Mother.

The Patriarch of Jerusalem, an aged man of four-score years of age, had secured a safe-conduct from the Saracens, and had come to the King to help him ransom his freedom. Now it is the custom between Christians and Saracens, that when the King or the Sultan dieth, those that are acting as envoys whether in heathendom or Christendom, are captive and enslaved; and since the Sultan that had given safe-conduct to the Patriarch was dead, the said Patriarch was prisoner as we were. When the King had given his answer, one of the Emirs said that the counsel had been given him by the Patriarch; and said to the paynim, 'If ye will trust me, I will force the King to swear; for I will cause the head of the Patriarch to leap into his lap.'

They would not take heed to him, but laid hands on the Patriarch and took him from before the King, and bound him to a tent-pole with his hands behind his back, so straitly that his hands were swollen as big as his head, and the blood started from the nails. The Patriarch cried out to the King: 'Sir, for God's sake swear in safety; for I will take all the sin upon my soul of the oath that ye take, since ye have intent to keep it.' I know not how the oath was arranged; but the Emirs were well content with the oath of the King and of the other men of substance that were there.

LXXII

FROM the time that the Sultan was killed, they brought the Sultan's instruments before the King's tent, and men told him that the Emirs had had a great mind and wish to make him Sultan of Cairo. And he asked me if I believed that he would have taken the Kingdom of Cairo an they had offered it to him. And I told him that so would he have acted as a fool, since they had slain their lord; and he told me that verily he would not have refused it.

And know ye that they said that it stayed for no other reason than that they said that the King was the most steadfast Christian that could be found. And they brought forward this example, that when he left his lodging, he would lay himself crosswise on the ground, and make the sign of the cross all over his body. And they said that if Mahomet had suffered them to endure such hurt, they would never more put faith in him; and they said that if these folk made him Sultan, he would slay them all or they would turn Christian.

After the covenants were agreed by the King and the Emirs, and sworn, it was agreed that they should set us free on the day after Ascension Day; and that so soon as Damietta was handed over to the Emirs, they should deliver the King's person and the men of substance that were with him, as hath been told before. The Thursday, *5 May 1250* in the evening, those that steered our four galleys came to anchor in the midst of the stream before the bridge of Damietta, and had a pavilion pitched before the bridge, where the King went ashore.

At sunrise my lord Geoffrey of Sargines went into the town and gave up the town to the Emirs. On the towers of the town they set the Sultan's banners. The Saracen knights took possession of the city, and began to drink the wine and were soon all drunken; of whom one came to our galley and drew his sword stained with blood, and said that for his part he had slain six of our men.

Before Damietta was given back they had taken the Queen aboard our ships, and all our folk that were in Damietta, except the sick that were in Damietta. The Saracens were to keep them according to their oath; they killed them all. The King's engines of war, that they were also to keep, they hacked to pieces. And the salt meats that they were to keep, since they did not eat pork, they did not keep; but made a pile of engines, a pile of salted pigs, and another of dead men, and set fire thereto; and there was so great a blaze that it lasted the Friday, the Saturday, and the Sunday.

LXXIII

THE King and the rest of us, whom they were to set free as soon as the sun rose, did they keep until the sun set; nor did we ever eat, or the Emirs either, but were in debate the whole day. And an Emir spake for those that were of his faction: 'Lords, if ye will trust me, me and those here present of my party, we will slay the King and these rich men that are here; for then for forty years we need have no vigilance: for their children are young, and we have Damietta before us; wherefore may we do it the more surely.'

Another Saracen, that was named Ṣabri and was born in Spain, spake against him and said thus: 'If we slay the King after we have slain the Sultan, men will say that the Egyptians are the most evil men and the most treacherous that there are in the world.'

And he who would have had them kill us spake against him: 'In sooth we were rid in over-evil fashion of the Sultan whom we have slain, for we have gone against the commandment of Mahomet, who biddeth us to guard our lord as the apple of our eye: and here in this book behold the law written. Now hearken', said he, 'to the other commandment of Mahomet which cometh after.' He turned over a leaf of the book that he held, and showed them the other commandment of Mahomet, which was this: 'For the safeguard of the faith, kill the enemy of the law.' 'Now see how we have sinned against the commandments of Mahomet in that we have slain our lord; and we should do yet worse an we kill not the King, whatsoever safeguard we may have given him; for he is the strongest enemy that the paynim law hath.'

Our death was all but agreed on; wherefore it befell that an Emir that was our adversary thought that they should kill us all, and came to the river and began to cry out in the Saracen tongue to them that steered the galleys, and took off the cloth from his head and made a sign with the head-cloth. And forthwith they raised the anchor and took us back a full league towards Cairo. Then did we think ourselves altogether lost, and shed many a tear.

LXXIV

BY the will of God, who never forgetteth his own, it was agreed about sunset that we should be set free. Then they rowed us back and brought the four galleys to land. We made request that they should let us go. They told us that they would not until we had eaten, 'for it would be shame upon the Emirs if ye left our prisons fasting'. And we asked that they should give us meat and we would eat; and they told us that men had gone to seek it in the camp. The food that they gave us was round cakes of cheese which were roasted in the sun so that worms should not come therein, and eggs hard boiled, four or five days old, and in our honour they had dyed them divers colours outside.

They put us ashore; and we went to the King whom they brought down to the river from the pavilion where they had kept him; and there came full twenty thousand Saracens, girt with their swords, after him on foot. On the river before the King was a Genoese galley on which there appeared but one man on deck. So soon as he saw the King by the stream, he sounded his whistle; and at the sound of the whistle there leapt from the hold of the galley four-score crossbowmen, well arrayed, their crossbows mounted, and forthwith set their bolts in the nocks. So soon as the Saracens saw them, they took to flight like sheep; so that none of them remained with the King but two or three.

They let down a plank to the land to pick up the King and the Count of Anjou, his brother, and my lord Geoffrey of Sargines and my lord Philip of Nemours, and the Marshal of France that they called du Mez, and the Master of the Trinity and me. The Count of Poitiers they held in prison until the King had caused them to be paid the hundred thousand crowns that he was to pay them as ransom before he left the river.

7 May 1250 The Saturday after Ascension, which Saturday was the day after we were set free, there came to take leave of the King the Count of Flanders and the Count of Soissoins and many of the rich men that had been taken in the galleys. The King spake to them thus, that it appeared

BOOK TWO

to him that they would do well to wait until the Count of Poitiers, his brother, should be set free. And they said that they could not, for the galleys were all made ready. They went aboard their galleys and went back to France and took with them the good old Count Peter of Brittany, who was so ill that he only lived for three weeks, and died at sea.

LXXV

THEY began to make up the payment on the Saturday in the morning and they took the Saturday and all the Sunday until nightfall to make the payment; for they paid by weight in the balance, and each weighing was of five thousand crowns. When it came to vespers on Sunday, the King's men, that were making up the payment, sent word to the King that a full fifteen thousand crowns were still lacking. And with the King there were then only the King of Sicily and the Marshal of France, the Master of the Trinity and I; and all the others were making up the payment.

Then said I to the King that it were well that he should send to fetch the Commander and the Marshal of the Templars (for the Master was dead) and that he should make request to them that they should lend him the fifteen thousand crowns to deliver his brother. The King sent for them, and the King told me what I was to say to them. When I had said it, Brother Stephen of Otricourt, who was the Commander of the Temple, said to me: 'Lord of Joinville, this counsel that ye give the King is neither good nor reasonable; for ye know that we receive what is entrusted to us in such wise that by our oath we may not hand it over but to them who entrusted it to us.' There was enow of hard words and anger between him and me.

And then spake Brother Reynold of Vichiers, that was

Marshal of the Temple, and said thus: 'Sir, let be the dispute betwixt the Lord of Joinville and our Commander; for, even as our Commander saith, we can hand over naught but by breaking our oath. And as for what the Seneschal counselleth you, that, if we will not lend, ye should take, he sayeth naught that is strange, and ye shall do what ye will therein; and if ye take of our goods, we have fully enough of yours in Acre wherefrom ye may make restitution to us.'

I told the King that I would go, an he would; and he bade me go. I went into one of the galleys of the Temple, into the master galley, and when I would go down into the hold of the galley, there where the treasure was, I asked the Commander of the Temple to come to see what I took; and he never deigned to come. The Marshal said that he would come to see the violence I did him.

So soon as I had got down there where the treasure was, I asked the Treasurer of the Temple, who was there, if he would hand over to me the keys of a chest which was before me; and he, that saw me thin and fleshless from my sickness and in the habit that I had worn in prison, said that he would not give them to me. And I saw a hatchet which was lying there, so I picked it up and said that I would make it the King's key. When the Marshal saw this, he took me by the hand and said, 'Sir, we see well that ye would do us violence, and we will hand over the keys.' Then he bade the Treasurer hand them over, which he did. And when the Marshal told the Treasurer who I was, he was much abashed.

I found that this chest that I opened belonged to Nicholas of Choisy, a sergeant of the King's. I threw out of it what money I found therein, and went to sit at the prow of our vessel that had brought me. And I took the Marshal of France aboard and left him with the money and put the Master of the Trinity on the galley. The

Marshal handed down the money to the Master in the galley, and the Master handed it to me in the vessel in which I was. When we came to the King's galley, I began to halloo to the King, 'Sir, Sir, look how I am provided!' And the saintly man saw me with much gladness and mirth. We handed over what I had brought to them that were making up the payment.

LXXVI

WHEN the payment was made up, the King's Council that had made it up came to him and told him that the Saracens would not set his brother free until such time as they had the money in front of them. There were some of the Council that advised the King that he should not hand over the money until he had his brother back. And the King answered that he would hand it over, for so he had covenanted; and they would keep their covenants also if they thought to do right. Then my lord Philip of Nemours told the King that they had misreckoned against the Saracens a measure of five thousand crowns.

And the King was very wroth and said that his will was that they should restore the five thousand crowns, for he had covenanted to pay them the hundred thousand crowns before he left the river. And then I touched my lord Philip on the foot, and said to the King that he should not heed him, for he was not speaking truth; for the Saracens were the most skilled reckoners that there were in the world. And my lord Philip said that I spake truth, for he spake thus only in mockery. And the King said that such mockery was ill placed, 'And I command you,' said the King to my lord Philip, 'on the faith that ye owe me as my liegeman that ye are, that if these five thousand crowns be not paid, ye have them paid without fail.'

Many folk had advised the King that he should withdraw to his ship, which awaited him at sea, to take himself out of the hands of the Saracens. Never would the King take heed to them; but said that he would not leave the river, as he had covenanted, until such time as he had paid them an hundred thousand crowns. So soon as the payment was made, the King, without any man's asking, told us that henceforth his oaths were fulfilled, and that we were to leave that place and go into the ship that was at sea.

Then our galley went forward and we went for a full league before any man spake to another, because of the disquiet which we felt concerning the imprisonment of the Count of Poitiers. Then came my lord Philip of Montfort in a galleon, and cried to the King, 'Sir, Sir, speak to your brother, the Count of Poitiers, that is in this other vessel.' Then cried the King, 'Light up! Light up!' And so they did. Then was the joy great as could be amongst us. The King got into his ship, and we with him. A poor fisherman went to tell the Countess of Poitiers that he had seen the Count of Poitiers freed; and she had him given ten crowns.

LXXVII

I WOULD not forget certain matters that befell in Egypt while we were there. First of all I will tell you of my lord Walter of Châtillon. A knight, that was named my lord John of Monson, recounted to me that he saw my lord of Châtillon in a street of the village in which the King was taken prisoner; and this street passed straight through the village, so that one saw the fields at the one end and the other. In this street was my lord Walter of Châtillon with his bare sword in his hand. When he saw that the Turks were coming into the street, he ran at them sword in hand, and drove them out of the village; and, as they fled before him, the Turks (that shoot as well behind as before them) covered him with darts. When he had driven them out of the village, he plucked himself free of their darts which were on him, and put on again his surcoat, and stood up in his stirrups and stretched out his arm with the sword and cried, 'Châtillon, knights! Where are my brave men?' When he turned round and saw that the Turks had entered at the other end, he attacked them again, sword in hand, and drove them out; and thus did he do thrice in the manner aforesaid.

When the admiral of the galleys had me brought to those that had been taken prisoner on the land, I made inquiry of those who were about him; nor did I find any that could tell me how he was taken, except that my lord John Fouinon, the good old knight, told me that when they were taking him towards Mansourah, he encountered a Turk that was mounted on the horse of my lord Walter of Châtillon; and the crupper of the horse was all bloody. And he asked him what he had done with him to whom the horse belonged; and he answered that he had cut his throat while on horseback, as appeared by the crupper that was stained with the blood.

There was a very valiant man in the camp who was named my lord James of Castel, Bishop of Soissons. When he saw that our men were giving way on the side of Damietta, he who had a great wish to be with God, nor desired to go back to the land wherein he was born, therefore made haste to go to God, and set spur to his horse and attacked the Turks all by himself, who slew him with their swords and set him in the fellowship of God, numbered with the martyrs.

As the King awaited the paying over which his men were making to the Turks for the deliverance of his brother the Count of Poitiers, a Saracen, very well arrayed and very fair of person, came to the King and offered to him milk in pots, and flowers of divers colours and sorts, on behalf of the children of Malik an Nāṣir Dā'ūd that had been Sultan of Cairo; and he made him the present in French. And the King asked him where he had learned French; and he said that he had been a Christian; and the King said to him: 'Go ye hence, for I will speak no more with you.' I took him on one side and asked him his folk. And he told me that he had been born in Provins, and had come to Egypt with King John, and that he had taken himself a wife in Egypt and was a great man and rich. And I said to him: 'Know ye not well that if ye die in this case, ye shall be damned and go to hell?'

And he answered 'Yea,' (for he was certain that no law was so good as the Christian) 'but an I come over to your side, I fear the poverty in which I shall be, and the reproach. Every day will they say to me, "Behold the renegade!" I had liefer live rich and at my ease than put myself in such case as I foresee.' And I told him that the reproach would be greater on the Day of Judgement, when all men should behold his sin, than that of which he spake. Many good words did I speak to him which were of no avail. So he departed from me, nor did I ever see him more.

LXXVIII

NOW have ye heard of the great afflictions that the King suffered and we with him, which afflictions the Queen likewise did not escape, as ye shall hear hereafter. For three days before she was brought to bed, news came that the King was taken captive; by which news she was so affrighted that each time that she fell asleep in her bed it seemed to her that her whole chamber was full of Saracens, and she cried out

'Help! Help!' And so that the child should not perish that she bare, she had an old knight of four-score years of age lie at the foot of her bed, who held her by the hand. Each time that the Queen cried out, he said, 'Madam, have no fear, for I am here.'
Before she was delivered she had all the room emptied except for the knight, and knelt before him and asked of him a favour: and the knight granted it by his oath. And she said to him: 'I ask of you,' said she, 'by the troth that ye have plighted me, that if the Saracens take this town, ye will cut off my head before they take me prisoner.' And the knight made answer: 'Be ye certain that I will do it willingly; for I had it in my mind that I would kill you before they took us.'
The Queen was brought to bed of a son that was called John; and they called him Tristan, for the great sorrow wherein he was born. The very day that she was brought to bed, they told her that the folk of Pisa and Genoa and the other free cities were minded to escape thence. The day after she was brought to bed, she sent for them all before her bed, so that all the chamber was full, and said to them, 'Lords, for the love of God, leave not this town; for ye see that my lord the King would be lost, and all they that are prisoners, if the town were lost. And if this please you not, may ye take pity on this feeble creature that lieth here, so that ye wait until I be afoot again.'
And they answered: 'Madam, how should we do this? For we are dying of hunger in this town.' And she told them that never should they depart thence for famine, 'for I will buy all the victuals in this town, and maintain you henceforward at the King's expense'.
They took counsel together and came back to her and vouchsafed her that they would stay of their free will; and the Queen (whom God assoil) had all the victuals

in the town bought, that cost her an hundred and eighty thousand crowns and more. She had to get up before her time because the city had to be given back to the Saracens. The Queen went away to Acre to await the King.

LXXIX

As the King awaited the deliverance of his brother, he sent Brother Raoul, the Friar Preacher, to an emir that was called Fārisu-d-dīn 'Uqṭayy, one of the most loyal Saracens that ever I saw. And he sent him word that he marvelled much how he and the other emirs suffered their truce to be so basely broken; for they had slain the sick men whom they were to keep, and made firewood of his engines, and had burnt the bodies of the sick and the salt pork which they should have kept likewise.

Fārisu-d-dīn 'Uqṭayy made answer to Brother Raoul and said: 'Brother Raoul, tell the King that by my law I may not give him redress therein; wherefore is my heart heavy. And warn him from me that he make no showing that it annoyeth him, so long as he is in our hands; for he would be dead.' And he advised that so soon as the King was come to Acre, he should bear the matter in mind.

When the King came to his ship, he found that his people had naught made ready for him, neither bed nor robes; but he had to lie, until we were in Acre, on the mattresses that the Sultan had given him and to wear the dress that the Sultan had given and had made for him, which was of black satin, furred with ermine and grey squirrel; and there was on it great plenty of buttons all of gold.

So long as we were at sea, for six days, I who was ill sate always beside the King. And then he told me how he had been taken prisoner, and how he had purchased his ransom and ours, by the help of God. And he had me tell him how I had been taken prisoner on the water; and afterwards he told me that I should show great gratitude to Our Lord, for that He had delivered me from such great perils. Much did he mourn the death of the Count of Artois his brother and said that the Count would not have endured not to come and see him in his galley, as had not the Count of Poitiers.

Of the Count of Anjou, who was in his ship, did he also complain to me that he bare him no company. One day he asked what the Count of Anjou was doing and they told him that he was playing at backgammon with my lord Walter of Nemours. And he went thither, tottering from the weakness of his malady; and took the dice and the tables and cast them into the sea; and was very wroth with his brother for that he had so soon betaken himself to playing at dice. But my lord Walter was the better paid thereby; for he threw all the money that was on the board (whereof there was great plenty) into his lap and bare it away.

LXXX

AFTER this shall ye hear of many afflictions and tribulations which I bare at Acre, wherefrom God, in Whom was and is my trust, delivered me. And these things will I have written that they that hear them may have trust in God in their afflictions and tribulations; and God shall aid them even as me.

Then let us tell that when the King came to Acre, all Acre came in procession down to the sea to receive him at his coming, with passing great joy. They brought me a palfrey. So soon as I was mounted thereon, my heart failed me and I said to him that had brought me the palfrey that he must hold me lest I fall. With much ado

14 May 1250

did they make me mount the stairs of the King's Hall. I sate myself by a window and a child by me (and he was about ten years old) that was called Bartholomew and was a bastard son of my lord Ami of Montbeliard, lord of Montfaucon.

As I sate there, where none heeded me, a chamberlain came to me in a scarlet coat charged with two yellow stripes, and bowed to me, and asked me if I knew him; and I told him nay. And he told me that he came from Oiselay, my uncle's castle. And I asked him whose man he was, and he told me that he served no one, and that he would remain with me, if I would; and I said that I was very willing. He went forthwith to seek me white caps, and combed me very well.

And then the King sent for me to eat with him and I went in the tunic that they had made me in prison of the bits cut from my coverlet; and my coverlet I left for the child Bartholomew, and four ells of camlet that they had given me for charity in the prison. Guillemin, my new chamberlain, came to carve before me, and got food for the child while we were eating.

My new chamberlain told me that he had found me a lodging hard by the baths, to wash me from the filth and sweat that I had brought from prison. When evening came and I was in the bath, my heart failed me and I swooned, and with much ado did they get me out of the bath into my bed. The next day, an old knight that was called my lord Peter of Bourbonne came to see me and I kept him to be with me; he stood surety for me in the town for what I needed for dress and adornment.

When I was ready, full four days after we had come there, I went to see the King; and he reproved me and told me that I had done ill to have tarried so long in coming to see him; and he bade me, as I held him dear, to eat with him henceforth both noon and night until he had settled what we should do, whether to go to France or to remain.

I told the King that my lord Peter of Courtenay owed me two hundred crowns of my pay, which he would not pay me. And the King answered that he would have me paid out of the money that he owed the Lord of Courtenay; and thus he did. By the counsel of my lord Peter of Bourbonne, we took twenty crowns for our expenses and the remainder we entrusted for keeping to the Commander of the Palace of the Templars. When the time came that I had spent the twenty crowns, I sent the father of John Caym of Sainte Menehould, whom I had as retainer oversea, to fetch another twenty crowns. The commander answered him that he had not a penny of mine and knew me not.

I went to Brother Reynold of Vichiers, that was Master of the Temple by the help of the King, because of the courtesy that he had shown the King in prison (of which I have told you) and made accusation to him against the Commander of the Palace, who would not give me back my money that I had entrusted to him. When he heard this, he was sore dismayed and said to me, 'Lord of Joinville, I love you well; but be ye sure that if ye will not abstain from this claim, I will love you no more; for ye would have men understand that our brethren are thieves.' And I told him that God willing I would not abstain.

In this disquiet of heart was I for four days, like a man who hath no more money at all to spend. After these four days the Master came to me laughing, and told me that he had found my money again. The manner in which it was found was this, that he had changed the Commander of the Palace and had sent him to a village that is called as-Sāfiriyya; and this man gave me back my moneys.

LXXXI

THE Bishop of Acre that then was (who had been born at Provins) had me lent the house of the priest of Saint Michael's. I had kept Caym de Sainte Menehould with me, who served me very well for two years, better than any man that ever I had with me in the country; and several men had I also as retainers. Now it so happened that there was at my bed's head a closet through which one went into the church.

Now it befell that a continual fever laid hold on me, wherefore I took to my bed, and all my household likewise. Nor ever a day all day had I any there that could help me nor lift me up; and I awaited naught but death by a sign that was ever in my ears; for there was no day that they did not bring a full score of dead or more into the church; and from my bed each time that they brought them in, I heard them chant *Libera me Domine*. Then I wept and gave thanks to God and spake to Him thus: 'Lord, be Thou adored for this suffering which Thou bringest upon me; for much unthriftiness have I had in my downlying and uprising. And I pray Thee, Lord, that Thou help me and deliver me from this sickness.' And so did He, me and my people.

After these things I asked Guillemin, my new squire, that he should render account; and so did he. And I found that he had mulcted me of ten florins and more. And he told me when I asked him that he would pay them me back when he could. I gave him his dismissal, and told him I gave him what he owed me, for he had well deserved it. I found from the knights of Burgundy, when they came back out of prison (for him had they brought in their company), that he was the most courteous thief that ever was, for whenever a knight lacked knife or strap, gloves or spurs, or other matter, he would go and steal it and then give it to him.

At the time that the King was in Acre, the King's brothers betook themselves to playing at dice; and the Count of Poitiers played in such courteous fashion that when he had won, he had the hall thrown open and summoned the gentlemen and gentlewomen, if any were there, and gave away in handfuls his own money as well as that which he had won. And when he had lost, he bought back at a guess the stakes of those with whom he had played, both from his brother the Count of Anjou and from others; and gave all, his own and the rest.

LXXXII

AT this time that we were in Acre, the King sent for his brothers and the Count of Flanders, and the other men of substance, on a Sunday, and spake to them thus: 'Lords, Madam the Queen my mother hath sent word to me and besought me, as earnestly as she can, that I go hence to France, for my realm standeth in great peril; for I have neither peace nor truce with the King of England. Those of this land with whom I have spoken of it, tell me that if I go hence this land is lost; for all in Acre will go hence after me since none will dare stay with so few folk. I beg you,' said he, 'give your minds to it; and since the matter is weighty, I give you respite, to give me what answer shall seem good to you, in eight days from now.'

In these eight days the Legate came to me, and spake me thus, that he understood not how the King should be able to tarry; and prayed me very instantly that I should go thence in his ship. And I answered him that I could not; for I had nothing, as he knew, since I had lost all in the river where I was taken captive.

And this answer did I make him not because I would not have gone with him very willingly, but because of a saying that my lord of Borlaymont, my cousin german (God rest his soul), made to me when I was setting out across the seas. 'Ye go oversea,' he said; 'now take ye heed to your coming back; for no knight, whether rich or poor, can come back without dishonour if he leave in the hands of the Saracens the meaner folk of Our Lord in whose company he set forth.' The Legate was wroth with me, and told me that I should not have refused him.

LXXXIII

THE Sunday after, we came back before the King; and then the King asked his brethren and the other barons and the Count of Flanders, what counsel they gave him, whether his going or his tarrying. They all answered that they had charged my lord Guy Mauvoisin with the counsel that they would give the King. The King bade him speak the message wherewith they had charged him; and he spake thus:

'Sir, your brethren and the men of substance here present have had regard to your estate, and have seen that ye are not able to tarry in this land to your own honour nor to that of your Kingdom; for of all the knights that came in your company (whereof ye brought to Cyprus two thousand and eight hundred) there are not an hundred remaining in this town. So they counsel you, Sir, that ye go hence to France, and get together men and money, wherewith ye may speedily come back to this land, to take vengeance on the enemies of God that have kept you in their prison.'

The King would not be content with what my lord Guy Mauvoisin had said; but made inquiry of the Count of

BOOK TWO

Anjou, the Count of Poitiers, and the Count of Flanders, and of divers other men of substance that sate by them; and all agreed with my lord Guy Mauvoisin. The Legate asked of the Count John of Jaffa, who sate near them, how these things seemed to him. The Count of Jaffa begged him to refrain from this question, 'for,' said he, 'my castle is on the marches; and if I counsel tarrying to the King, men will think that it was for my own profit.'

Then the King asked him, as directly as he could, to say how it seemed to him. And he said that if the King were able to do so much as to lie encamped in the fields for a year, it would do him great honour that he stayed. Then the Legate made inquiry of those that sate by the Count of Jaffa; and all agreed with my lord Guy Mauvoisin.

I was seated fourteenth counting from the Legate. He asked me how it seemed to me; and I gave him answer that I agreed fully with the Count of Jaffa. And the Legate asked me, very wroth, how it could be that the King could hold the field with so few men as he had. And I answered as if wroth likewise, for meseemed that he said it to anger me, 'Sir, I will tell you, since it pleaseth you. They say, Sir (I know not if it be true), that the King hath not yet spent any of his own moneys, but only the moneys of the clergy. Let the King disburse his moneys and let the King send into the Morea and beyond the seas to seek knights; and when men hear the news that the King payeth well and generously, knights will come to him from all parts, whereby he may hold the field for a year, if God will. And by his staying will the poor prisoners be delivered who have been taken captive in God's service and his, who will never come out if the King goes hence.'

There was no man there that had not near friends in

prison, wherefore no man took me up, but all turned to weeping.

After me the Legate asked how it seemed to my lord William of Beaumont, who was then Marshal of France; and he said that I had spoken passing well; 'and I will tell you,' said he, 'the reason why . . . .'. My lord John of Beaumont, the good old knight, who was his uncle and had a great wish to return to France, cried out to him very frowardly and said to him: 'Filthy prater, what would ye say? Sit ye down again and hold your tongue.' The King said to him, 'My lord John, ye do ill. Let him have his say.' 'Faith, Sir, that will I not.' He had to hold his peace; nor did any man after agree with me, but only the lord of Chatenay. Then said the King to us: 'Lords, I have hearkened to you, and I will make answer to you of what it shall please me to do, in eight days from now.'

LXXXIV

WHEN we had gone thence, the assault upon me began from all sides: 'Now, Lord of Joinville, is the King a fool, if he give heed to you against all the council of the realm of France.' When the tables were laid, the King had me sit next him at meat, where he used ever to have me sit if his brethren were not there. Never did he speak to me so long as the meal lasted, which was not his custom, for he used always to take notice of me while we were eating. And I thought truly that he was wroth with me for that I had said that he had not yet disbursed any of his moneys, and that he should spend freely.

As the King was hearing grace, I went to a barred window that was in an embrasure by the head of the King's bed; and I put my arms through the bars of the window and

BOOK TWO

thought that if the King went back to France I would go to the Prince of Antioch (who counted me kin and had sent for me) until such time as another expedition should take me to the country, whereby the prisoners might be set free, according to the counsel that the lord of Borlaymont had given me.

At this instant that I was there the King came and leant upon my shoulder and held me with his two hands on my head. And I thought that it was my lord Philip of Nemours who had given me annoyance enow for the counsel that I had given the King; and I spake thus: 'Leave me in peace, my lord Philip.' By misadventure, at the turning of my head, the King's hand fell across my face; and I knew that it was the King by an emerald that he had on his finger. And he said to me: 'Keep ye quiet; for I would ask you how ye are so bold that ye, who are a young man, didst dare to counsel my staying against all the great men and wise of France who counselled my going.'

'Sir,' said I, 'had I evil in my heart, I would not advise you for aught to do it.' 'Say ye,' said he, 'that I should do evil were I to go?' 'God help me, Sir,' said I, 'aye.' And he said to me, 'If I stay, will ye stay?' And I told him, 'Yea, if I can, whether at mine own expense or at another's.' 'Then be ye content,' said he, 'for I owe you thanks for that which ye counselled me; but tell no one all this week.'

I was the easier in my mind for this saying and defended myself the more boldly against them that attacked me. They call the peasants of that country *poulains* or colts; wherefor my lord Peter of Avallon, that dwelt at Tyre, heard say that men called me a colt because I had counselled to the King his staying with the colts. So my lord Peter of Avallon sent me word that I should defend myself against them that called me colt, and say to them that I had liefer be a colt than a broken-down charger such as they were.

LXXXV

ON the next Sunday we all came back before the King; and when the King saw that we were all come, he made the sign of the Cross on his mouth and spake to us thus (after that he had called upon the help of the Holy Spirit, as I take it; for Madam my Mother told me that every time that I wished to say aught, I should call upon the help of the Holy Spirit, and make the sign of the Cross upon my mouth).
The words of the King were these: 'Lords,' said he, 'I thank you much, all you that have counselled my going to France; and render thanks likewise to them that have counselled my staying; but I am of opinion that if I stay I see no danger that my realm should be lost, for Madam the Queen hath men to defend it. And I have heeded also what say the barons of this country, that if we go the Kingdom of Jerusalem is lost since no man will dare tarry after me. I have seen that never at any cost will I leave the Kingdom of Jerusalem to perish which I have come hither to protect and conquer; such is my mind, that I stay here as heretofore. So I say to you, men of substance that are here, and to all other knights that would remain with me, that ye should come and speak with me boldly; and I will give you so much that the fault shall not be mine, but yours, if ye will not stay.' Many were there that heard these words, that were dismayed; and many were there that wept.

BOOK TWO

LXXXVI

THE King gave orders, so men say, that his brethren should return to France. I know not if it were at their request or by the King's wish. This saying of the King's concerning his staying was about the time of the feast of Saint John. Now it befell that on the day of Saint James, whose pilgrim I was and who had brought me many benefits, the King had come back into his chamber after Mass, and sent for his council that remained with him; that is to say, my lord Peter the Chamberlain, who was the most loyal man and the most upright that ever I saw in the household of a King; my lord Geoffrey of Sargines, the good old knight and a man of worth; my lord Giles the Black, both a brave knight and a man of worth, to whom the King had given the Constableship of France, after the death of my noble lord Imbert of Beaujeu. To them spake the King in a loud voice, as if he were wroth: 'Lords, it is already a month since my staying was known, nor have I yet had news that ye have engaged any knights in my service.' 'Sir,' said they, 'we can do naught therein; for every man rateth himself so dear, because they would go back to their own country, that we dare not give them what they ask.' 'And whom', said the King, 'would ye find cheaper?' 'In sooth, Sir,' said they, 'the Seneschal of Champagne; but we dare not give him what he asketh.' I was at that moment in the King's chamber and heard these words. Then said the King: 'Summon me the Seneschal.' I went to him and knelt before him; and he made me sit and spake to me thus: 'Seneschal, ye know that I have loved you much, and my people tell me that they have found you stubborn. How is this?' 'Sir,' said I, 'I can do no other; for ye know that I was taken prisoner on the water, and naught remaineth to me, but

25 July 1250

I have lost all that I had.' And he asked what I was asking; and I told him that I asked a thousand crowns until Easter for the two-thirds of the year. 'Now tell me,' said he, 'have ye made a bargain with any knights?' And I said, 'Aye, my lord Peter of Pontmoulain with two bannerets, who will each cost two hundred crowns till Easter.' And he counted on his fingers. 'That maketh', said he, 'six hundred crowns that your new knights will cost.' 'Now see, Sir,' said I, 'if it will not cost me four hundred crowns to mount me and arm me and to victual my knights; for ye would not have us eat in your house.' Then said he to his people: 'Truly,' said he, 'I see naught outrageous herein'; and 'I will engage you', said he to me.

LXXXVII

AFTER these things the brethren of the King made ready their fleet, and the other rich men that were in Acre. At their departure from Acre, the Count of Poitiers borrowed jewels from them that were going back to France; and to us that were staying he gave of them freely and generously. Much did they beseech me, the one brother and the other, that I should look after the King; and told me that there remained no man in whom they had more trust. When the Count of Anjou saw that he must betake himself to the ship, he showed such grief that all marvelled thereat; and all the same went thence to France.

It was not long after the King's brethren had departed from Acre that the envoys of the Emperor Frederick came to the King and brought him letters of credence, and told the King that the Emperor had sent them for our deliverance. To the King they showed letters that the Emperor was sending to the Sultan that was dead (which the Emperor knew not), and the Emperor bade him give heed to his envoys for the King's deliverance. Many men said that it had been no help to us if the envoys had found us in prison; for men thought that the Emperor had sent his envoys rather to hinder us than to set us free. The envoys found us freed so they went their way.

At the time that the King was in Acre the Sultan of Damascus sent his envoys to the King and made great accusation against the Emirs of Egypt, that had slain his cousin the Sultan; and promised the King that if he would lend him aid, he would hand over to him the Kingdom of Jerusalem that was in his hands. The King was of a mind to make answer to the Sultan of Damascus by his own envoys, that he sent to the Sultan. With the envoys that went thither went Brother Yves le Breton, of the Order of Friars Preachers, who knew the Saracen tongue.

As they went from their lodging to the Sultan's house, Brother Yves saw an old woman that was going across the street, and she carried in her right hand a vessel full of fire, and in her left a phial full of water. Brother Yves asked her, 'What dost thou with these?' She answered him that with the fire she would burn up Paradise, so that there should be none ever again, and with the water quench Hell, so that there should be none ever again. And he asked her, 'Why would ye do this?' 'Because I would not that any should do good to have the guerdon of Paradise nor for the fear of Hell; but only to have the love of God that is of passing worth and can do to us all good.'

LXXXVIII

JOHN the Armenian, that was bowyer to the King, went then to Damascus to buy horns and glue to make crossbows; and he saw an old man, very aged, sitting in the market of Damascus. This old man called him and asked him if he were a Christian; and he told him aye. And he said to him, 'Much hate must there be betwixt you Christians; for once upon a time I saw King Baldwin of Jerusalem, that was a leper, discomfit Saladin; and he had no more than three hundred men-at-arms and Saladin three thousand; now are ye so overwrought by your sins that we drive you down the fields like beasts.'

Then John the Armenian told him that he should hold his peace concerning the sins of Christians, because of the sins which the Saracens committed, which were much greater. And the Saracen answered that he had made answer foolishly. And John asked him why. And he told him that he would tell him, but first he would ask him a question. And he asked if he had a child. And he said, 'Aye, a son.' And he asked him which would annoy him the more, if a man were to give him a blow, whether the Saracen or his son. And he said he would be the more wroth with his son if he did it than with him. 'Now will I give thee,' said the Saracen, 'my answer in this wise: that among you Christians ye are Sons of God, and by His name of Christ are ye called Christian; and such courtesy hath He shown you that He hath given you teachers through whom ye may know when ye do well and when ye do ill. Wherefore God beareth you more grudge for a little sin when ye do it, than He doth to us for a great one who know naught, and who are so blind that we think to be quit of our sins if we can wash ourselves in water ere we die, because Mahomet tells us that at death we may be saved by water.'

John the Armenian was in my company after I had come back from beyond the seas, and I was going to Paris. While we were eating in the pavilion a great crowd of poor folk asked alms of us for the love of God, and made a great brawl. One of our people that was there gave orders and said to a groom: 'Up with you, and drive these beggars out.'

'Ah!' said John the Armenian, 'ye have spoken over-ill; for if the King of France were to send us each by his messengers an hundred marks of silver, we should not drive them away; and ye drive away these envoys that will give you all that they can: that is to say, that they ask that ye give to them for God's sake, which meaneth that ye will give them of your goods, and they will give you God. And God said it out of His own mouth, that they have power to give Him to us; and the saints say that the poor may accord us with Him in such wise that even as water quencheth fire, so doth almsgiving quench sin. Therefore let it never befall you', said John, 'that thus ye drive away poor folk; but give to them and God will give to you.'

LXXXIX

AS the King tarried in Acre, the envoys of the Old Man of the Mountain came to him. When the King came back from Mass he had them come before him. The King had them sit in such wise that there was an Emir before, well dressed and well arrayed: and behind this Emir came a squire well arrayed, who held three knives in his hand, of which one fitted into the handle of the next, because if the Emir had been refused he would have offered the King these three knives in defiance. Behind him that held the knives was there another that held a winding-sheet wound about his arm that he would likewise have presented to the King for his burial, if he had refused the request of the Old Man of the Mountain.

The King told the Emir to tell him his will; and the Emir handed to him a letter of credence and spake thus: 'My Lord sendeth me to you to ask if ye know him.' And the King answered that he knew him not, for he had never seen him, but that he had heard tell of him. 'And since ye have heard tell of my Lord,' said the Emir, 'I marvel much that ye have not sent to him so much of your goods as would have kept him your friend, as do the Emperor of Germany, the King of Hungary, the Sultan of Cairo, and the rest every year, for they are assured that they cannot live but so long as it shall please my lord.

'And if it please you not to do this, make him acquitted of the toll that he oweth to the Hospital and to the Temple, and he will count himself quits with you.' To the Temple and the Hospital did he then pay toll, because they had no fear of the Assassins, since the Old Man of the Mountain gained naught if he had the Master of the Temple or of the Hospital killed; for he knew that if he had one killed, they would forthwith put in his place another as good. Wherefore he would not sacrifice his Assassins in a cause wherein there was naught for him to gain. The King gave answer to the Emir that he should return in the afternoon.

When the Emir was come back, he found the King seated in such wise that the Master of the Hospital sate on one side and the Master of the Temple on the other. Then the King told him to say to him again what he had said in the morning; and he said that he was not of a mind to rehearse it again save before them that had been with the King in the morning. Then the two Masters told him: 'We order you to say it.' And he said that he would say it since they bade him. Then the two Masters had him told, in the Saracen tongue, that he was to come to speak with them at the Hospital on the morrow; and so it was done.

Then the two Masters caused him to be told that his lord was passing rash when he sent such stubborn words to the King; and they had him told that were it not for the honour of the King, to whom they had come as envoys, they would have them drowned in the foul sea of Acre, in their lord's despite. 'And we command you that ye go back to your master, and within a fortnight that ye be back here again, and bring to the King such letters and such jewels from your Master that the King shall account himself appeased and that he have you in his good grace.'

XC

WITHIN the fortnight the envoys of the Old Man came back to Acre and brought to the King the Old Man's shirt; and told the King, on behalf of the Old Man, that it signified that as the shirt is nearer to the body than any other garment, so would the Old Man hold the King closer in love than any other King. And he sent him his ring that was of very fine gold, and thereon his name was written; and sent him word that by his ring did he make alliance anew with the King, for his will was that thenceforward they should be as one.

Among the other jewels that he sent to the King, he sent him an elephant of crystal very well made, and a beast that is called a giraffe, likewise of crystal, balls of divers sorts of crystal, and games of backgammon and chess; and all these things were scented with ambergris, and the amber was fixed upon the crystal with fair filigree of fine gold. And know ye that so soon as the envoys opened their caskets wherein these things were, it seemed that all the chamber was perfumed, so sweet did they smell.

The King sent back his envoys to the Old Man, and returned him great plenty of jewels, scarlet cloth, golden cups, and a silver bridle; and with the envoys he sent Brother Yves le Breton that knew the Saracen tongue. And he found that the Old Man of the Mountain had no faith in Mahomet, but believed the law of Ali that was uncle to Mahomet.

This Ali brought Mahomet to the honour in which he was; and when Mahomet was established in the lordship of the people, he held his uncle in scorn and withdrew from him. And Ali, when he saw this, drew to himself such men as he might, and taught them another belief than that which Mahomet had taught; wherefore it still is, that all they that believe in the law of Ali say that they that believe in the law of Mahomet are misbelievers; and likewise all they that believe in the law of Mahomet say that all they that believe in the law of Ali are misbelievers. One of the points of the law of Ali is that when a man letteth himself be killed by the commandment of his lord, his soul goeth into a gentler body than it had before; and therefore the Assassins are fain to be killed when their lord commandeth, since they believe that they shall be by that much more at ease, when they are dead, than they were before.

The other point is this, that they think that no man can die until the day that is appointed for him; and this should no man believe, for God hath power to lengthen our lives and to shorten them. And in this point do the Bedouins have faith; and therefore will they not arm themselves when they go into battle, for they think to act against the commandment of their law. And when they curse their children, they say to them, 'Be thou curst like the Franks, who bear armour for fear of death.' Brother Yves found a book at the head of the Old Man's bed, wherein were written many sayings that Our Lord said to Saint Peter, when He was on earth. And Brother Yves said to him, 'Ah, Sir, for God's sake read ye often in this book; for these are passing good words.' And he said that he was wont so to do; 'For I hold very dear my lord Saint Peter; for in the beginning of the world, the soul of Abel, when he was killed, went into the body of Noah; and when Noah was dead, it went into the body of Abraham; and from the body of Abraham, when he died, it went into the body of Saint Peter when God came to earth.'

When Brother Yves heard this, he showed him that his belief was not good, and taught him many good precepts; but he would put no faith in them. And these things did Brother Yves explain to the King, when he had come back to us. When the Old Man rode out, he had a crier before him that bare a Danish axe with a long haft all covered with silver, with any number of knives stuck into the haft, and cried: 'Turn ye from before him that beareth between his hands the death of Kings.'

XCI

I HAVE forgot to tell you the answer that the King made to the Sultan of Damascus, which was this: that he was not of a mind to go with him until he knew if the Emirs of Egypt would give him redress for the treaty that they had broken; and that he was sending envoys about it to them, and if they would not make redress for the treaty that they had broken, he would willingly help him to take vengeance for his cousin, the Sultan of Cairo, whom they had killed.

While the King was in Acre he sent my lord John of Valenciennes into Egypt, who made request to the Emirs that they should make restoration for the outrages and the scathe that they had done unto the King. And they said that they would do so willingly if so be that the King would ally himself with them against the Sultan of Damascus. My lord John of Valenciennes reproached them much for the great outrages which they had done unto the King, which have been told ere this; and advised them that it would be well that, to assuage the heart of the King towards them, they should send him all the knights that they held in prison. And so they did; and over and above this they sent all the bones of Count Walter of Brienne to lay in consecrated earth.

When my lord John of Valenciennes had returned to Acre together with two hundred knights that he had brought out of prison, not counting the other people, my lady of Sidon, that was cousin of Count Walter and sister of my lord Walter of Reynel (whose daughter John, Lord of Joinville, took to wife when he came back from beyond the seas), the said lady of Sidon took the bones of Count Walter and had them buried in the Hospital at Acre. And she had the service performed in such wise that each knight offered a candle and a silver penny, and the King offered a candle and a besant of gold, all in the money of my lady of Sidon. Whereat men marvelled that the King should do this, for men had never seen him make offering but of his own money; but he did it of his courtesy.

XCII

AMONG the knights that my lord John of Valenciennes brought back, I found full forty of the Court of Champagne. I had coats and mantles of green cut for them, and led them before the King and prayed him that he would do so much for them that they should remain with him. The King heard what they asked, and was silent.

And a knight of his Council said that I did not well when I brought such tidings to the King, wherein he was abused for three thousand five hundred crowns. And I told him that by ill hap could he say so, and that we of Champagne had lost full thirty-five knights banneret of the Court of Champagne; and I said: 'The King will not do well if he heed you, in the need that he has of knights.' After this saying I began to weep bitterly; and the King told me to hold my peace, and he would give them what I had asked. The King took them into his service as I wished, and put them in my squadron.

The King gave answer to the envoys from Egypt that he would make no treaty with them, if they did not send him all the heads of Christians that hung round the walls of Cairo, from the time that the Count of Bar and the Count of Montfort were taken; and if they did not send him likewise all the children that they had, that had been taken prisoner young and had denied their faith; and if they did not acquit him of the hundred thousand crowns which he still owed. With the envoys to the Emirs of Egypt the King sent my lord John of Valenciennes, a brave man and wise.

At the beginning of Lent, the King made ready, with all the men that he had, to go to fortify Caesarea, which the Saracens had destroyed, which was twelve leagues from

1 March 1251

Acre towards Jerusalem. My lord Raoul of Soissons, who, being sick, had remained in Acre, was with the King to fortify Caesarea. I know not how it was, unless by the will of God, that never did the Saracens do hurt to us all that year. While the King was fortifying Caesarea, the envoys came back to us from the Tartars, and the news that they brought to us will I tell you.

XCIII

AS I have told you ere this, while the King was sojourning in Cyprus, the envoys of the Tartars came to him, and gave him to understand that they would help him to conquer the Kingdom of Jerusalem from the Saracens. The King sent them his envoys in return, and by his envoys that he addressed to them sent a set of chapel hangings that he had made for them of scarlet cloth (and to incline them to our faith, he had had wrought for them in the chapel hangings all our belief, the Annunciation by the Angel, the Nativity, the Baptism whereby God was baptized, and all the Passion and the Ascension and the Coming of the Holy Ghost); chalices and books and all that is needed to sing Mass, and two Friars Preachers to sing Mass before them.

The envoys of the King came to the port of Antioch; and from Antioch to the great King they took a full year's going, riding ten leagues a day. They found all the land subject to the Tartars, and many cities that they had destroyed, and great heaps of the bones of dead men.

They made inquiry how they had come to such authority whereby they had so many men dead and confounded; and the manner was this, as they brought word to the King: that they were born and bred on a great plain of sand where no good thing would grow. This plain had its beginning in certain very great and wonderful rocks,

BOOK TWO

which are at the end of the world towards the East, which rocks hath no man ever crossed, according to the testimony of the Tartars; and they say that therein are enclosed the peoples of Gog and Magog, who shall come at the end of the world when Antichrist shall come to destroy all things.

In this plain was the nation of the Tartars, and they were subject to Prester John and to the Emperor of Persia, whose lands came after theirs, and to several other heathen Kings, to whom they gave tribute and service each year in consideration of the pasturing of their beasts; for they lived by naught else. This Prester John and the Emperor of Persia and the other Kings held the Tartars in such despite that when they brought them their rent they would not receive them face to face, but turned their backs upon them.

Among them was there a wise man that sought through all the plains and spake with the wise men of the plains and of the dwellings, and showed them the servitude wherein they lived, and asked them all that they should take counsel together how they should escape from the servitude wherein men held them. So much did he that he assembled all of them together at the end of the plain, nigh the land of Prester John, and made demonstration to them of these things; and they answered that he should make a plan and they would execute it. And he spake thus, that they had no power to achieve aught, save they had a King and Lord over them; and he taught them the manner in which they might have a King, and they put their trust in him.

And the manner was this, that of the fifty-two tribes among them, each tribe should bring an arrow which bare the sign of their name; and by accord of all the people, it was agreed that they should set these fifty-two before a child of five years; and that which the child first took, of that lineage should they make the King. When the child had picked up one of the arrows, the wise man made all the other tribes withdraw; and it was ordained in such fashion that the tribe wherefrom they were to make the King chose among them fifty-two of the wisest and best men that they had. When they were chosen, each man brought thither an arrow with the sign of his name.

Then was it agreed that of the arrow that the child picked up, of that man should they make the King. And the child picked up one, of that very man of wisdom who had taught them this; and the people were so glad thereat that each man rejoiced. He bade them be silent and said to them: 'Lords, if it be your will that I be your King, ye shall swear to me by Him that hath made heaven and earth, that ye will keep my commandments.' And they sware it.

The ordinances which he made for them were to keep the people in peace; and were these: that no man should steal aught from another, nor any man strike another, unless he would lose his hand; that no man should have company with another man's wife or daughter, unless he would lose his hand or his life. Many other good ordinances did he give them to keep the peace.

XCIV

AFTER he had ordered and arrayed them, he said to them, 'Sirs, the strongest enemy that we have is Prester John. And I command you that tomorrow ye be all ready to ride against him; and if it be that he discomfit us (which Heaven forfend) let each man do the best he can. And if we discomfit him, I command that the pursuit endure for three days and three nights, and that no man be so bold as to lay his hand on any plunder, but only to slay men; for after we have gained the victory, I will divide the plunder among you so fairly and so loyally that each man shall hold himself satisfied.' To this did they all agree.

The next day they rode against their enemy, and, as God willed, discomfited them. All that they found with weapons of defence they slew; but all that they found in religious habits, priests, and other men of religion, did they not slay. The other folk of the land of Prester John, who were not in the host, gave themselves up.

One of the princes of one of the tribes before named was lost a full three months, that no man had news of him; and when he came back he had neither hunger nor thirst, for he thought to have tarried but one night at the most. The tidings that he brought back were these: that he had climbed upon a hill that was passing high, and thereon had found great number of folk, the fairest folk ever that he had seen, the best dressed and the best arrayed; and at the top of the hill he saw a King fairer than the rest, better dressed and arrayed, that sate on a throne of gold.

On his right hand sate six crowned Kings, well arrayed with precious stones, and on his left as many. Near him on his right hand was there a Queen kneeling, who spake to him and besought him to have thought for her people. To his left hand there knelt a man, very fair to see, who had two wings shining like the sun; and round the King was there great plenty of beauteous folk with wings.

The King called this prince and said to him: 'Thou art come from the Tartar host?' And he answered, 'Sir, I am come thence.' 'Thou shalt go to thy King, and shalt tell him that thou hast seen Me, who am Lord of Heaven and Earth; and thou shalt tell him to give Me thanks for the victory that I have given him over Prester John and over his people. And thou shalt tell him also, from Me, that I bestow upon him power to put all the earth in subjection.' 'Sir,' said the prince, 'how shall he believe me?'

'Thou shalt tell him he should believe thee, by these signs: that thou shalt go to combat the Emperor of Persia with three hundred men, and no more, of thy folk; and that thy great King may believe that I have power to do all things, I will give thee victory, to discomfit the Emperor of Persia, who will give thee battle with three hundred thousand men-at-arms and more. Before thou goest to give him battle, thou shalt ask thy King that he give thee the priests and men of religion that he hath taken in the battle; and what they testify to thee shalt thou steadfastly believe, thou and all the people with thee.'

'Sir,' said he, 'I know not how to go hence unless Thou have me guided.' And the King turned towards a great crowd of knights so well armed that it was marvel to behold; and called one, and said: 'George, come hither.' And he came thither and knelt. And the King said to him: 'Rise up and lead me this man to his lodging safely.' And so did he at the dawning of a day.

So soon as the people saw him, they made such rejoicing, and all the host with them, as no man can recount. He asked for the priests from the great King, and he gave them to him; and this prince and all the people received their teachings with so good a grace that they were all baptized. After these things he took three hundred men-at-arms, and had them confessed and made ready, and went to give battle to the Emperor of Persia, and discomfited him and drove him forth from his Kingdom, who went in flight to the Kingdom of Jerusalem; and it was this Emperor that discomfited our folk and took Count Walter of Brienne, as ye shall hear tell hereafter.

BOOK TWO

XCV

THE nation of this Christian King was so great that the envoy of the King told us that they had in their camp eight hundred chapels on wagons. The manner of their life was this, that they ate no bread and lived on flesh and milk. The best meat that they have is horseflesh, and they set it to lie in brine and to dry thereafter, until they cut it like black bread. The best drink that they have and the strongest is mare's milk steeped with herbs. Some one had given the great King of the Tartars a horse laden with flour that had come on a journey three months long; and he gave it to the King's messengers.

There are among them many Christian people that believe in the law of the Greek Church, as well as those of whom we have spoken and others. These they send against the Saracens when they would make war against them; and the Saracens they send against the Christians when they have to do with them. All manner of women that are childless go into battle with them; so that they give pay to the women as to the men, according as they are lusty. And the King's envoys recounted that the men soldiers and the women soldiers ate together in the quarters of the rich men whom they served; and the men dared in no wise touch the women by reason of the law that their first King had given them.

All manner of beasts that die in their camp do they eat. The women that have their children tend them and keep them and dress meat for them that go into battle. The raw flesh they set between their saddles and their skirts; when the blood is well out of it, they eat it quite raw. What they cannot eat they cast into a leathern bag; and when they are hungry, they open the bag, and eat always the oldest piece first. Thus I saw a Khwarizmī that was of the Emperor of Persia's folk, that guarded us in the prison; and when he opened his bag, we stopped our noses; for we could not endure it, for the stench that came out of the bag.

Now come we back to our tale and tell how that when the great King of the Tartars had received the envoys and the presents, he sent under safe conduct for several Kings that had not yet put themselves at his mercy, and had the chapel pitched for them, and spake to them in this wise: 'Sirs, the King of France is at our mercy and come under our vassalage, and behold the tribute that he sendeth; and if ye put not yourselves at our mercy, we will send to fetch him to confound you.' There were enow of them that for fear of the King of France put themselves at the mercy of that other King.

With the envoys of the King came theirs likewise; and they brought letters from their great King to the King of France, that said thus: 'A fair thing is peace; for in a land of peace they that go on four feet eat the grass in quiet; and they that go on two till the land (whence come riches) in quiet. And this do we send thee to give thee counsel; for thou canst not have peace an thou have it not with us. For Prester John rose against us, and these Kings and these (and he named many); and we have put them all to the sword. So we send thee word that thou shalt send us so much of thy gold and of thy silver every year, that thou mayest keep us thy friend; and if thou dost not, we will destroy thee and thy people as we have those aforenamed.' And know ye that the King repented sore that he had ever sent envoys thither.

BOOK TWO

XCVI

NOW come we back to our tale and tell that as the King was fortifying Caesarea, there came to the camp my lord Alenard of Senaingan, who told us that he had built his ship in the realm of Norway, that is at the end of the world towards the West; and in the journey that he made to the King he had gone round the whole of Spain, and had been forced to pass through the straits of Morocco. Through great peril did he come ere he came to us. The King took him into his service, and nine knights under him. And he told us that in the land of Norway the nights were so short in summer that there was no night when a man did not see at once the light of the day at sunset and the light of dawn.

He betook himself, he and his men, to hunting lions, and they caught several very perilously; for they used to go to shoot at them, spurring their horses as hard as they could. And when they had shot, the lion came at them; and thereupon would have overtaken them and devoured them, if it had not been that they let fall a piece of foul cloth; and the lion stopped thereat, and tore this cloth, and ate it; for it thought to be holding a man. As it tore at this cloth, the others came back to shoot at it; and the lion left the cloth and came upon them; and so soon as they let fall a piece of cloth, the lion took heed to the cloth again. And doing thus, they slew the lion with their arrows.

XCVII

WHEN the King was fortifying Caesarea, there came to him my lord Philip of Toucy. And the King said that he was his cousin, for he was descended from one of the sisters of King Philip, that the Emperor Andronicus had to wife. The King took him into his service, for a year, and nine knights under him; and then he went away, and went back to Constantinople whence he had come. He told the King that the Emperor of Constantinople and he, and the other rich men that were in Constantinople at that time, had allied themselves with a people that are called Comans, so that they might have their help against Vataces, that was then Emperor of the Greeks.

In order that the one should aid the other faithfully, it was needful that the Emperor and the other rich men that were with him should be bled and should give their blood into a great cup of silver. And the King of the Comans and the other rich men that were with him did likewise and mixed their blood with the blood of our folk and tempered it with wine and water, and drank thereof, and our men likewise; and then they said that they were blood-brothers. Further, they made a dog cross from our folk to theirs and cut up the dog with their swords, and so did our men likewise; and said that thus should they be cut up if they failed one another.

Further he told us a great marvel that he saw while he was in their camp: that a rich knight lay dead, and they had made him a great grave and wide in the ground, and had set him very nobly and well arrayed in a chair, and they put with him the best horse that he had and the best man-at-arms, both alive. The man, before he was put in the grave with his lord, took his leave of the King of the Comans and of the other rich lords; and at the leave-taking that he made with them, they put in his scarf great plenty of gold and of silver, and told him: 'When I come into the other world shalt thou give me back what I entrust to thee.' And he said, 'So will I, right willingly.'

The great King of the Comans gave him a letter for their first King, which brought him word that this worthy man had led a good life and had served him passing well, and that he should give him the guerdon of his service. When this was done, they put him in the grave with his lord and with the horse, all alive; and then threw over the mouth of the grave planks well joined, and all the host ran for stones and earth; and before they slept had they made in remembrance of those that they had buried a great mound above them.

XCVIII

WHILE the King was fortifying Caesarea, I went into his lodging to see him. So soon as he saw me come into his chamber, where he was speaking with the Legate, he arose and drew me aside, and said to me, 'Ye know', said the King, 'that I hold you in my service only until Easter; I pray you that ye tell me what I am to give you to be with me until Easter year.' And I told him that I would have him give me no more of his money than he had given me already; but that I was of a mind to strike another bargain with him.

'Since', said I, 'that ye are wroth when a man ask anything of you, would I have a covenant with you, that if I ask you aught in all this year, ye be not wroth; and if ye refuse me, I will not be wroth either.' When he heard this, he began to laugh aloud, and told me that he would keep me in his service by this covenant; and took me by the hand, and led me before the Legate and in front of his Council, and bare record to them of the bargain that we had made; and they were mirthful thereat, for I was the richest man in the host.

Hereafter will I tell you how I ordered and arranged my affairs in the four years that I tarried there, after the King's brethren had gone. I had two chaplains with me, who

Easter 1251

said my Hours to me; one of them sang Mass for me so soon as the dawn of the day appeared, and the other waited until my knights and the knights of my squadron were up. When I had heard my Mass, I went out with the King. When the King had a mind to ride, I bare him company. Sometimes it chanced that messengers came to him, wherefore it behoved us to work in the morning. My bed was made in my pavilion in such wise, that no man could enter therein, but he saw me lying in my bed; and this did I to remove all wrong beliefs concerning women. When it came near the feast of Saint Remi, I used to buy my sty of pigs and my sheepfold of sheep, and flour and wine, to victual my dwelling for the whole winter; and this did I because provisions grow dearer in winter, because of the sea which is more froward in winter than in summer. I used to buy a full hundred barrels of wine, and always to have the best drunk first; and I used to have the men's wine tempered with water, and less water in the wine of the squires. At my own table they used to serve for my knights a great vial of wine and a great vial of water, and they watered their wine as they liked.

The King had given me in my squadron forty knights; each time I ate, I used to have ten knights at my table with my own ten, and they used to eat one opposite the other, according to the custom of the country, and used to sit on mats on the floor. Every time that they called us to arms, I sent the four knights that they called captains of ten, for there was one in every ten. Every time that we rode forth armed, all forty knights ate at my house on our return. At all yearly feasts I invited all the men of substance in the host; wherefore the King had sometimes to borrow men whom I had invited.

BOOK TWO

XCIX

HEREAFTER ye shall hear the sentences and judgements which I saw given at Caesarea, while the King was sojourning there. First I will tell you of a knight that was taken in the brothel, to whom a choice was offered, according to the custom of the country. The choice was this: either that the harlot should lead him through the camp, in his shirt, shamefully bound by a cord; or that he should lose his horse and his armour and be driven out of the host. The knight left his horse with the King, and his armour, and went away from the camp.

I went to the King to beg him to give me the horse for a poor gentleman that was in the host. The King answered me that this request was not reasonable, for the horse was still worth two score crowns. And I answered him: 'How is it that ye break your covenant with me, when ye are wroth at that which I have asked of you?' And he told me, laughing: 'Say what ye will, and I will not be wroth.' But all the same I did not get the horse for the poor gentleman.

The second sentence was this, that the knights of our squadron were hunting a wild beast that is called a gazelle, that is like a kid. The brethren of the Hospital came suddenly upon them, and thrust them aside and drove them away. I complained to the Master of the Hospitallers, and the Master of the Hospitallers made answer to me that he would do me justice according to the custom of the Holy Land, which was this, that he would make the brethren who had done the insult eat sitting on their mantles, until such time as those whom they had insulted should raise them up.

The Master fully kept his word; and when we saw that they had eaten for a time sitting on their mantles, I went to the Master and found him at meat, and begged him to have the brethren that ate sitting on their mantles stand up before him; and the knights to whom the insult had been done asked him likewise. And he answered that he would do naught therein; for he would not that his brethren should behave scurvily to them that came on pilgrimage to the Holy Land. When I heard this, I sat me down with the brethren and began to eat with them; and told him I would not rise until the brethren rose. He told me that I used force with him, and granted my request; and made me and my knights that were with me, eat with him; and the brethren came to eat with the rest at a high table.

The third sentence that I saw given at Caesarea was this, that a man-at-arms of the King's, that was called the Glutton, laid hands on a knight of my squadron. I went to complain to the King. The King told me that I must endure it, as it seemed to him; for he had only jostled him. And I told him that I would in no wise endure it; and that if he did not do me justice, I would leave his service, since his men-at-arms could jostle knights.

He had justice done me, and the judgement was this, according to the custom of the country, that the man-at-arms came to my lodging barefoot, in his shirt and drawers, and no more, a naked sword in his hand, and knelt before the knight, took the sword by the point and held out the hilt to the knight, and said to him: 'Sir, I make amends to you for having laid my hands upon you; and have brought you this sword that ye may cut off my hand, an it please you.' And I begged the knight to pardon his misdeed; and so he did.

The fourth penalty was this, that Brother Hugh of Jouy, who was Marshal of the Temple, was sent to the Sultan of Damascus on behalf of the Master of the Temple, to compass how the Sultan of Damascus might come to an agreement concerning a great estate that the Templars had been used to hold, of which the Sultan wished the Temple to hold one half and he the other. These covenants were made in a certain manner, provided that the King should assent to them. And Brother Hugh brought back an Emir from the Sultan of Damascus, and brought the covenants in writing that is called credential.

The Master told these things to the King; whereat the King was sore dismayed, and told him that he was passing bold in that he had made any covenants or parleys with the Sultan without telling him; and the King wished to have redress. And the redress was this, that the King had the flaps of three of his tents raised, and therein were all the common people of the host that had a mind to come; and thither came the Master of the Temple and all the Order, all barefoot, right through the camp, since their lodging lay outside. The King made the Master of the Temple and the Sultan's envoy sit before him, and the King spake in a loud voice to the Master: 'Master, ye shall tell the envoy of the Sultan that it grieveth you that ye have made treaties with him without telling me; and since ye have not spoken thereof to me, ye release him from whatsoever he hath agreed with you and give him back all his covenants.' The Master took the covenants and handed them to the Emir, and then the Master spake thus: 'I render you the covenants that I have wrongly made; wherefore is my heart heavy.' And then the King bade the Master rise, and have all his brethren rise; and so did he. 'Now get ye to your knees, and make amends to me for that ye have gone against my will.'

The Master knelt and held out the end of his mantle to the King, and gave up whatsoever they had, to take as fine as he had a mind to decide. 'And I say', said the King, 'first of all, that Brother Hugh, who hath made the covenants, be banished from all the Kingdom of

Jerusalem.' Neither the Master, who was godfather with the King of the Count of Alençon, that was born at Châtel-Pèlerin, nor even the Queen, nor any other, could help Brother Hugh, nor save him from having to leave the Holy Land and the Kingdom of Jerusalem.

C

WHILE the King was fortifying the city of Caesarea, the envoys from Egypt returned to him, and brought him the treaty, as the King had devised it, as has been told ere this. And the covenants between them and the King were such that the King was to go, on a day appointed, to Jaffa; and on this day that the King was to go to Jaffa were the Emirs of Egypt to be at Gaza by their oath, to deliver to the King the Kingdom of Jerusalem. The treaty, such as the envoys had brought it, did the King and the men of substance in the host swear to, and by our oaths we were bound to help them against the Sultan of Damascus.

May 1252 When the Sultan of Damascus knew that we were allied with them of Egypt, he sent full four thousand Turks well arrayed to Gaza, whither they from Egypt were to come, since he well knew that if they could come to us, he might lose much thereby. All the same, the King did not give up setting out to go to Jaffa. When the Count of Jaffa saw that the King was coming, he arrayed his castle in such wise that it seemed indeed to be a defensible place; for at each battlement (and there were full five hundred) there was a shield of his arms and a pennon; which thing was fair to see, for his arms were *or* a cross patée *gules*.

We lodged round the castle in the fields, and surrounded the castle, that lieth on the sea, from one shore to the other. Meanwhile, the King undertook to fortify a new settlement all round the old castle, from one shore to the other. The King himself have I often seen there bearing a hod to the trenches, to have remission of his sins.

The Emirs of Egypt failed us in the covenants that they had promised; for they durst not come to Gaza because of the folk of the Sultan of Damascus that were there. None the less they kept their covenant with us, in so far as they sent to the King all the heads of Christians that they had hung on the walls of the Castle of Cairo, from the time that the Count of Bar and the Count of Montfort were taken; the which the King had laid in holy ground. They sent him also the children that had been taken when the King was captured, which thing they did against their will, for the children had already forsworn their faith. And with these things they sent to the King an elephant that the King sent to France.

As we sojourned at Jaffa, an Emir that belonged to the faction of the Sultan of Damascus came to reap corn at a village three leagues from the camp. It was agreed that we should ride out against him. When he saw us coming, he took to flight. As he fled, a young gentleman squire took to pursuing him, and bare two of his knights to the ground without breaking his lance; and the Emir struck him in such wise that he brake his spear upon his body.

The envoys of the Emirs of Egypt besought the King that he should appoint a day on which they could come to the King, and they would come without fail. The King was of opinion that he should not refuse them, and gave them a day; and they gave him their covenant, on their oath, that on that day they would be at Gaza.

CI

As we awaited this day that the King had appointed with the Emirs of Egypt, the Count of Eu, that was a squire, came to the camp, and brought with him my lord Arnoul of Guines, the good old knight, and his two brothers, ten all told. He remained in the King's service, and the King knighted him.

At this moment the prince of Antioch returned to the camp, and the princess his mother; to whom the King did great honour, and knighted him very nobly. His age was no more than sixteen years, but a wiser youth I never saw. He asked the King that he would grant him a hearing in his mother's presence. The King vouchsafed it. The words that he spake to the King before his mother were these:

'Sir, it is very true that my mother should hold me yet four years more in her ward; but for all that it is not right that she should let my land be lost or minish; and these things, Sir, do I say because the city of Antioch perisheth in her hands. So I beseech you, Sir, that ye will ask her that she hand over to me money and men, wherewith I may go to succour my folk that are there, and bring them aid. And, Sir, she should indeed do it; for if I tarry with her in the city of Tripoli, it will not be without great expense, and the great expenditure that I should make would serve for naught.'

The King heard him right willingly, and worked upon his mother with all his might that she should hand over as much as the King could get out of her. So soon as he left the King he went to Antioch, where he did much for his patrimony. By the King's favour he quartered his arms, which are *gules*, with the arms of France, because the King had made him knight.

With the prince came three minstrels from Great

Armenia; and they were brethren, and were going to Jerusalem on pilgrimage; and they had three horns, whereof the sound came from the side of their faces. When they began to play, ye would have said that it was the sound of swans that were leaving a pool; and they made the sweetest melodies and the most gracious, that it was marvel to hear them. The three used to make marvellous leaps; for they set a cloth under their feet, and tumbled as they stood, so that their feet came down as they stood upon the cloth. The two used to tumble with their heads backwards, and the eldest likewise; when he had to tumble with his head forwards, he crossed himself, for he was afraid lest he should break his neck in tumbling.

CII

SINCE it is a good thing that the memory of the Count of Brienne, that was Count of Jaffa, be not forgotten, will we presently tell you concerning him, for he held Jaffa for many years, and by his vigour defended it long time; and lived in great part on what he used to take from the Saracens and from the enemies of the faith. Whence it befell once that he discomfited a great number of Saracens that were bringing great plenty of cloth of gold and of silk, all which he took; and when he had brought it to Jaffa, he divided everything among his knights, so that naught of it was left him. His way was this, that when he had left his knights, he would shut himself up in his chapel, and would be a long time in prayer before he would go at night to lie with his wife, that was a passing good lady and wise, and sister to the King of Cyprus.

The Emperor of Persia, that was called Bārbaqān, that one of the princes of the Tartars had discomfited, as I have told ere now, came thence with his host to the

Kingdom of Jerusalem; and took the castle of Tiberias, that my lord Odo of Montbéliard, the Constable, had fortified, that was Lord of Tiberias in right of his wife. Very great hurt did he do to our folk; for he destroyed all that he found outside Châtel-Pèlerin, and outside Acre, and outside Ṣafad, and outside Jaffa likewise. And when he had done this harm, he withdrew to Gaza to the Sultan of Cairo, that was to come thither to vex and annoy our folk.

The barons of the country were of opinion, and the Patriarch with them, that they should go forth to give him battle ere the Sultan of Cairo should come. And to bear them aid they sent to seek the Sultan of Homs, one of the best knights there was in all paynimry, to whom they showed such honour in Acre that they spread cloths of gold and silk wheresoever he was to go. They came *1244* thence as far as Jaffa, our men and the Sultan with them. The Patriarch held Count Walter excommunicate, because he would not give him back a tower that he held in Jaffa, which men called the Patriarch's Tower. Our folk begged Count Walter to go with them to give battle to the Emperor of Persia; and he said that he would gladly, but on condition that the Patriarch would absolve him until their return. Never would the Patriarch do aught in the matter; yet all the same Count Walter set out and went with them. Our folk made three squadrons, whereof Count Walter had one, the Sultan of Homs another, and the Patriarch and the men of the land the other; in the host of the Count of Brienne were the Hospitallers.

They rode out until they could see their enemies before their eyes. So soon as our people saw them, they halted, and the enemy formed three squadrons likewise. While the Khwarizmī were arraying their hosts, Count Walter came to our people and cried out to them: 'My lords, for God's sake let us go at them; for we are giving them time, since we have come to a halt.' But there was never a one that would take heed to him.

When Count Walter saw this, he went to the Patriarch and asked him absolution in the manner aforesaid; but the Patriarch would have none of it. With the Count of Brienne there was a valiant clerk, that was Bishop of Ramleh, that had done many fair and knightly deeds in the Count's company; and he said to the Count: 'Trouble not your conscience whether the Patriarch absolve you; for he is in the wrong, and ye are in the right; and I absolve you in the name of the Father and of the Son and of the Holy Ghost. Now go we at them.'

Then they struck spurs into their horses and encountered the host of the Emperor of Persia, that was the last. Great plenty of men was there dead on one side and the other, and Count Walter was there taken prisoner; for all our own men took to flight in such scurvy fashion that there were many that from despair drowned themselves in the sea. This despair came upon them because one of the hosts of the Emperor of Persia encountered the Sultan of Homs, the which defended himself so long against them, that of two thousand Turks that he led there, there remained but four-score when he left the field.

CIII

THE Emperor took counsel to go to beleaguer the Sultan in the Castle of Homs, since it seemed to him that the Sultan could not long hold it by reason of his men that he had lost. When the Sultan discovered this, he went to his people and told them that he was going forth to give the Emperor battle; for if he let himself be beleaguered, he would be lost. He ordered his affairs in such wise that all his men that were armed, he sent by a sheltered valley; and so soon as they heard the drums of the Sultan, they were to attack the camp of the Emperor from the rear and set to killing the women and children.

And so soon as the Emperor, that had gone into the field to give battle to the Sultan whom he saw before his eyes, heard the cry of his people, he turned back to the camp to succour their women and children; and the Sultan came against them, he and his men; which fell out so well, that of twenty-five thousand that they had been, there remained neither man nor woman, but all were put to the sword and slain.

Before the Emperor of Persia came to Homs, he had brought Count Walter before Jaffa; and they hanged the Count by the arms to a gibbet, and told him that they would not take him down until they held the Castle of Jaffa. And as he hung by the arms, he cried out to them that were in the Castle, that they were not to give up the town for any harm they did him, and that if they gave it up, he himself would slay them.

When the Emperor saw this, he sent Count Walter to Cairo and made a present to the Sultan of him, and of the Master of the Hospital, and of divers other prisoners that he had taken. They that brought the Count to Cairo were full three hundred, and were not slain when the Emperor died before Homs. And these Khwarizmī encountered us on the Friday that they came to attack us, and we were on foot. Their banners were scarlet and were jagged right up to the staves; and on the staves were there heads made of hair that seemed like the heads of devils.

Divers merchants of Cairo cried after the Sultan that he should grant them justice against Count Walter, for the great hurts that he had done them; and the Sultan gave him up to them so that they might take their vengeance upon him. And they went to slay him in the prison and to martyr him; wherefore should we have faith that he is in Heaven among the number of the martyrs.

The Sultan of Damascus took his men that were at Gaza and went into Egypt. The Emirs came to give him battle. The host of the Sultan discomfited the Emirs that it encountered, and the other host of the Emirs of Egypt discomfited the rearguard host of the Sultan of Damascus. So the Sultan of Damascus withdrew to Gaza, wounded in the head and in the hand. And before he left Gaza, the Emirs of Egypt sent their envoys and made peace with him, and broke all their covenants with us; and thenceforward we were in a state of having no truce nor peace either with them of Damascus or with them of Cairo. And know ye that when we were at our most for men-at-arms, we were never more than fourteen hundred.

CIV

WHEN the King was encamped before Jaffa, the Master of the Order of Saint Lazarus had espied nigh Ramleh, almost twelve miles off, cattle and other things whereby he thought to have great gain, and he, that held no rank in the host but did as he would in the camp, went thither without having speech of the King. When he had gathered in his booty, the Saracens came up against him and discomfited him in such wise that of all the men that he had with him in his squadron, there escaped but four.

So soon as he was come into the camp, he began to call to arms. I went to arm, and begged the King that he would let me go thither; and he gave me leave and bade me take with me the men of the Temple and the Hospital. When we were come thither, we found that other stranger Saracens had come suddenly into the valley wherein the Master of Saint Lazarus had been discomfited. As these stranger Saracens looked at the dead, the master of the King's crossbowmen attacked them; and before we were come thither, our men had discomfited them and had slain divers of them.

A man-at-arms of the King's and one of the Saracens bare each other to the ground by strokes of their spears. Another of the King's men-at-arms, when he saw this, took the two horses and led them away to purloin them; and so that no man should see him, he gat himself between the walls of the city of Ramleh. As he led them, an old cistern over which he was passing gave way beneath him; the three horses and he with them went to the bottom, and men told me of it. I went thither to see, and saw that the cistern was still falling down upon them, and that it wanted little for them to be all buried. So we returned without loss, save for them that the Master of Saint Lazarus had lost there.

CV

SO soon as the Sultan of Damascus had made peace with them of Egypt, he sent word to his folk, that were at Gaza, that they were to come back to him; and so they did. And they passed before our camp at a distance of less than two leagues, but never durst attack us; and they were full twenty thousand Saracens and ten thousand Bedouins. Before they came nigh our camp, the master of the King's crossbowmen and his squadron guarded it for three days and three nights that they should not come against our camp unawares.

6 May 1253 On Saint John's Day, which fell after Easter, the King was hearing the sermon. As the preaching went on, a man-at-arms of the master of the crossbowmen came all armed into the King's chapel and told him that the

Saracens had hedged in the master crossbowman. I asked the King that he would let me go thither, and he vouchsafed it, and told me that I was to take with me up to four or five hundred men-at-arms, and named to me those that he wished me to take. So soon as we came forth out of the camp, the Saracens that had set themselves between the master of the crossbowmen and the camp went to an Emir that was on a hillock before the master of the crossbowmen with full a thousand men-at-arms. Then the brawl began between the Saracens and the men of the master of the crossbowmen, whereof there were full fourteen score. As soon as the Emir saw that his men were pressed he sent them aid and so many men that they drove our men-at-arms right into the master's squadron. When the master saw that his folk were pressed, he sent them a hundred or six score men-at-arms, that drove them back again right into the host of the Emir. While we were there, the Legate and the barons of the country that had stayed with the King, told the King that he did great folly when he sent me into jeopardy; and by their counsel the King sent to bring me back again, and the master of the crossbowmen likewise. The Turks made their way thence, and we came back to the camp. Many men marvelled that they did not come to give us battle, and some said that they would not have abstained but by reason that they and their horses had all been starving at Gaza, where they had sojourned for nearly a year.

CVI

WHEN these Saracens were gone from before Jaffa, they came before Acre and sent word to the Lord of 'Arṣūf, that was Constable of the Kingdom of Jerusalem, that they would destroy the gardens of the town an he send them not fifty thousand besants; and he sent word to them that he would not send them one. Then they had their squadrons arrayed, and went right across the sands of Acre, so close to the city as one might have shot with a swivel crossbow. The Lord of 'Arṣūf came out of the town and set himself on Saint John's Hill, where is the cemetery of Saint Nicholas, to defend the gardens. Our foot-soldiers came forth from Acre and began to provoke them with bows and crossbows.

The Lord of 'Arṣūf summoned a knight of Genoa, that was named my lord John the Great, and bade him withdraw the lesser folk that had come forth from Acre, that they should not put themselves in peril. As he brought them to the rear, a Saracen began to cry out to him in the Saracen tongue that he would joust with him an he would; and he said that he would do so gladly. As my lord John went towards the Saracen to joust, he looked to his right hand; and saw there a little troop of Turks, wherein there were as many as eight men, who had come to a halt to see the joust.

He left the joust of the Saracen against whom he was to ride, and went towards the troop of Turks that stayed quite still to watch the jousting, and struck one of them through the body with his lance and laid him dead. When the others saw this, they came at him while he was coming back towards our people, and one of them struck him a great blow with a mace on his steel cap; and as he passed, my lord John struck him with his sword on a cloth that he had wound round about his head, and made the turban fly off into the fields. They used to wear these turbans when they were meaning to give battle, because they take the brunt of a great sword-stroke.

One of the other Turks spurred up to him, and would have given him his spear between the shoulders; but my lord John saw the spear coming, and turned aside; and as the Saracen passed, my lord John gave him a backhand stroke with his sword through the arm, so that he made his spear fly into the fields. And so he returned and brought back his foot-soldiers; and these three fair blows did he give before the Lord of 'Arṣūf and the men of substance that were in Acre, and before all the women that were on the walls to see these folk.

CVII

WHEN this great number of Saracen folk that were before Acre, and durst not give us battle, as ye have heard, nor those of Acre either, heard tell (and it was truth) that the King was having the city of Sidon fortified, and by few good men, they drew off to those parts. When my lord Simon of Montléart, that was master of the King's crossbowmen and chieftain of the King's people at Sidon, heard tell that these folk were coming, he retired to the Castle of Sidon, that is very strong and is shut in by the sea on every side; and this did he since he well saw that he was not able to resist them. With him he gave shelter to what folk he could, but there were few of them for the castle was over small.

The Saracens rushed into the town, where they encountered no defence, for it was not wholly walled. More than two thousand of our people did they slay; and with all the plunder that they took there went off to Damascus. When the King heard these tidings, greatly was he wroth thereat (if that had helped matters!); and the barons of the country did well out of it, for the King had been of a mind to go to fortify a hillock where there had once been an old castle in the time of the Maccabees. This castle standeth as one goeth from Jaffa to Jerusalem.

The barons of oversea were not agreed to fortify the

castle anew, because it was five leagues off from the sea; wherefore no victuals could reach us from the sea, but the Saracens would take them, that were stronger than we. When these tidings came to the camp from the town of Sidon that was destroyed, the barons of the land came to the King, and told him that it would be more to his honour to fortify anew the town of Sidon, that the Saracens had overthrown, than to make a new fortress; and the King agreed with them.

CVIII

WHILE the King was at Jaffa he was told that the Sultan of Damascus would suffer him to go to Jerusalem, and with good safe-conduct. The King held a great council thereon; and the end of the council was this, that no man advised the King that he should go there, for he would have had to leave the city in the hands of the Saracens.

They showed the King a precedent, that was this: that when the great King Philip went from before Acre to go to France, he left all his men to stay in the camp with Duke Hugh of Burgundy, grandfather of the Duke that is newly dead. While the Duke was sojourning at Acre, and King Richard of England likewise, tidings reached them that they could take Jerusalem on the morrow an they would, because all the force of horsemen of the Sultan of Damascus were gone to him, for a war that he had with another Sultan. They arrayed their host, and the King of England had the first squadron, and the Duke of Burgundy the next, together with the men of the King of France.

When they were purposing to take the city, word was sent from the Duke's host that the King of England go not forward; for the Duke was turning back, in order (and no more) that men should not say that the English

SIDON. THE CHÂTEAU DE LA MER
(*Phot. J. E.*)

had taken Jerusalem. As they spake thus, one of his knights cried out: 'Sir, Sir, come hither and I will show you Jerusalem.' And when the King heard this, he cast his surcoat before his eyes, weeping, and said to Our Lord: 'Fair Lord God, I pray Thee that Thou suffer me not to see Thine holy city, since I may not deliver it from the hands of Thine enemies.'

This precedent did they show the King, by reason that if he, that was the greatest King in Christendom, made his pilgrimage without delivering the city from the enemies of God, all the other Kings and the other pilgrims that should come after him would hold themselves content to make their pilgrimage even as the King of France had done, and would make no endeavour for the deliverance of Jerusalem.

King Richard did such feats of arms overseas what time that he was there, that when the Saracens' horses were afeared of a bush, their masters would say to them: 'Thinkest thou', would they say to their horses, 'that it be King Richard of England?' And when the Saracens' children used to bawl, the women would say to them: 'Hush, hush, or I will go for King Richard who will kill thee.'

CIX

THE Duke of Burgundy, of whom I have spoken, was a passing good knight of his hands; but he was never held wise either for God or for the world; and so he appeareth in the deed aforesaid. Whereof spake the great King Philip, when men told him that Count John of Chalon had a son, and he was called Hugh after the Duke of Burgundy, and he said: 'God make him as brave a man as the Duke after whom he is called Hugh.'

And they asked him why he had not said as worthy a

man: 'Because', said he, 'there is a great difference between a brave man and a man of worth, a *preux-homme* and a *prud'homme*. For there are many brave men, knights in the land of the Christians and of the Saracens, that never believed in God or in His Mother. Wherefore I tell you', said he, 'that God giveth a great gift and great grace to the Christian knight whom he suffereth to be valiant in body and that he endureth in his service keeping him from mortal sin; and he that thus demeaneth himself should men call *prud'homme*, a man of worth, for this prowess cometh to him from God. And them of whom I have spoken may men call brave men, *preux-hommes*, for they are valiant in body, and fear neither God nor sin.'

Of the great moneys that the King laid out to fortify Jaffa it is not fitting to speak, for they were uncounted; for he fortified the town from one sea to the other, and therein there were full four and twenty towers; and the fosses were cleared of mud within and without. Three gates were there, whereof the Legate made one, and a piece of wall.

And to show you the cost that the King laid out therein, will I have you know that I asked the Legate how much this gate and this piece of wall had cost him; and he asked me how much I thought they had cost; and I reckoned that the gate that he had caused to be built would have cost him full two thousand five hundred crowns, and the piece of wall a thousand five hundred crowns. And he told me that, as God helped him, the gate and the wall had cost him full fifteen thousand crowns.

CX

WHEN the King had completed the fortress of the town of Jaffa, he took counsel that he should go to fortify anew the city of Sidon, that the Saracens had overthrown. He set out to go

PLATE 5

SIDON. THE CHÂTEAU DE SAINT LOUIS
(*Phot. J. E.*)

BOOK TWO

thither on the feast day of the Apostles Saint Peter and 29 June
Saint Paul, and the King and his host lay before the castle 1253
of 'Arṣūf, that is very strong. That night the King summoned his people, and told them that if they agreed, he would go to take a city of the Saracens that is called Naplous, which city the ancient Scriptures call Samaria. The Templars and the Hospitallers and the barons of the land answered him with one consent, that it was well to essay to take the city; but they in no wise agreed that he should go there in person, because if aught befell him, all the land would be lost. And he said that never would he let them go thither if he went not in person with them. And so this emprise went no farther, since the lords of the land would not agree that he should go thither.

By day's marches we came to the sands of Acre, where we pitched camp, the King and the host. Thither in that place came to me a troop of many people from Great Armenia, that were going on pilgrimage to Jerusalem, having paid a great toll to the Saracens that guided them. By an interpreter that knew their language and ours, they begged me that I would show them the saintly King. I went to the King where he sate in a pavilion, leaning against the pole of the pavilion; and he sate on the sand, without carpet or any other thing under him. I said to him: 'Sir, there is without a band of many folk from Great Armenia, that are going to Jerusalem, and they pray me, Sir, that I have them shown the saintly King; but I have no wish yet to kiss your bones.' And he laughed aloud and told me to go to fetch them; and so I did. And when they had seen the King, they commended him to God, and the King them.

On the morrow the host lay at a place that is called Passe-Poulain, which is to say the Colt's Crossing, where there is very good water wherewith they water the plant whence sugar cometh. When we were lodged there, one of my knights said to me: 'Sir', said he, 'now have I lodged you in a fairer place than ye were in yesterday.' The other knight that had chosen the place before, leapt up all dismayed, and said to him aloud: 'Ye are over bold when ye speak of a matter that I have done.' And he leapt upon him and seized him by the hair. And I arose and struck him with my fist between the shoulders, and he let go; and I said to him: 'Now out of my house; for (as God may help me!) with me shall ye not be again.' The knight went away mourning much and brought to me my lord Giles the Black, the Constable of France; and he, by reason of the great repentance that he saw that the knight felt for the folly he had done, begged me, as instantly as he might, that I would take him back into my household. And I answered that I would not take him back unless the Legate would absolve me from mine oath. They went to the Legate and told him the tale; and the Legate answered them that he could not absolve me, because the oath was reasonable; for the knight had well deserved it. And these things do I make clear to you, that ye may keep yourselves from taking an oath that it is not fitting to take reasonably; for, as the Wise Man saith: 'Whoso sweareth easily, easily forsweareth himself.'

CXI

ON the morrow the King went to lie before the city of Sur, that is called Tyre in the Bible. There the King summoned the men of substance of the host, and asked counsel of them whether it would be well that he should go to take the city of Bāniyās before he went to Sidon. We all advised that it was well that the King should send some of his people thither; but no man counselled that he should go there in person; and with much ado did men turn him from it. It was agreed thus, that the Count of Eu should go, and my lord Philip of Montfort, the lord of Tyre, my lord Giles the Black, Constable of France, my lord Peter the Chamberlain, the Master of the Temple and his Order, and the Master of the Hospital and his brethren likewise.

We armed ourselves at nightfall, and came a little after daybreak into a plain that is before the city that is called Bāniyās; and the ancient Scripture calleth it Caesarea Philippi. In this city riseth a fountain that men call Jor; and among the plains that surround the city riseth another very fair fountain that is called Dan. Now so it is, that when the two streams of these two fountains meet together, men call the river Jordan, wherein God was baptized.

By consent of the Templars and of the Count of Eu, of the Hospital and of the barons of the land there present, it was agreed that the King's squadron (in which squadron I then was, since the King had kept the forty knights that were in my squadron with him), and my lord Geoffrey of Sargines, the noble knight, likewise, should get between the castle and the city; and the lords of the land should enter the city on the left hand, and the Hospital on the right, and the Temple should get into the city straight ahead by the way that we had come.

We set forth until we were come nigh the city, and found that the Saracens that were in the town had discomfited the men-at-arms of the King and had driven them forth out of the town. When I saw this, I went to the men of worth that were with the Count of Eu, and said to them: 'My lords, if ye go not whither we are ordered, between the castle and the town, the Saracens will slay our men that have gone into the city.' The going thither was passing perilous; for the place whither we were to go was very parlous in that there were three double dry walls to cross, and the slope was so steep that a horse could hardly stand thereon; and the hillock that we were to make for was held by great plenty of Turks on horseback. As I spake to them, I saw that our foot-soldiers were breaking down the walls. When I saw this, I said to them with whom I was speaking, that orders had been given that the King's squadron should go thither where the Turks were; and since those were the orders I would go. I made my way, I and my two knights, towards them that were breaking down the walls, and saw that a mounted man-at-arms had thought to cross the wall, and that his horse had fallen on his body. When I saw this, I dismounted and took my horse by the bridle. When the Turks saw us coming, as God would, they left the place whither we were to go. From this place where the Turks had been a sheer rock went down into the city.

When we had got there and the Turks had gone thence, the Saracens that were in the city were discomfited and left the town to our people without dispute. As I stood there, the Master of the Temple heard tell that I was in danger, and came thither uphill towards me. While I was standing at the top of the hill, the Germans that were in the squadron of the Count of Eu followed me; and when they saw the Turks on horseback that were flying towards the castle, they set out to go after them; and I said to them: 'My lords, ye do not well; for we are here where we have been ordered to be, and ye go beyond your orders.'

CXII

THE castle that standeth above the city is called Ṣubayba, and standeth full half a league up in the mountains of Lebanon; and the foothill that goeth up to the castle is strewn with great rocks as big

THE HEIGHTS OF ṢUBAYBA
(Phot. American Colony Photographers, Jerusalem)

as chests. When the Germans saw that it was folly to pursue, they came back to the rear. When the Saracens saw this, they made at them on foot, and gave them great blows with their maces from above the rocks, and tore away the housings of their horses.

When our men-at-arms that were with us saw the mischief, they began to be dismayed; and I told them that if they went thence I would have them cast forth out of the King's pay for ever afterwards. And they said to me: 'Sir, the lots have fallen uneven between us; for ye are on horseback, if ye fly; and we are on foot, and the Saracens will slay us.' And I said to them: 'Sirs, I give you my word that I will not fly; for I will stay afoot with you.' I dismounted and sent my horse to be with the Templars, that were a good crossbow-shot behind.

As the Germans came back, the Saracens struck a knight of mine, that was called my lord John of Bussey, with a quarrel through the throat; and he fell dead just before me. My lord Hugh of Écot, who had proved himself worthy in the Holy Land, and was his uncle, said to me: 'Sir, come help us to bring in my nephew down the hill.' 'An ill turn will he do', said I, 'that helpeth you therein: for ye have gone up there without my orders; and if ill hath befallen you therefrom, it is with good reason. Take him down to the town ditch, for I will not go hence until they send for me back.'

When my lord John of Valenciennes heard of the plight in which we were, he went to my lord Oliver of Termes and to those other chieftains of Languedoc, and said to them: 'My lords, I beg and command you, in the King's name, that ye lend me your aid to seek the Seneschal.' As he endeavoured thus, my lord William of Beaumont came to him and said to him: 'Ye labour for naught, for the Seneschal is dead.' And he answered: 'Dead or alive, I will bring tidings of him to the King.' Then he set out and came towards us, where we were up on the hill; and when he was come to us, he sent word to me to come to speak with him; and so I did.

Then Oliver of Termes said to me that we were in great peril in that place; for if we went down by the way that we had come, we could not do it without great loss, for the hillside was too steep, and the Saracens would leap down upon our bodies: 'But if ye would give heed to me, I will deliver you without loss.' And I told him that he should devise what he would, and I would do it.

'I will tell you', said he, 'how we may escape. We will go', said he, 'all along this slope as if we were going towards Damascus; and the Saracens that are there will think that we mean to take them in the rear. And when we are in the plains, we will set spur to our horses round the city and we shall have crossed the brook before they can reach us; and so shall we do them great hurt; for we will set fire to this threshed grain that is lying about in the fields.'

We did even as he devised; and he had them take canes such as men make flutes of, and had live coals put therein, and set them in the grain. And thus God led us back into safety by the counsel of Oliver of Termes. And know ye that when we came to the lodging where our people were, we found them all disarmed; for there was never a man that had taken heed for us. So we came back on the morrow to Sidon, where was the King.

CXIII

WE found that the King himself had caused the Christians to be buried that the Saracens had slain, as has been told above; and he himself in person bare the corpses, all rotten and stinking, to lay them in the earth in the graves, and never stopped his nose, although the others stopped theirs. He caused workmen to come from all parts, and began again to fortify the city with high walls and great towers. And when we came into the camp, we found that he himself had measured out the places where we were to lodge; my place had he chosen nigh the place of the Count of Eu, for he knew that the Count of Eu loved my company.

I will tell you of the pranks that the Count of Eu played upon us. I had a house made wherein I used to eat, I and my knights, by the light of the door. Now the door was on the side of the Count of Eu; and he, that was very subtle, had a little engine for throwing stones made, which cast within; and he espied when we were seated at meat, and trained his engine along the table, and had it shoot, and brake our pots and our glasses. I had stocked myself with hens and capons; and some one (I know not who) had given him a young she-bear, which he let come at my hens; and it had killed a dozen quicker than a man could get there; and the woman that looked after them beat the bear with her distaff.

CXIV

WHILE the King was fortifying Sidon, merchants came to the camp that spake with us and told that the King of the Tartars had taken the city of Bagdad and the Pope of the Saracens, that was lord of the city, whom men called the Caliph of Bagdad. The merchants told us the manner whereby they took the city of Bagdad and the Caliph: and the manner was this, that when they had the city of the Caliph beleaguered, the King of the Tartars sent word to the Caliph that he would readily have marriages made between the Caliph's children and his own; and the council of the Caliph advised him to agree to the marriage.

And the King of the Tartars sent word to him demanding that he should send him as many as forty persons of his Council, and those from among the greatest folk, to depose to the treaty of marriage; and so the Caliph did. Again the King of the Tartars sent word that he should send him forty of the richest and noblest men that he had; and so the Caliph did. The third time he sent word that he was to send him forty of the best men of his company; and so he did. When the King of the Tartars saw that he held all the chief men of the city, he bethought himself that the lesser folk of the town would not be able to defend themselves without leaders. He had all the six-score great men beheaded, and then assaulted the town and took it, and the Caliph likewise.

To cover his treachery, and to throw on the Caliph the blame for the taking of the city that he had achieved, he had the Caliph taken and set in an iron cage, and caused him to fast for as long as a man may without dying; and then he asked him if he were hungry. And the Caliph said, 'Aye'; which was no marvel. Then the King of the Tartars had a great charger of gold brought, laden with jewels set with precious stones, and said to him: 'Knowest thou these jewels?' And the Caliph answered: 'Aye; they were mine.' And he asked him if he loved them well; and he answered, 'Aye.'

'Since thou lovest them so much', said the King of the Tartars, 'then take of them such portion as thou wilt, and eat.' The Caliph answered that he could not, for they were not meat that a man might eat. Then said the King of the Tartars: 'Now thou mayest see thy fault; for if thou hadst given thy treasure (whereby thou canst not have succour in this hour) to the men-at-arms, thou wouldst have been well defended against us by thy treasure, an thou hadst disbursed it, that faileth thee now in the greatest need in which thou hast ever been.'

CXV

WHILE the King was fortifying Sidon, I went to his Mass at daybreak, and he bade me wait for him, for he was of a mind to ride; and so I did. When we were out in the fields, we came by a little church and saw, as we rode, a priest that was singing Mass. The King told me that this church had been built in honour of the miracle that God wrought on the devil that he cast out of the body of the widow woman's daughter; and he told me that an I would, he would hear in that place the Mass that the priest had begun, and I told him that it meseemed it were a good thing to do.

When it came to giving the pax, I saw that the clerk that served the Mass was tall, black-avised, thin, and bristle-haired, and I feared that if he bare the pax to the King, that maybe he was an Assassin, an evil man, and might slay the King. I went to take the pax from the clerk and bare it to the King. When Mass was sung, and we were mounted on our horses, we found the Legate in the fields; and the King drew near to him and called me and said to the Legate: 'I make complaint to you of the Seneschal, who brought me the pax himself, and would not have the poor clerk bring it me.'

And I told the Legate the reason wherefore I had done this; and the Legate said that I had done very well. And the King made answer: 'Nay, forsooth.' Great dispute was there between the two of them and I stayed in peace. And this tale have I told you, that ye may see the great humility of the man. Of this miracle that God wrought upon the daughter of the widow woman the Gospel speaketh, and saith that God, when he wrought the miracle, was *in parte Tyri et Syndonis*; for then the city of Sur that I have named to you, was called Tyre; and the city of Sayette that I have named to you before, Sidon.

CXVI

WHILE the King was fortifying Sidon, there came to him envoys from a great lord of farthest Greece, that called himself the Great Comnenus and lord of Trebizond. They brought to the King divers jewels as a present. Among the rest they brought bows of horn, whereof the nocks were set by a screw within the bow; and when one thought them outside, one found that they were within, well-edged and very well made.

They made request from Comnenus that the King should send him a maiden from his palace, and he would take her to wife. And the King made answer that he had brought none from oversea; and advised them that they should go to Constantinople to the Emperor, that was cousin to the King, and ask him to hand over a wife for their lord, such as was of the King's lineage and of his own. And this did he, that the Emperor might have an alliance with this great and rich man against Vataces that was then Emperor of the Greeks.

The Queen, that was newly uprisen after the birth of my lady Blanche, of whom she had lain in at Jaffa, landed at Sidon, for she had come by sea. When I heard tell that she had come, I rose up from before the King and went to meet her and brought her to the castle.

And when I came back to the King, that was in his chapel, he asked me if the Queen and the children were well; and I told him Yea. And he said to me: 'I well knew when ye arose from before me, that ye went to meet the Queen; and therefore have I waited for you for the sermon.' And these things do I recount to you, because I had then been five years in his company, and never yet had heard him speak to me of the Queen or of his children, nor, as I heard, to any other; and this was not good usage, as it seemeth to me, to be stranger to wife and children.

CXVII

ON All Saints' Day I invited all the men of substance in the camp to my house, that was by the sea; and then a poor knight came to shore in a little ship, and his wife and four sons that they had. I had them come to meat in my house. When we had eaten, I called the rich men that were there, and said to them: 'Let us make a great almsgiving, and take over the charge of his children from this poor man; and let each man take his, and I will take one of them.' Every man took one, and they strove with each other to have one. When the poor knight saw this, he and his wife, they began to weep for joy.

1 November 1253

Now it so befell, that when the Count of Eu came back from eating in the King's house, he came to see the men of substance that were at my house, and took from me my child, that was twelve years old, who served the Count so well and so loyally that when we came back to France the Count arranged a marriage for him and made him a knight. And every time that I was where the Count was, scarcely could he leave me, and would say to me; 'Sir, God render it to you again! For to this honour have ye brought me.' I know not what befell the other three brethren.

CXVIII

I BESOUGHT the King that he would let me go on pilgrimage to Our Lady of Tortosa, where there was a very great pilgrimage, since it is the first altar that ever was made in honour of the Mother of God on earth.

And there used Our Lady to work passing great miracles; and among the rest was there a man out of his mind that had the Devil in his body. In that place when his friends that had brought him thither prayed to Our Lady that she would give him health, the enemy that was within him made answer to them: 'Our Lady is not here, but is in Egypt, to succour the King of France and the Christians that on this day land in that country, on foot, against the paynim on horseback.' The day was put in writing and was brought to the Legate, as he himself told me out of his own mouth. And be ye sure that she succoured us; and would have helped us more had we not angered her, and her Son likewise, as I have told before.

The King gave me leave to go thither, and told me in his great Council that I was to buy him an hundred pieces of grogram of divers colours, to give to the Grey Friars when we came to France. Then was my heart lightened, for I well surmised that he would not tarry long. When we came to Tripoli, my knights asked me what I was of a mind to do with the cloth, and begged that I would tell them: 'Maybe', said I, 'have I stolen it for gain.'

The prince there (God rest his soul) did us as great joy and honour as he could; and would have given me and my knights great gifts, an we would have taken them. We would take naught, except it were relics, which I bare to the King with the cloth that I had bought him.

Likewise I sent to Madam the Queen four pieces of grogram. The knight that presented them to her bare them wound in a white sheet. When the Queen saw him come into the chamber in which she was, she knelt before him, and the knight in his turn knelt before her; and the Queen said to him: 'Rise up, Sir knight; ye should not kneel, that are bearing relics.' But the knight said: 'Madam, these are not relics, but grogram that my lord sendeth you.' When the Queen heard this, and her

PLATE 7

TORTOSA. THE CHURCH OF OUR LADY
(*Phot. Mrs. Charles Wrinch*)

damsels, they began to laugh; and the Queen said to my knight: 'Tell your lord that evil days befall him, for that he hath made me kneel to his grograms.'
While the King was at Sidon, men brought him a stone that came off in scales, the most marvellous in the world; for when one took off a scale, one found between the two stones the shape of a sea-fish. The fish was of stone; but there wanted nothing in its shape, neither eyes, nor little bones, nor colour, nor aught that made it other than as if it were alive. The King gave me a stone and therein I found a tench, brown and of such fashion as a tench should be.

CXIX

TO Sidon came tidings to the King that his mother was dead. Such mourning did he make for her that for two days no man could have speech of him. After that he sent to fetch me by one of his chamberlains. When I came before him in his chamber, where he was all alone, he saw me, and stretched out his arms, and said to me: 'Ah, Seneschal, I have lost my mother!'
'Sir, I marvel not thereat,' said I, 'for she had to die; but I marvel that ye that are a wise man should have made such mourning; for ye know that the Sage saith that the distress that a man hath in his heart should not appear upon his face; for he that showeth it thereby rejoiceth his enemies and grieveth his friends.' Many fair services did he cause to be holden for her beyond the seas; and thereafter he sent a messenger to France laden with letters of prayer to the churches, that they should pray for her.
My lady Mary of Vertus, a passing good lady and a very holy woman, came to tell me that the Queen was making great mourning, and besought me to go to her to give her comfort. And when I went thither, I found that she

wept, and I told her that he spake truth that said that none should put faith in a woman. 'For she was the woman that ye hated most that is dead, and yet ye make such mourning thereat!' And she told me that it was not for her that she wept, but for the distress that the King had from the mourning that he made, and for her daughter (that afterwards was Queen of Navarre) that was left in the ward of men.

The harshness that Queen Blanche showed to Queen Margaret was this, that Queen Blanche, so far as it lay in her power, would not suffer that her son should be in the company of his wife, except at night when he went to lie with her. The house wherein it pleased him best to stay was at Pontoise, for his sake and the Queen's, for the chamber of the King was above, and the chamber of the Queen below. And they had so planned the matter that they used to hold converse together in a winding staircase that went from one chamber to the other; and they had their affairs so arranged, that when the door-keepers saw the Queen coming to the chamber of the King her son, they used to strike on the door with their wands, and the King would come running into his chamber so that the Queen might find him there; and so in turn did the door-keepers of the chamber of Queen Margaret when Queen Blanche was coming thither, that she might find Queen Margaret therein.

Once the King was by the side of the Queen his wife, and she was in passing great peril of death, for being great with child, she had miscarried. Thither came Queen Blanche, and took her son by the hand, and said to him: 'Come ye hence, ye do naught here.' When Queen Margaret saw that the mother was leading the King away, she cried out: 'Alas! ye will not let me see my lord whether I am dead or alive.' And then she swooned, and they thought that she was dead; and the King, that thought that she was dying, turned back; and with much ado they brought her round.

CXX

AT the moment that the city of Sidon was already almost wholly fortified, the King had several processions made in the camp; and at the end of the processions the Legate had prayer made that God would order the affairs of the King according to His will, that thereby the King might do that which was better in the favour of God, whether to go back to France, or to tarry in that place.

After the processions had been made, the King called me from where I was sitting with the rich men of the land into a courtyard, and made me turn my back towards them. Then said the Legate to me: 'Seneschal, the King glorieth much in your service, and would gladly prosecute your profit and your honour; and to set your heart at ease,' said he to me, 'doth he bid me tell you that he arrangeth his affairs to go to France at this Eastertide that cometh.' And I made answer to him: 'God grant that he may do His will therein!' *1254*

Then the Legate arose and bade me escort him as far as his house, which I did. Then he shut himself into his closet, he and I and no more, and put my two hands betwixt his own, and began to weep very bitterly; and when he could speak, he said to me: 'Seneschal, I rejoice much, and give thanks to God, that the King and ye and the other pilgrims are escaping from the great peril wherein ye have been in this land. And much am I in distress of heart that it behoveth me to leave your holy company, and to go to the Court of Rome, among the treacherous folk that are there. But I will tell you what I am of a mind to do: I still think to contrive to tarry a year after you; and desire to spend all my moneys in fortifying the suburbs of Acre, so that I may make manifest to them that I bear back no money with me; so will they not run to seek aught at my hands.'

I recounted once to the Legate two sins whereof a priest of mine had told me; and he made answer to me in this wise: 'No man knoweth as much of the disloyal sins that men do in Acre, as do I; wherefore it is fitting that God avenge them in such wise that the city of Acre be washed in the blood of them that dwell there, and that there come thereafter other men that shall inhabit it.' The prophecy of the faithful man is fulfilled in part, for the city hath indeed been washed in the blood of them that dwelt therein; but they that should inhabit it are not yet come; and may God send them worthy and such as be according to His will!

CXXI

AFTER these things, the King sent to seek me and bade me go and arm myself, and my knights likewise. I asked him wherefor; and he told me to lead the Queen and her children as far as Tyre, that was seven leagues off. I answered him never a word; and the order was indeed full of peril, for we had then neither truce nor peace either with them of Egypt or with them of Damascus. By the mercy of God, we got thither all in peace, with no hindrance, and as night fell, although we had twice to dismount in the country of our enemies to make a fire and cook meat, to feed the children and to give them suck.

When the King left the city of Sidon, that he had fortified with great walls and great towers and great fosses cleared within and without, the Patriarch and the barons of the country came to him, and spake to him in this wise:

'Sir, ye have fortified the city of Sidon, and that of Caesarea, and the town of Jaffa, that is greatly to the benefit of the Holy Land; and the city of Acre have ye greatly strengthened by the walls and towers that ye have there had made. Sir, we have taken counsel among ourselves, that we see not that henceforward your tarrying could bring any profit to the Kingdom of Jerusalem; for which reason we commend and counsel you that ye go to Acre at this Lent which is coming, and arrange your passage, whereby ye may go hence to France after this Easter.' By the counsel of the Patriarch and the barons, the King left Sidon and came to Tyre, where was the Queen; and thence we came to Acre at the beginning of Lent. *25 February 1254*

All Lent the King had his ships arrayed to return to France, whereof there were thirteen, ships as well as galleys. The ships and galleys were made ready in such wise that the King and Queen went aboard their ship on St. Mark's Eve after Easter, and we had a fair wind at the start. *24 April 1254* On St. Mark's Day, the King told me that on that day he had been born; and I told him that likewise he might well say that on that day had he been born again, for it was near enough to being born again when he escaped out of that perilous land.

CXXII

ON the Saturday we sighted the island of Cyprus, and a mountain that is in Cyprus which is called the mountain of the Cross. That Saturday a fog arose from the land, and came down from the land on to the sea; wherefore the mariners thought that we were farther from the island of Cyprus than we were, for they saw the mountain through the mist. And therefore they went forward recklessly, whereby it happed that our ship struck upon a bank of sand that was in the sea. Now it happened so that if we had not found this bit of sand whereon we struck, we should have struck full upon rocks that were hidden, whereon our ship would have been broken to pieces and we all in jeopardy and drowned.

At the moment that our ship had struck, a great cry arose in the ship, for each man cried 'Alas!' and the shipmen and the others wrung their hands, for every man was afraid of drowning. When I heard this, I arose from my bed whereon I was lying, and went to the ship's castle with the mariners. When I came thither, Brother Raymond that was a Templar and master over the shipmen, said to one of his varlets: 'Cast the lead.' And so did he. And so soon as he had cast it, he cried out and said: 'Alas! we are aground.' When Brother Raymond heard this, he rent his shirt to the belt, and began to tear at his beard, and to cry: 'Alack! Alack!'

At this instant one of my knights that was called my lord John of Monson, father of Abbot William of Saint Mihiel, did me a great courtesy, which was this, that he brought me without words a furred surcoat of mine, and cast it over my back, for I had put on naught but my coat. And I cried out and said to him: 'What have I to do with your surcoat, that ye bring me when we are drowning?' And he said to me: 'On my soul, Sir, I had rather that we were all drowned than that a sickness laid hold on you from the cold, whereof ye might die.'

The shipmen cried out: 'Galley here! to pick up the King.' But of four galleys that the King had there, never a one was there that came nigh; wherein they were no more than wise, for there were full eight hundred persons in the ship who would all have leapt into the galleys to save their bodies, and thus would have sunk them.

The man that had the lead, cast it a second time, and came back to Brother Raymond and told him that the ship was no longer aground. And then Brother Raymond went to tell it to the King, that was lying cross-wise on the deck of the ship, barefoot, in his shirt only and all dishevelled, before the Body of Our Lord that was in the ship, like one that thought to drown. So soon as it was day we saw the rock before us whereon we should have struck if the ship had not run against the bank of sand.

CXXIII

ON the morrow the King sent to fetch the master mariners of the ships, who sent four divers down into the sea; and they dived into the sea, and when they came up again, the King and the master mariners hearkened to them one after the other, in such wise that one diver did not know what another had said. Howbeit they found from the four divers that at the grating that our ship had made against the sand, the sand had ripped away full four and twenty feet of the keel on which the ship was built.

Then the King called the master mariners before us, and asked them what counsel they had to give concerning the blow that his ship had received. They took counsel together, and advised the King that he should leave the ship in which he was and go aboard another.

'And this counsel do we commend to you, for we hold it certain that all the planks of your ship are loosened; wherefore we fear that when your ship shall come into the deep water she shall not be able to endure the blows of the waves, without falling in pieces. For even so did it befall us when ye came from France, that a ship struck thus; and when she came to the high seas, she could not endure the blows of the waves, but brake in pieces; and all perished that were in the ship, save a woman and her child that escaped therefrom on a piece of the ship.' And I bear witness to you that they spake truth: for I saw the woman and the child in the house of the Count of Joigny in the city of Paphos, whom the Count nourished for the love of God.

Then the King asked of my lord Peter the Chamberlain, and my lord Giles the Black, Constable of France, and my lord Gervase of Escraines, that was the King's Master Cook, and the Archdeacon of Nicosia, that bare his seal, and was afterwards Cardinal, and of me, what we advised him in these matters. And we made answer to him that in all earthly matters a man should take heed to them that know most therein: 'wherefore we advise you, for our part, that ye do what the shipmen commend.'

Then said the King to the shipmen: 'I ask you, on your loyalty, if the ship were yours and were laden with your merchandise, if ye would leave her?' And they answered him, all together, Nay; for they had liefer put their bodies in jeopardy of drowning, than buy a ship for two thousand crowns and more. 'And why then do ye counsel me that I should leave her?' 'Because', said they, 'the stakes are not equal; for neither gold nor silver can appraise your person, and your wife's and your children's that are here, and therefore we counsel you not that ye put yourself or them in peril.'

Then said the King: 'Sirs, I have heard your counsel and the counsel of my people; now will I in my turn tell you mine, which is this: that if I leave the ship, that there are therein these five hundred folk and more that will stay in the island of Cyprus, for fear of the peril of their bodies (for there is no man here but loveth his life as much as I do mine) and that never, perchance, will they get back to their own land. Wherefore I had liefer put my body and my wife and my children into the hands of God, than do such harm to so many people as are here.'

BOOK TWO

The great harm that the King would have done to the folk that were in his ship, may men see by Oliver of Termes that was in the King's ship; who was one of the boldest men that ever I saw and that had best approved himself in the Holy Land; and he durst not remain with us for fear of drowning, but tarried in Cyprus, and had such hindrances that it was over a year and a half ere he came back to the King; and he was a great man and a rich, and could well pay his passage. Now consider how lesser folk would have fared that had not the wherewithal to pay, when such a man had such great hindrance.

CXXIV

OUT of this peril, wherefrom God had granted us escape, we ran into another; for the wind that had blown us to Cyprus, where we might have been drowned, arose so strong and so terrible, that it drove us by force upon the island of Cyprus; for the mariners dropped their anchors against the wind, but could never stop the ship until they had brought up five of them. The walls of the King's chamber had they to break down, nor was there any there that dared remain therein, lest the wind should carry them into the sea. At this time the Constable of France, my lord Giles the Black, and I, were lying in the King's cabin; and at this moment the Queen opened the door of the cabin, and thought to find the King in his room.

And I asked her what she had come to seek; she said that she had come to speak to the King, that he should promise to God, or to his saints, some pilgrimage, wherefore God might deliver us out of the peril in which we were; for the shipmen had said that we were in danger of drowning. And I said to her: 'Madam, promise the journey to my Lord Saint Nicholas of Varengéville, and

I stand pledge for him that God will bring you back to France, and the King and your children.' 'Seneschal,' said she, 'truly I would do it gladly; but the King is so wayward that if he knew that I had promised it without him, he would never let me go.'

'Ye shall do one thing, that if God bring you back to France, ye shall promise him a ship of silver of five marks' worth, for the King, for yourself and your three children; and I will stand pledge to you that God will bring you back to France; for I promise Saint Nicholas that if he bring us out of this peril in which we have been this night, I will make pilgrimage to him from Joinville on foot and unshod.' And she told me concerning the silver ship of five marks' worth, that she promised it to Saint Nicholas, and told me that I should stand pledge thereto; and I told her that so would I, very gladly. She went from thence, and stayed away but a little time; and came back to us and told me: 'Saint Nicholas hath saved us from this danger; for the wind is fallen.'

When the Queen (God rest her soul) was come back to France, she had the silver ship made in Paris. And there were in the ship, the King, the Queen, and the three children, all of silver; the sailors, the masts, the rudder, and the ropes, all of silver; and the sails all sewn with silver thread. And the Queen told me that the making had cost fifty crowns. When the ship was made, the Queen sent it to me at Joinville to have it taken to Saint Nicholas, and so I did; and saw it again at Saint Nicholas when we took the King's sister to Hagenau, to the King of Germany.

CXXV

NOW come we back to our matter, and tell how that after we had escaped out of these two perils, the King sate himself on the bulwark of the ship, and made me sit at his feet, and spake to me thus: 'Seneschal, well hath God manifested to us His great power; for one of His little winds (not one of the four master winds) hath all but drowned the King of France, his wife, and his children and all his company. Now do we owe Him grace and thanksgiving for the peril from which He hath delivered us.'

'Seneschal,' said the King, 'of such tribulations, when they befall men, or of great maladies, or of other afflictions, do the saints say that they are the threats of Our Lord. For even as God saith to them that escape out of great illness: "Now see ye well that I might have had you dead an I had wished"; even so might He say to us: "Ye see well that I might have had you all drowned an I had wished." '

'Now should we', said the King, 'look to ourselves, that there be naught that displeaseth Him wherefore He hath thus affrighted us; and if we find aught that displeaseth him, let us cast it out; for if we did otherwise after this threat that He hath made to us, He will strike us either with death or with other great mischance, to the hurt of body and soul.'

The King said: 'Seneschal, the saint saith: "Lord God, wherefore dost Thou threaten us? For if Thou hadst us lost altogether, Thou wouldst not be any the poorer thereby; and if Thou hadst gained us altogether, Thou wouldst be none the richer thereby. So we may see", said the saint, "that these threats that God maketh to us, are not to advance His own profit, nor to avert His harm; but only for the great love that He beareth us, He awaketh us by His threats, that we may see clearly into our faults, and that we may cast out of us that which displeaseth Him." Now so let us do,' said the King, 'for we should do but wisely.'

CXXVI

WE set sail from the island of Cyprus after we had taken aboard in the island fresh water and other things of which we were in need. We came to an island that is called Lampedusa, where we caught any number of rabbits; and we found an ancient hermitage among the rocks, and found the garden that the hermits that lived there of old time had made: olive-trees, fig-trees, vine-stocks, and other trees were therein. The brook from the spring ran through the garden. We and the King went up to the end of the garden, and found a chapel, whitewashed in the first bay, and with a cross of red earth.

We came into the second bay, and found two bodies of men dead, whereof the flesh was all rotted away; the sides still held together, and the bones of the hands were on their breasts; and they were lying towards the east, as one layeth bodies in the ground. At our gathering together on the ship, one of our sailors was missing, whom the master of the ship thought had tarried there to be a hermit; and for this reason Nicholas of Soisy, that was master sergeant of the King, left three sacks of biscuit on shore, that he might find them and live thereon.

CXXVII

WHEN we had gone thence, we saw a great island in the sea, that was called Pantelleria, and was peopled by Saracens that were in subjection to the King of Sicily and to the King of Tunis. The Queen besought the King that he would send three galleys thither to get fruit for her children; and the King granted it, and bade the master of the galleys that when the King's ship should pass before the island they should be all ready to come out to her. The galleys came to the island by a harbour that is there; and it befell that when the King's ship passed before the harbour, we heard no tidings of our galleys.

Then the shipmen began to whisper one to the other. The King had them called, and asked them what they thought of this hap; and the sailors told him that it seemed to them that the Saracens had taken his men and his galleys. 'But we commend and counsel you, Sir, that we await them not; for ye are betwixt the Kingdom of Sicily and the Kingdom of Tunis, that love you not, neither one nor the other; and if ye let us sail on, we shall this very night have got you out of danger, for we shall have passed this strait.'

'Truly,' said the King, 'never will I believe you that I should leave my folk in the hands of the Saracens, and not do at least what I can to deliver them. And I order you that ye back your sails, and that we go against them.' And when the Queen heard this, she began to make great mourning, and said: 'Alas! all this is my fault!'

As they shifted the sails of the King's ship and of the others, we saw the galleys come forth from the island. When they were come to the King, the King asked the shipmen why they had done this, and they answered that they could not help it, for the children of citizens of Paris, six of them, had stayed to eat the fruit in the gardens; wherefore they could not find them, and would not desert them. Then the King ordered that the culprits should be put in the ship's boat; and then they began to cry and bawl: 'Sir, for God's sake, fine us all that we have, but put us not there where they put murderers and thieves; for ever afterwards will it be a reproach to us.'

The Queen and the rest of us did all we could that the King might be of a mind to allow it; but never would the King listen to any one; and there were they put and remained there until we came to land. In such a plight were they, that when the sea rose, the waves flew over their heads and they had to crouch down lest the wind should bear them into the sea. And it served them right; for their gluttony did us such harm that we were delayed a good eight days because the King had the ships turned about.

CXXVIII

ANOTHER hazard befell us at sea, before we came to land, which was this, that one of the Queen's waiting-women, when she had the Queen put to bed, heedlessly cast the cloth that she had wound about her head on to the end of the iron pan wherein the Queen's nightlight was burning; and when she was gone to bed in the chamber underneath the Queen's chamber, where the women lay, the candle burnt so far down that the flame caught at the cloth, and from the cloth caught at the sheet wherewith the Queen's robes were spread. When the Queen awoke, she saw all the chamber alight with the fire, and leapt up all naked, and took the cloth and cast it burning into the sea, and took the sheets and quenched them. Those that were in the ship's boat cried down below: 'Fire! Fire!' I lifted my head and saw that the cloth burned still with a clear flame upon the sea, that was very quiet. I put on my coat as quickly as I could, and went to sit with the shipmen.

As I sate there, my squire, that used to lie at my feet, came to me and told me that the King was awake and had asked where I was. 'And I told him that ye were in the privy; and he said to me: "Thou liest."' Whilst we were speaking there, behold thereupon Master Geoffrey, the

Queen's clerk, that said to me: 'Be not dismayed, for it has happened so.' And I said to him: 'Master Geoffrey, go tell the Queen that the King is awake, and that she go to him to set his mind at peace.'

On the morrow the Constable of France and my lord Peter the Chamberlain and my lord Gervase the pantler, said to the King: 'What befell last night, that we heard tell of fire?' And I said never a word. And then said the King: 'It must be that by ill luck the Seneschal is more secret than I am; and I will tell you', said the King, 'how it was that we ought all to have been burnt last night.'

And he recounted how it was and said to me: 'Seneschal, I order you that ye never go to bed henceforth until ye have all the fires here put out, except for the great fire that is in the hold of the ship; and know that I will never go to bed until ye are come back to me again.' And so did I for so long as we were at sea; and when I had come back, the King would go to bed.

CXXIX

ANOTHER hazard befell us at sea; for my lord Dragonet, a rich man of Provence, was sleeping one morning in his ship, that was a full league in front of ours, and called a squire of his and said to him: 'Stop up that hole for me, for the sun striketh on my face.' The squire saw that he could not stop up the hole unless he went outside the ship; and so he went out on the ship's side. While he went to stop the hole, his foot failed him, and he fell into the water; and that ship had no boat, for the ship was small; and in a moment the ship was far away. We that were in the King's ship saw him, and thought that it was a bundle or a barrel, for he that was fallen into the water strove not to help himself.

One of the King's galleys picked him up and brought

him to our ship, where he told us how it had befallen him. I asked him how it was that he had taken no thought to save himself by swimming or otherwise. He answered me that he had no occasion or need to help himself; for so soon as he began to fall, he commended himself to Our Lady of Vauvert, and she held him up by the shoulders from the time he fell until the King's galley picked him up. In honour of this miracle I have had it painted at Joinville in my chapel, and in the windows at Blécourt.

CXXX

AFTER we had been ten weeks at sea we came to land at a harbour that is at two leagues' distance from a castle that is called Hyères, the which belonged to the Count of Provence that was afterwards King of Sicily. The Queen and all the Council were agreed that the King should go ashore there, since the land belonged to his brother. The King made answer to us that never would he land from his ship until he had come to Aigues Mortes that was on his own land. To this point the King kept us on the Wednesday and the Thursday, so that we might never shake him.

On these ships of Marseilles are there two rudders which are attached to two tillers so marvellously, that just as a man may turn a war-horse, so may a man turn the ship to right or left. On one of the tillers of the rudders sate the King on the Friday, and called me to him and said to me: 'Seneschal, what think you of this pass?' And I said to him: 'Sir, it would be just that it should befall you as it befell my lady of Bourbon, that would not land at this place, but set out to sea again to get to Aigues Mortes and tarried seven weeks thereafter at sea.'

Then the King called his Council, and told them what I had told him, and asked them what they counselled him to do; and all were of opinion that he should land, for he would do less than wisely to put his person, his wife, and his children in jeopardy of the sea, after he had come out therefrom. To the counsel that we gave him the King agreed, whereat the Queen was very joyful.

CXXXI

AT the castle of Hyères the King landed from the sea, and the Queen and his children likewise. As the King tarried at Hyères to procure horses to come into France, the Abbot of Cluny, that afterwards was Bishop of Oliva, presented him with two palfreys that to-day would be worth full two hundred and fifty crowns, one for himself and one for the Queen. When he had presented them, he said to the King: 'Sir, I will come on the morrow to speak with you of my needs.' When the morrow came, the Abbot came again; the King heard him very diligently for very long. When the Abbot had gone thence, I came to the King and said to him: 'I would ask you, an it please you, if ye have heard the Abbot of Cluny with a better grace, since yesterday he gave you these two palfreys?'

The King thought for a long while, and said to me: 'In sooth, aye.' 'Sir,' said I, 'know ye why I have asked this question of you?' 'Why?' said he. 'Because, Sir,' said I, 'I commend and counsel you that ye forbid all your sworn councillors, when ye shall be come to France, that they take aught from those that have business to bring before you; for be ye certain, an they take, that they will hear more gladly and more diligently them that have made them gifts, even as ye have heard the Abbot of Cluny.' Then the King summoned all his council and recounted to them forthwith what I had said to him; and they said that I had given him good counsel.

CXXXII

THE King heard tell of a Grey Friar, that was called Brother Hugh; and for the great renown that he had the King sent to fetch this Grey Friar, to see him and hear him speak. The day that he came to Hyères we were looking at the road by which he was coming, and saw that a passing great crowd of men and women followed him on foot. The King had him preach. The beginning of the sermon was on men of religion and ran thus: 'Sirs,' said he, 'I see too many men of religion in the King's court, in his company.' After these words: 'I to begin with,' said he, 'and say therefore that they are not in a state to save themselves, or the Scriptures lie to us, which cannot be.'

'For the Holy Scriptures tell us that a monk cannot live outside his cloister without mortal sin, any more than a fish can live without water. And if the religious that are with the King say that this is a cloister, I tell them that it is the widest that ever I saw; for it stretcheth from this side the sea to the other. If they say that in this cloister men may lead an austere life to save their souls, in that do I put no faith in them; but I say unto you that I have eaten with them great plenty of divers dishes of meat, and have drunk good wines, both strong and clear; wherefore am I certain that had they been in their cloister, they had not been as easeful as they are with the King.'

To the King he taught in his sermon how he should keep himself in the favour of his people; and at the end of his sermon said this, that he had read the Bible and the books that go against the Bible, but never had he seen either in the books of believers or in the books of the misbelievers, that any realm or any lordship had ever been lost, nor changed its lordship for another, nor from one King to another, but by want of justice. 'Now,' said he, 'let the King take heed, since he is going hence to France, that he do such justice to his people that thereby he keep the love of God, in such wise that God will not take from him the realm of France in his lifetime.' I said to the King that he should not let him go from his company, for as long as he could; he told me that he had already besought him, but that he would do naught for him. Then the King took me by the hand, and said to me: 'Let us go to beg him again.' We came to him, and I said to him: 'Sir, do that which my lord beseecheth you, to stay with him as long as he shall be in Provence.' And he answered me very wroth: 'Faith, Sir, I will not; but will go into a place where God will love me better than in the King's company.' One day did he stay with us, and on the morrow he went. Men have told me that he lieth buried in the city of Marseilles, where he worketh very fair miracles.

CXXXIII

THE day that the King left Hyères, he went down on foot from the castle, because the hill was too steep; and went so far on foot that, since he could not have his own palfrey, it behoved him to mount on mine. And when his palfrey came, he turned on Ponce the groom very bitterly; and when he had soundly rated him, I said to him: 'Sir, ye must endure much from Ponce the groom; for he hath served your grandfather and your father and you.'

'Seneschal,' said he, 'he hath not served us, but we have served him when we have endured him about us, with the evil blemishes that he hath. For King Philip my grandfather told me that a man should give guerdons to his household, to one more and to another less, according as they serve; and he said likewise that no man could be a good governor of land, if he did not know how to gainsay as boldly and hardily as he knew how to give. And these things', said the King, 'do I teach you, because the world is so greedy in asking, that few are the folk that look to the salvation of their souls nor to the honour of their persons, when they can filch aught from before the face of another, whether by wrong or by right.'

CXXXIV

THE King went through the county of Provence as far as a city that is called Aix-en-Provence, where men said that the body of Magdalene lay; and we went into a high vault of rock, where they said that the Magdalene had been a hermit for seventeen years. When the King came to Beaucaire and I saw him in his own land and dominion, I took my leave of him, and went by way of the Dauphine of Viennois my niece, and by way of the Count of Chalon my uncle, and by the Count of Burgundy his son.

And when I had stayed a time at Joinville and had done my business, I set out towards the King, whom I found at Soissons; and he made such joy for me that all that were there marvelled thereat. There found I Count John of Brittany, and his wife the daughter of King Thibault, who offered her homage to the King for such rightful possession of land as she might have in Champagne; and the King adjourned it to the High Court of Paris, and King Thibault II (that was there) likewise, to hear them and do justice to the parties.

To the High Court came the King of Navarre and his councillors, and the Count of Brittany likewise. At this Court King Thibault asked for my lady Isabel, the King's daughter, to take to wife. And in spite of the things that our folk of Champagne said behind my back, by reason of the love that they had seen that the King showed me at Soissons, I did not forbear to go to the King of France to talk of the said marriage. 'Go,' said the King, 'make your peace with the Count of Brittany, and then we will make our marriage.' I told him that for that reason he should not give it up. And he made answer to me that at no price would he arrange the marriage until peace was made, so that no man should say that he married his children by the disinheritance of his barons.

I carried back these words to Queen Margaret of Navarre and to the King her son, and to their other councillors; and when they heard them, they made haste to make peace. And after peace had been made, the King of France gave his daughter to King Thibault; and the wedding was held at Melun, largely and lavishly; and thence King Thibault brought her to Provins, whither they came amid a great crowd of barons.

CXXXV

AFTER that the King was come back from beyond the seas, he bare himself so devoutly that never again did he wear ermine or minever, or scarlet, or gilded stirrups or spurs. His robes were of grogram or of watchet cloth; the furs of his coverlets and of his robes were of wild goat, or hare's legs, or lamb. He was so temperate of his mouth that never did he give thought to ask concerning his food, but what his cooks dressed for him, and they set before him, he ate. His wine he watered in a goblet of glass; and according as was the wine, he put in water by measure and held the goblet in his hand while they watered the wine from behind his table. Every day he gave meat to his poor folk, and after meat had them given money.

When the minstrels of rich men came there and brought

their fiddles after dinner, he waited to hear grace said until the minstrel had done his lay; then he would rise, and the priests would stand before him that were wont to say grace for him. When we were there privately, he would sit at the foot of his bed; and when the Preaching Friars and the Grey Friars that were there suggested some book that he might like to hear, he would answer them: 'Ye shall not read to me; for there is no book so good after meat as *Quo libet*, which is to say that each man speak as he will.' When any rich strangers ate with him, he was good company to them.

Of his wisdom will I tell you. There was a time that men bare witness that there was none so wise as he in all his Council. And it appeared in that whensoever men spoke to him of aught, he did not say: 'I will take counsel in the matter'; but when he saw the right clear and manifest, he gave answer straightway without his Council; so have I heard that he gave answer to all the prelates of the realm of France to a request that they had made him, which was this.

Bishop Guy of Auxerre told him on behalf of them all: 'Sir,' said he, 'these Archbishops and Bishops here present have charged me to tell you that Christendom falleth into decay and crumbleth in your hands, and will fall yet farther if ye concern not yourself therewith, for to-day no man feareth excommunication. We ask you, Sir, that ye should order your judges and your officers that they constrain the excommunicate that have borne their sentence for a year and a day, that they make satisfaction to the Church.' And the King made answer to them without counsel that he would willingly order his judges and his officers to constrain the excommunicate as they asked, provided that they gave him cognizance of the sentence, whether it were rightful or not.

And they took counsel together and made answer to the

BOOK TWO

King, that in what concerned Christianity they could not give him cognizance. And the King answered them in turn, that in what concerned himself he would never make them cognizant, nor ever order his officers to constrain the excommunicate to seek absolution from them, whether right or wrong. 'For were I so to do, I should act against God and against justice. And I will show you a precedent, which is this: that the Bishops of Brittany have held the Count of Brittany full seven years in excommunication, and then he hath had absolution from the Court of Rome; and had I had him constrained from the first year, I should have constrained him wrongly.'

CXXXVI

IT befell that when we were come back from beyond the seas, the monks of Saint Urbain elected two abbots; Bishop Peter of Châlons (whom God assoil) drove them both out, and blessed my lord John of Mimery as abbot, and gave him the crozier. I did not wish to receive him as abbot, because he had wronged Abbot Geoffrey, who had appealed against him and had gone to Rome. I held the Abbey in my hands until such time as the said Geoffrey had borne off the crozier, and he to whom the Bishop had given it had lost it; and as the dispute went on the Bishop had me excommunicated. Whereby at a High Court held in Paris there was great vexation between me and Bishop Peter of Châlons, and between Countess Margaret of Flanders and the Archbishop of Rheims, to whom she gave the lie.

At the Court that came after, all the prelates besought the King that he would come to have speech with them all alone. When he came back from speaking with the prelates, he came to us that awaited him in the Court of Pleas, and told us laughing of the troubles he had had with the prelates, of which the first was this, that the Archbishop of Rheims had said to the King: 'Sir, what justice will ye do me for the wardenship of Saint Remi of Rheims that ye take from me? For by the holy relics that are here, I would not bear such a sin as ye do, for all the realm of France.' 'By the holy relics that are here,' said the King, 'ye would do as much for Compiègne, for the covetousness that is in you. Now is one of us forsworn.'

'The Bishop of Chartres asked me', said the King, 'that I would cause to be restored to him what I held of his. And I told him that I would not, until my dues had been paid. And I told him that he was liegeman of my hands and that he bore himself neither well nor loyally towards me when he tried to disinherit me.'

'The Bishop of Châlons said to me,' said the King, ' "Sir, what justice will ye do me for the Lord of Joinville, that taketh from this poor monk the Abbey of Saint Urbain?" "Lord Bishop," ' said the King, ' "between you ye have ordained that no excommunicate person should be heard in a lay court; and I have seen by letters sealed with thirty-two seals that the Lord of Joinville be excommunicate; wherefore I will not hear your case until he be absolved." ' And these things do I recount to you, that ye may see clearly how he delivered judgement alone by his own sense in what he had to do.

The Abbot Geoffrey of Saint Urbain, after I had done his business, returned me evil for good, and appealed against me. To our saintly King he let it be understood that he was in his ward. I made request to the King that he would cause the truth to be discovered, whether the ward were his or mine. 'Sir,' said the Abbot, 'this will ye not do, please God; but hear us in ordered assize betwixt us and the lord of Joinville; for we had liefer have our Abbey in your ward, and not in his whose freehold it is.' Then said the King to me: 'Speak they sooth, that the ward of the Abbey is mine?' 'Faith, Sir,' said I, 'it is not, but mine.'

Then said the King to me: 'It may well be that the freehold is yours, but that with the wardship of your abbey ye have naught to do.' And to the Abbot: 'But it is fitting, an ye will, and according to what ye say and according to what the Seneschal saith, that it remain either with me or with him. Never will I give it up for aught that ye say, unless I have the truth made known; for if I put it to a fixed assize, I should transgress against him who is my liegeman, if I put his right in plea, of which right he offereth me to make known the truth clearly.' He had the truth discovered; and, the truth once known, he handed over to me the wardship of the abbey and gave me his charter for it.

CXXXVII

IT befell that the holy King wrought to such effect *1258* that the King of England, his wife, and his children came to France to make the treaty of peace betwixt him and them. The men of his Council were altogether against this peace, and spake to him thus: 'Sir, we marvel much that your will is this, that ye would give to the King of England so great a portion of your land, that ye and those that went before you have conquered from him by his forfeit. Wherefore it seemeth to us that if ye understand that ye have no right thereto, that ye make not fair restitution to the King of England unless ye give him back all the conquests that ye and your forerunners have made; and if ye understand that ye have a right thereto, it seemeth to us that ye lose as much as ye give back to him.'

To this the saintly King made answer in this wise: 'My lords, I am certain that the forerunners of the King of

England have altogether lost of right the conquests that I hold; and the land that I owe him, I owe him not for aught wherein I am bound to him or to his heirs, but to put love between my children and his, that are cousins german. And meseemeth that of this that I give him do I make good use herein, since he is not now my liegeman, and thus cometh into mine homage.'

He was the man that in all the world toiled most to have peace between his subjects, and especially among the rich men that were neighbours and the princes of the realm, as between the Count of Chalon, uncle to the lord of Joinville, and his son the Count of Burgundy, that had a great strife when we came back from overseas. And to have peace between father and son, he sent men from his Council to Burgundy, and at his own expense; and by his diligence was peace made between father and son. Thereafter was there a great feud between the second King Thibault of Champagne, and Count John of Chalon and the Count of Burgundy his son, for the Abbey of Luxeuil. To make peace in this feud, my lord the King sent thither my lord Gervase of Escraines, that was then Master Cook of France; and by his diligence he made peace between them.

After this feud that the King appeased there arose yet another war between Count Thibault of Bar and Count Henry of Luxembourg, that had his sister to wife; and it so befell that they fought one against the other below Prény, and Count Thibault of Bar took Count Henry of Luxembourg prisoner, and took the castle of Ligny, which belonged to the Count of Luxembourg in right of his wife. To make peace in this war, the King sent my lord Peter the Chamberlain, the man in the world in whom he most believed, and at the King's expense; and the King did so much that they made peace.

Of these stranger folk between whom the King had made

peace, some of his Council told him that he did not well when he did not suffer them to make war; for if he let them impoverish themselves, they would not attack him so soon as if they were rich. And to them the King made answer, and said that they spake not well. 'For if the princes our neighbours saw that I suffered them to make war, they might take counsel together, and say: "The King of his malice suffereth us to make war." So it would befall that by reason of the hatred that they would have for me, they would come to assail me, when I might well lose, apart from the hatred of God that I should gain, Who saith: "Blessed are the peacemakers." '
Whence it so happed that the men of Burgundy and Lorraine that he had pacified, loved him so much and obeyed him so well that I have seen them come to make their pleas before the King, concerning the disagreements that they had between them, at the King's Court at Rheims, at Paris, and at Orleans.

CXXXVIII

THE King so loved God, and His sweet Mother, that all those that he could attaint that they had said of God or of His Mother any foul thing or scurvy oath, he had them punished grievously. Thus have I seen him have a goldsmith put in the pillory at Caesarea, in his drawers and shirt, the guts and haslet of a hog around his neck, and in such abundance that they came up to his nose. I heard say that after I had come back from oversea, he had the nose and the lip of a citizen of Paris burned therefor; but I saw it not. And the saintly King said: 'I would be branded by a hot iron, if by that covenant all evil swearing might be driven out of my realm.'
I was full two and twenty years in his company, and never

heard him swear by God, or by His Mother, or by His saints; and when he was of a mind to affirm aught, he would say: 'Truly it was thus', or 'Truly it is so.' Never did I hear him name the Devil, save it were in some book where it behoved him to name him, or in the life of saints whereof the book spake. And it is great shame to the Kingdom of France and to the King that he suffer it, that now scarcely can a man speak but he say: 'The Devil take it!' And it is a great fault of speech, when a man convert to the Devil's use the man or woman that have been given to God from the time they were baptized. In my house of Joinville, whosoever speaketh such a word getteth a box on the ear or a blow on the hand; and this bad language is there almost altogether overcome.

CXXXIX

HE asked me if I were wont to wash the feet of the poor on Maundy Thursday, and I answered him nay, that it seemed not good to me. And he told me that I should not hold it in despite, for God had done it. 'Very loath would ye be to do what the King of England doth, that washeth the feet of lepers and kisseth them.'

Before he went to bed, he was wont to have his children come before him, and used to recount to them the deeds of good kings and good emperors, and to tell them that from such men should they take example. And he used to recount to them likewise the deeds of evil rich men who by their lusts and by their robberies and by their avarice had lost their realms. 'And these things', he used to say, 'I bring to your mind, that ye may keep yourselves therefrom, that God be not wroth with you therefor.' He made them learn the Hours of Our Lady, and had them say before him the Hours of the day, to accustom them to hear their Hours when they should hold their own lands.

The King was so great an almsgiver, that wheresoever he went in his realm he had gifts made to poor churches, to lazar-houses, to almshouses, to hospitals, and to poor gentlemen and gentlewomen. Every day he gave meat to a great number of poor folk, without counting those that ate in his chamber; and many a time I saw that he himself cut their bread and gave them to drink.

In his time were built many abbeys: that is to say, Royaumont, the Abbey of St. Anthony near Paris, the Abbey of the Lily, the Abbey of Maubuisson, and many another religious house of Friars Preachers and Grey Friars. He built the Hospital at Pontoise, the Hospital at Vernon, the Hospital for the Blind in Paris, and the nunnery of Grey Sisters of Saint-Cloud, that his sister my lady Isabel founded by his grant.

As any benefice in Holy Church fell in to the King, before he gave it he took counsel with good men of religion and others; and when he had taken counsel, he would give the benefices of Holy Church in good faith, loyally and according to the will of God. Nor would he give any benefice to any clerk, except he renounced the other benefices of churches that he held. In all the towns of his kingdom where he had never been before, he used to go to the Friars Preachers and the Grey Friars, if any were there, to ask them for their prayers.

CXL

AFTER that King Louis was come back to France from beyond the seas, he bare himself very devoutly towards Our Lord, and very righteously towards his subjects; and considered and bethought himself that it were a very fair thing and good to amend the realm of France. First, he established a general ordinance over his subjects throughout the realm of France, in the manner that followeth:

'We, Louis, by the grace of God King of France, ordain that all our judges, castellans, provosts, mayors, and all others, in whatsoever business it be, or in whatsoever office they be, shall take oath that so long as they are in office or in authority they shall do justice to all, without exception of persons, as well to the poor as to the rich, and to the stranger as to the citizen, and they shall keep the usages and customs that are good and proved.

'And if it befall that the judges or the castellans or others, as officers or rangers, do aught contrary to their oath, and are attainted therefor, our will is that they shall be punished in their property, and in their persons if the misdeed require it; and the judges shall be punished by us, and the others by the judges.

'Henceforth the other provosts, the judges, and the officers shall swear that they will loyally keep our revenues and our rights, nor suffer our rights to be filched or taken away or minished; and therewith shall they swear that they will not take or receive on their own behalf or on another's, gold or silver or indirect benefits, nor aught else, unless it be fruit, or bread, or wine, or other present up to the sum of a shilling, and that the said sum be not exceeded.

'And therewith shall they swear that they will not take or have taken any gift, whatsoever it be, for their wives, or their children, or their brothers, or their sisters, or any other person that be of their family; and so soon as they know that such gifts have been received, they shall have them given back as soon as they can. And therewith shall they swear that they will receive no gift, whatsoever it be, from a man that is of their bailiwick, nor from any other that hath a suit or that pleadeth before them.

'Henceforth they shall swear that they will neither give nor send a gift to any man that is of our Council, nor to their wives, nor to their children, nor to any soul that belongeth unto them, nor to any that receive their accounts on our behalf, nor to any inquisitors that we may send into their bailiwicks or into their jurisdictions, to make inquisition into their deeds. And therewith shall they swear that they will take no part in any sale that may be made of our revenues, our jurisdiction, or our mint, or of aught else that pertaineth to us.

'And they shall swear and promise that if they know that any official, officer, or provost that is under them be disloyal, robber, usurer, or full of other vices wherefore they should lose our service, that they will not sustain them for gift, or for promise, or for love, or for aught else, but will punish them and judge them in good faith. Henceforth our provosts, our castellans, our mayors, our rangers, and our other officers on foot or on horse, shall swear that they will give no gifts to their lords, nor to their wives, nor to the children that belong to them.

'And since we would that these oaths should be firmly stablished, our will is that they be taken in full assize, before all men, by both clerks and laymen, knights and men-at-arms, albeit that they may already have sworn them before us; so that they may fear to incur the vice of perjury, not only for the fear of God and of us, but also for shame before the world.

'We desire and decree that all our provosts and our judges shall forbear from swearing any word that tendeth to the despite of God, or of Our Lady, or of all the saints, and shall keep themselves from dicing and taverns. Our will is that the fashioning of dice be forbidden throughout our realm, and that wanton women be turned out of houses; and whosoever shall rent a house to a wanton woman, shall pay back to the provost or magistrate a year's rent of the house.

'Next we forbid that our judges should purchase for themselves or for others undue possessions or lands that are in their bailiwicks, or in another's, so long as they are in our service, without our leave; and if such purchases be made, our will is that they be and remain in our hands.

'We forbid our judges that so long as they are in our service they make marriages for sons and daughters that they may have, or for other persons that belong to them, to any other person of their bailiwick, without a special leave; and therewith, that they put them into a religious house in their bailiwick, or get them benefices in Holy Church, or other occupation; and therewith, that they get their living or take any procuration in a religious house, or near one, at the expense of the religious. This injunction against making marriages and acquiring possessions, in the manner we have said, we would not extend to provosts, nor to mayors, nor to others in lesser offices.

'We ordain that neither judge nor provost nor any other, should keep too great abundance of sergeants and bedels, that the people be not oppressed thereby; and our will is that the bedels be nominated in full assize, or else be not held to be bedels. When our officers are sent to any distant place or to a strange land, our will is that trust be not put in them without letters from their sovereign lord.

'We order that judges or provosts that hold office under us oppress not our good people with their judgements beyond what is justice; nor that any of those that are under us be put in prison for debts that they owe unless it be for debts to ourselves.

'We ordain that none of our judges shall enforce a fine for a debt that our subjects owe, nor for ill doing, unless it be in open court, or that the fine be tried and assessed, and by counsel of good men and true, even when it hath been already distrained before them.

'And if it hap that he that be accused of aught is not of a mind to await the judgement of the court that is offered him, but offer a certain sum of money for the fine, such as hath commonly been received, our will is that the court receive the sum of money if it be reasonable and convenient; or if not, our will is that the fine be assessed, in the manner that is told above, although the culprit leave it to the will of the court. We forbid that the judges, or mayors, or provosts, constrain our subjects by threat, by fear, or by any pettifogging, to pay a fine in secret or in public, and that they accuse them without reasonable cause.

'And we ordain that they that hold provostships, castellanies, or other jurisdictions, that they may not sell them to another without our leave; and if several together buy the offices above named, our will is that one of the buyers fill the office on behalf of all the others, and make use of the exemption that pertaineth to posting-horses, to taxes, and to common charges, as the custom is.

'And we forbid that they sell the said offices to brothers, to nephews, and to cousins after they shall have bought them from us; and that they shall demand any debt that is owed them on their own behalf, unless it be debts that pertain to their office; but their own debts shall they demand by the authority of the judge as if they were not in our service.

'We forbid that judge or provost vex our subjects in suits that they have brought before them, by moving from one place to another; but hear the business that they have before them, in the place where they are wont to hear it, so that they let not their justice be sought by labour or expense.

'Henceforth, we command that they dispossess no man

of seisin that he hold without taking cognizance of cause, or without special commandment from us; and that they oppress not our people by new exactions and taxes or new tolls; nor summon them to ride to arms to have their money; for our will is that no man that oweth service be summoned to the host without needful cause; and they that are of a mind to go to the host in their own person, be not constrained to redeem their going for money.

'Next, we forbid that judges or provosts ban the taking of corn or wine or other merchandise out of our realm, without needful cause; and when it behoveth that prohibition be made, our will is that it be made in common in the Council of sheriffs and without suspicion of fraud or deceit.

'Next, our will is that all former magistrates, castellans, provosts, and mayors, after they are out of office, be for forty days in the country wherein they have held office, in their own persons or by procuration, so that they may make answer to the new officers for aught wherein they may have done ill against those that would bring complaint against them.

'In all these things which we have ordained for the profit of our subjects and of our realm, we retain for ourselves the rights of explanation, emendation, adjustment, and minishing, according as our counsel may be.'

By this ordinance did he greatly better the realm of France, as many wise elders testify.

CXLI

THE provostship of Paris was at that time sold to the citizens, or to any man; and when it befell that men had bought it, they used to sustain their children and their nephews in their misdeeds, for the young men had trust in their parents and in their friends that held the provostship. For this reason were the lesser folk overmuch downtrodden, nor could they have justice against the rich men, because of the great gifts and presents that they used to make to the provosts.

Whosoever at that time spake truth before the provost, or was of a mind to keep his oath and not to be forsworn concerning any debt or any other thing that had to be answered for, the provost would levy a fine from him, and he would be punished. By the great perjuries and great robberies that were made within the jurisdiction of the provost, the lesser folk dared not stay on the King's land, but went to dwell in other jurisdictions and other lordships. And the King's land was so far waste that when the provost held his court, not more than ten or a dozen persons came thereto.

Therewith were there so many evil-doers and thieves in Paris and outside it, that all the country was full of them. The King, that looked very diligently to how the lesser folk were protected, knew the whole truth, and was no longer willing that the provostship of Paris should be sold, but gave good and ample pay to those that henceforward should hold it. And all the evil customs whereby the people might be oppressed did he overthrow; and had inquiry made throughout the realm and through all the land where he might find a man that did justice righteously and constantly, and that spared the rich man no more than the poor.

Stephen Boileau was pointed out to him, the which so maintained and defended the provostship that no malefactors, nor thieves, nor murderers dared stay in Paris, that were not forthwith hanged or overthrown; nor could family, nor lineage, nor gold, nor silver deliver them. The King's land began to amend, and folk came thither for the good justice that was done there. They so multiplied and bettered, that fees for the transferring of land, and of inheritances, the tax on purchases and other rights were worth twice what the King had received from them ere this.

CXLII

FROM the time of his childhood was the King pitiful to the poor and the suffering, and the custom was that the King, wheresoever he went, should forthwith have six score poor folk fed in his house with bread and wine and meat or fish, every day. In Lent and Advent the number of the poor increased; and oft-times it happed that the King would serve them, and put their food before them, and carve the meat before them, and give them money at their going by his own hand. Likewise at the solemn eves of the great festivals, he would serve these poor folk with all the things above said, ere he had meat or drink. With all these things, had he each day at dinner and at supper old men and broken near him, and had them given such meats as he himself used to eat; and when they had eaten, they took away a certain sum of money.

Over and above all these things, the King used to give each day such great and generous alms to poor folk in religion, to poor hospitals, to poor sick folk, and to other poor communities, and to poor gentlemen and gentlewomen and girls, to fallen women, to poor widow women and to those that lay in of child, and to poor minstrels that through old age or sickness could not work or make their living, that scarcely can the number thereof be told. Wherein we may well say that he was happier than Titus the Emperor of Rome, whereof the ancient writings tell that he was mournful and out of heart for a day wherein he had done no beneficence.

BOOK TWO

From the beginning when he came to hold his realm and knew himself of discernment, he began to build churches and many religious houses, among which the Abbey of Royaumont taketh first place in honour and excellency. He caused several hospitals to be built: the hospital of Paris, that of Pontoise, that of Compiègne and of Vernon, and gave them great revenues. He founded the Abbey of St. Matthew of Rouen, wherein he established women of the Order of Friars Preachers; and founded that of Longchamps, wherein he set women of the Order of Friars Minor, and gave them great revenues to live upon. And he granted leave to his mother to found the Abbey of the Lily near Melun-sur-Seine, and that near Pontoise that men call Maubuisson, and gave them great revenues and possessions thereafter. And he had the house for the blind built near Paris, to put therein the poor blind folk of the city of Paris; and had a chapel built for them to hear the services of God. And the good King had the Charterhouse built outside Paris, that is called Vauvert, and assigned sufficient revenues to the monks that dwelt there and served Our Lord.

Soon enough afterwards he had another house built outside Paris, on the road to Saint Denis, that was called the House of the Daughters of God; and he had a great multitude of women put in the hospice, that through poverty had given themselves to the sins of the flesh, and gave them two hundred crowns a year of revenue for their sustenance. And in many places in his kingdom he had houses of bedeswomen built, and gave them revenues for their living and ordered that they should receive therein women that were of a mind to set themselves to live in chastity.

Some of his household used to grumble that he gave such great alms, and therein spent much; and he would say: 'I had liefer that the abuse of great spending that I do were done in almsgiving for the love of God, than in pomp or in the vainglory of this world.' Yet in spite of the great sums that the King used to spend in almsgiving, he would allow much to be spent in his house every day. Amply and generously did the King bear himself to his magistrates' courts and to the assemblies of barons and knights; and used to have them served more graciously at his court, and more amply and abundantly, and more, than had long time been at the courts of those that went before him.

CXLIII

THE King loved all men that set themselves to serve God and that wore the habit of religion; nor did any come to him that failed to find the wherewithal to live. He provided for the Brothers of the Carmel and bought them a place on the Seine towards Charenton, and had a house built for them, and bought them vestments and chalices and such things as are needful to celebrate the service of Our Lord. And afterwards he provided for the Brethren of St. Augustine, and bought them the grange of a citizen of Paris and all the appurtenances thereof, and had a church built for them outside the gate of Montmartre.

The Brethren of the Sacks he provided for and gave them a place on the Seine near St. Germain des Prés, where they made their abode; but they tarried not long there, for they were soon suppressed. After the Brethren of the Sacks had been found a lodging, there came yet another sort of friars that they call the Order of White Mantles; and they made request to the King that he would lend them his aid so that they might stay in Paris. The King bought them a house and old buildings about it to give them an abode, near the old gate of the Temple at Paris, by the weavers' quarter. These White Mantles were suppressed at the Council of Lyons that Gregory X held.

Thereafter came friars of yet another sort, that had themselves called Brethren of the Holy Cross, and bare a cross on their breasts; and made request to the King that he would help them. Gladly did the King do so, and lodged them in a street that was called the Cross Roads of the Temple, which now is called Holy Cross Street. Thus did the good King surround the city of Paris with men of religion.

CXLIV

AFTER these things aforesaid, it befell that the King summoned all his barons to Paris one Lent. I excused myself to him by reason of a quartan fever that I then had, and begged him that he would let me bide; and he sent word to me that he wished beyond measure that I should come thither, for he had good physicians there, that well knew how to cure a quartan fever. *1267*

To Paris I went. When I came on the Eve of Our Lady in March, I found no one, neither the Queen nor any other, that could tell me why the King had sent for me. Now it chanced, as God willed, that I fell asleep at matins; and it seemed to me, as I slept, that I saw the King before an altar on his knees, and meseemed that many vested prelates invested him with a scarlet chasuble of Rheims serge. After this vision I called Sir William, my priest, that was very wise, and recounted the vision to him. And he spake to me thus: 'Sir, ye will see that the King will take the cross on the morrow.' I asked him wherefor he thought it; and he told me that he thought it because of the dream that I had dreamed; for the chasuble of scarlet serge signified the cross that was scarlet with the blood that God shed from His side and from His *24 March 1267* hands, and from His feet. 'That the chasuble was of Rheims serge signifieth that the Crusade will be of small achievement, as ye shall see if God give you life.'

When I had heard Mass at the Church of the Magdalene in Paris, I went to the King's chapel and found the King, who had mounted on the gallery of the relics, and had caused them to take down the True Cross. As the King came down, two Knights that were of his Council began to speak one to the other, and one said: 'Never believe me again, if the King take not the cross in this place.' And the other answered: 'If the King take the cross, this will be one of the most grievous days that ever were for France. For if we take not the cross, we shall lose the King's favour; and if we take the cross, we shall lose the favour of God, since we take not the cross for Him, but for fear of the King.'

25 March 1267 Now it befell thus, that the King took the cross on the morrow, and his three sons with him; and thereafter it befell that the crusade was of little achievement, according to the prophecy of my priest. I was much pressed by the King of France and the King of Navarre to take the cross.

To them I made answer, that while I had been in the service of God and the King across the seas, and since I came back thence, the officers of the King of France and the King of Navarre had ruined and impoverished my people for me; so that there was never a time but that I and they would be the worse for it. And I told them this, that if I meant to labour according to the will of God in this matter, that I would remain there to help and defend my people; for if I put my body in jeopardy of the pilgrimage of the Cross, wherein I saw full clearly that it would be to the hurt and harm of my people, I should make God wroth thereby, that gave His body to save His people.

PLATE 8

THE SAINTE CHAPELLE, PARIS. BUILT BY SAINT
LOUIS BETWEEN 1246 AND 1248
(*Phot. Giraudon*)

I held that they all did mortal sin that counselled his going, because at the point at which France stood, all the realm was at good peace with itself and with all its neighbours; nor ever after he had gone did the state of the realm do aught but worsen.

Great sin did they commit that counselled his going, in the great weakness in which his body was; for he could endure neither journeying in a cart, nor riding. His weakness was so great, that he suffered me to carry him in my arms from the house of the Count of Auxerre, where I took my leave of him, as far as the Grey Friars. And if, weak as he was, he had stayed in France, he might still have hoped to have lived long enow, and have done many fair and good deeds.

CXLV

OF the journey that he made to Tunis would I recount and say naught, since I was not there, thank God! For I would say naught nor put aught into my book whereof I be not certain. We will speak of our holy King and no more, and say that after he was come to Tunis before the Castle of Carthage, a sickness laid hold on him of a flux of the belly (and Philip, his eldest son, was ill of the same flux with a quartan fever), wherefor the King took to his bed, and felt that he was soon to pass from this world to the next.

Then he called my lord Philip his son, and commanded him to keep, as if according to his testament, all the precepts that he left him, which are hereinafter written in French, which precepts, as men tell, the King wrote with his own sainted hand.

'Fair son, the first thing that I teach thee, is that thou set thine heart to love God; for without this can no man be saved. Keep thyself from doing aught that is displeasing to God, that is to say, from mortal sin; but rather shouldst thou suffer all manner of torments, than fall into mortal sin.

'If God send thee adversity, receive it in patience and give thanks therefor to Our Lord, and bethink thee that thou hast deserved it, and that He will turn it altogether to thy profit. If He give thee prosperity, thank Him for it with humility, that thou be not the worse either by pride or other wise, through that whereby thou shouldst be the better; for one should not contend against God with his gifts.

'Confess thyself often, and choose a worthy man for thy confessor, that will know how to teach thee what thou shouldst do and from what thou shouldst keep thyself; and thou shouldst bear thyself in such wise that thy confessor and thy friends will dare to reprove thee for thy misdeeds. Hear thou the services of Holy Church with devotion and without mockery; but pray to God with both heart and tongue, especially at Mass when the sacring is done. Have a heart tender and pitiful to the poor, to the wretched, and to the afflicted, and comfort and aid them according to thy power.

'Maintain the good customs of thy realm, and overthrow the evil. Be not covetous towards thy people, neither burden them with exactions and imposition, unless it be for thy great need.

'If thou have any trouble of heart, tell it forthwith to thy confessor, or to any man of worth that is not full of idle words; thou shalt bear it the more lightly.

'Take heed that thou have in thy company men of worth and loyalty, whether religious or secular, that be not full of covetousness, and speak thou often with them; and flee and eschew the company of evil men. Hearken gladly to the word of God and bear it in thine heart; and gladly solicit prayers and pardons. Love that which is profitable and good, and hate all evil wheresoever it be.

'Let no man be so bold before thee that he speak words to thee that tempt and lead into sin, or that speak ill of another by slander behind his back; or suffer that any vile speech concerning God or His saints be said before thee. Give thanks to God often for all the benefits that He hath done thee, that thou mayest be worthy to have more.

'To keep right and justice be thou righteous and steady with thy people, without turning to the right hand or to the left, but straight forward, and uphold the poor man's suit until the truth be made manifest. And if any man have an action against thee, credit him not until thou knowest the truth; for thus thy counsellors will judge him more boldly according to the truth, on thy side or against thee.

'If thou hold aught that is another's, either on thine own behalf or on behalf of them that went before thee, if the matter be certain, restore it without delay; and if the matter be doubtful, have inquisition made by wise men, with diligence and dispatch.

'To this must thou set thy purpose, how thy people and thy subjects may live in peace and justice under thee. Especially the good towns and boroughs of thy realm do thou maintain in the state and liberties wherein thy forerunners have maintained them; and if there be aught to amend, amend and redress it, and hold them in favour and love; for by the strength and riches of the great towns will thy familiars and strangers fear to transgress against thee, and especially thy peers and thy barons.

'Honour and love all the persons of Holy Church, and take heed that men take not from them nor minish the gifts and alms that thy forerunners have given them. Men tell of King Philip, my grandfather, that on a time one of his counsellors told him that the men of Holy

Church did great wrongs and offences against him, in that they took from him his rights and lessened his jurisdictions; and it was great marvel that he endured it. And the good King made answer that he well believed it; but he considered the goodness and courtesy that God had shown him and would rather waive the question of his rights than have dispute with the men of Holy Church.

'To thy father and thy mother show honour and reverence, and keep their commandments. Give the benefices of Holy Church to men of virtue and clean life, and do it by the counsel of men of worth and clean living.

'Keep thyself from beginning war, without great deliberations, against a Christian; and if it behoveth thee to do it, protect Holy Church and them that have done naught wrong therein. If wars and dissensions arise among thy subjects, make peace between them as soon as lieth in thy power.

'Be thou diligent to have good judges and good provosts, and make inquiry often concerning them and those of thine household how they comport themselves: if there be any vice of over-great covetousness, or lying, or deceit. Strive thyself that all vile sin be driven out of thy land; especially base oaths and heresy do thou overcome according to thy power. Take heed that the expenses of thine household be reasonable.

'And finally, most sweet son, have thou Masses sung for my soul, and prayer made throughout thy realm; and grant me an especial and open part in all the good deeds that ye shall do. Fair and dear son, I give thee all the benisons that a good father may give his child. And may the blessed Trinity and All Saints guard thee and defend thee from all ill; and may God give thee grace ever to do His will, that He may be honoured by thee, so that thou and I, after this mortal life, may be together with Him and praise Him without end. Amen.'

CXLVI

WHEN the good King had given his precepts to my lord Philip, the infirmity that he had began greatly to worsen; and he asked for the Sacraments of Holy Church, and received them in sound mind and right understanding, as it appeareth; for when they anointed him and said the seven psalms, he repeated the verses in his turn.

And I have heard his son my lord the Count of Alençon say, that when he came near to death, he called upon the saints to aid and succour him, and especially upon my Lord Saint James, by saying his prayer that beginneth: '*Esto, Domine*', which is to say: 'God, be ye the sanctifier and keeper of your people.' Then called he my Lord Saint Denis of France to his aid, by saying the prayer that is as much as to say: 'Lord God, grant that we may so despise the prosperity of this world, that we may dread no adversity.'

And I then heard tell from my lord of Alençon (whom God assoil) that his father called upon my lady Saint Genevieve. Thereafter the holy King had himself laid upon a bed spread with ashes, and laid his hands upon his breast, and looking up to Heaven gave up his soul to our Creator, in the very hour that the Son of God died upon the Cross for the salvation of the world.

A pitiful thing, and one worthy to be wept over, is the passing of this saintly prince, that kept his kingdom in such holy and righteous fashion, and made such fair almsgiving therein, and instituted therein so many fair ordinances. And even as the scribe that hath made his book illumineth it with gold and blue, so did the said King illumine his realm with the fair abbeys that he there built, and with the great plenty of hospitals and houses of

Preaching Friars and Grey Friars and other religious that are named above.

25 August 1270 On the day after the feast of Saint Bartholomew the Apostle, there passed from this world the good King Louis, in the year of the Incarnation of Our Lord, the year of grace twelve hundred and seventy, and his bones were kept in a casket and brought and buried at Saint Denis in France, where he had chosen his sepulchre, in which place he was buried, where God hath since wrought many a fair miracle for him, according to his deserts.

CXLVII

1282 THEREAFTER, at the instance of the King of France and by command of the Pope, the Bishop of Rouen and Brother John of Samoys, that afterwards was bishop, came to Saint Denis in France, and tarried there long time to make inquisition into the life, the deeds, and the miracles of the holy King; and they sent me word that I was to go to them, and kept me for two days. And after that they had made inquiry of me and of others, what they had discovered was taken to the Court of Rome; and the Pope and the Cardinals examined diligently what they reported; and according *1297* to what they saw, they did him justice and set him among the number of the confessors.

Wherefor was there great joy (and so there should have been) in all the realm of France, and great honour to all his lineage that would take example in well-doing from him, and great dishonour to all them of his lineage that have no mind to follow him in good works: great dishonour, I say, to his lineage that are minded to do ill; for men will point the finger of scorn at them, and say that the holy King from whom they are descended would have been loath to do such wickedness.

BOOK TWO

After these good tidings had come from Rome, the King set aside the day after the feast of Saint Bartholomew, on which day the saint's body was taken up. When the holy body was taken up, the Archbishop of Rheims that then was (God rest his soul) and my lord Henry of Villers, my nephew, that was then Archbishop of Lyons, bare him before, and many others, both archbishops and bishops, came after, that I cannot name; and he was borne to the platform that they had set up.

25 August 1298

There Brother John of Samoys preached, and among the other great deeds that our holy King had done, he brought to mind one of the great deeds that I had testified to them upon my oath, and that I had seen; and spake thus:

'That ye may see that he was the most loyal man that ever lived in his time, will I tell you that he was so loyal that even with the Saracens would he keep the covenant that he had promised to the Saracens by his word alone; and so it was that if he had not kept it, he would have gained five thousand crowns and more.' And he recounted to them all the story as it is written above. And when he had told them the tale, he spake thus: 'Think not that I lie to you; for I see before me a man that hath testified to me on this matter on his oath.'

After the sermon was ended, the King and his brethren bare back the holy body into the church with the help of those of their lineage, to whom they owed honour; for a great honour hath been done them, an it abide not with them, as I have told you before. Let us beseech him that he will pray God that he may bestow upon us what we need in body and soul. Amen.

CXLVIII

FURTHER would I tell you hereafter certain things concerning our saintly King that shall be to his honour, that I saw concerning him while I slept: which is to say that meseemed in my dream that I saw him before my chapel at Joinville; and he was, as it seemed to me, marvellously gay and light of heart; and I myself was happy that I saw him at my castle, and said to him: 'Sir, when ye go hence, I will give you lodging at a house of mine that lieth in a town of mine that is called Chevillon.' And he answered me, laughing, and said: 'Lord of Joinville, on the faith I owe you, I am not of a mind to go hence so soon.'

When I awaked, I bethought myself; and meseemed that it would be pleasing to God and to him that I should give him lodging in my chapel, and so have I done; for I have set up an altar to the honour of God and of himself, where they shall sing for ever afterwards in his honour; and there is a perpetual revenue established to do this. And these things have I brought to the mind of my lord Louis that is heir of his name; and methinks that he would do according to the desire of God and the desire of our holy King Louis, if he procured relics of the true body of the saint, and sent them to the said chapel of Saint Lawrence at Joinville, that thereby those that come to his altar may have greater devotion.

CXLIX

I MAKE known to all men that I have herein set out a great part of the deeds of our holy King aforesaid, that I have seen and heard, and great part of his deeds that I have found, that are in a book written in French, that I have had written in this book. And these

BOOK TWO

things do I recall to you, that those that hear this book may firmly believe in what the book saith, that I have truly seen and heard; and the other things that are written there, I bear not witness to you that they are true, for I have not seen or heard them.

This was written in the year of grace thirteen hundred and nine, in the month of October.

NOTES

Like every editor of Joinville, I am deeply indebted to the edition published by Charles du Fresne, sieur du Cange, in 1678. Of subsequent editions I have chiefly made use of Natalis de Wailly, *Histoire de Saint Louis*, published in 1874, and Francisque Michel, *Mémoires de Jean Sire de Joinville*, published in 1881.

Other points I have taken from:

Gaston Paris, Review of de Wailly's edition in *Romania*, iii, 1874, p. 401.

Gaston Paris in *Histoire Litéraire de la France*, xxxii, 1898, p. 291 et seqq. I have taken the valuations of money from *La Vie du saint roi Louis, dictée et faite écrire par Jean, Seigneur de Joinville, et mise en nouveau langage par Henri Longnon*, 1928. A few passages of Joinville have been edited in *Extraits des Chroniqueurs français ... publiés ... par Gaston Paris et A. Jeanroy*, Paris (11th ed.), 1922; to this I owe certain topographical notes. The genealogical details are derived from Père Anselme, *Histoire généalogique et chronologique de la Maison Royale de France*, 1726-33.

PROLOGUE

This prologue, dating from 1309 at latest, was the last part of the book to be written.

Louis—Louis, son of Philippe le Bel and Jeanne of Navarre, succeeded his father as Louis X (le Hutin) in 1314, five years after this book was dedicated to him. At the date of this dedication he was King of Navarre and Count of Champagne and Brie by inheritance from his mother.

Seneschal—The Seneschal of Champagne presided over the courts of law known as the 'Grands Jours de Troyes' which corresponded in Champagne to the Exchequer Court of Normandy. He also presided over the ceremonial of the Court of Champagne. The office became hereditary in the House of Joinville after 1226.

his ready service—*son servise appareillié*: the formula of feudal homage.

Madam the Queen your Mother—Queen Jeanne of Navarre, wife of Philippe le Bel, who died April 2, 1305, aged barely 34.

that I would have a book written—*que je li feisse faire un livre*: that Joinville would dictate a book and have a fair copy made for her.

Our King Saint Louis: Louis IX, King of France, d. 1270. When Joinville finished this book, in 1309, the King had been canonized for twelve years.

of that true saint on earth: *du vrai cors saint*: my translation does not give Joinville's sense of the body of St. Louis as elevated to the status of relics.

NOTES

Count Peter of Alençon: the son of Saint Louis born at Châtel Pèlerin in Palestine. See Chapter XCIX.

did him not worship enow: they made him a Confessor but did not canonize him.

II

The first time: see Chapter XXXV.

The second time: see Chapter LXI.

The third time: see Chapter LXXXVII.

When at last the city was taken: when the Saracens captured Acre in 1291.

The fourth time: see Chapter CXXII.

three fathoms: *trois toises*.

the Count of Joigny: see Chapter XIX.

Oliver of Termes: see Chapter CXII.

BOOK I

III

six years: 1248 to 1254.

my lord Louis: the eldest son of Saint Louis, who died in 1260, aged 16.

Fontainebleau: the fortified castle of Fontainebleau (36 miles SE. of Paris) is first mentioned in the twelfth century.

give thought to the ordering of any dish: *devisier nulles viandes*. Fra Salimbene, however, gives us to believe that the King was not ill fed. On a *maigre* day in 1248 he had 'primo cerasas, postea panem, vinum . . . postea fabas recentes cum lacte decoctas; pisces et cancros; pastillos anguillarum; risum cum lacte amigdularum et pulvere cynamomi; anguillas assatas cum optimo salsamento; turtas et juncatas; fructus . . .'.

the discreet men of this world: *li preudome de cest siecle*. *Prud'homme* is always a stumbling-block to the translator of medieval French, for the conception is as national, and the connotation as wide, as that of the *honnête homme* of the seventeenth century.

the father of the King that now is: Philippe le Hardi, father of Philippe le Bel.

surcoats embroidered with arms: *les cotes brodées à armer*: this is ambiguous, as it may mean *cotes à armer*—that is, tunics worn over the armour—which are embroidered, or ordinary surcoats embroidered with coats of arms, such as are often represented in the illuminated manuscripts of the period.

sewn with his arms: *enforcié de ses armes*: I take this to mean worked in *appliqué*, which would be cheaper and simpler than working the arms in solid embroidery.

IV

Seneschal: it will be noted that it was the polite usage to call a man by the title of his office. Otherwise *sire* was the title given to bishops and between knights; Joinville uses it to the King, and the King to John of Valery (Chapter XXXVI) and to a clerk (Chapter XXVI).

V

Constableship: the Constable of France was the highest of the great officers of the Crown. After the office of Seneschal of France was suppressed in 1191, he became general commander of the army, with direct command over the vanguard.

Giles the Black: *Gilles le Brun*: he was born in the Imperial territory of Flanders, son of the Constable of Flanders, and held the fief of Trasignies. He was well known to Joinville, for he married Simonette, Joinville's younger sister. He succeeded Imbert of Beaujeu as Constable.

Master Robert of Sorbon: born at Sorbon in the Ardennes in 1201, canon of Cambrai in 1250 and of Paris in 1258. In 1250 he founded the hostel for students in Paris through which his name is perpetuated in the Sorbonne. He died in 1274. His conversations with Joinville must have taken place about 1260.

for discretion: *d'estre preudomme*. This illustrates the fact (which Joinville found it hard to accept) that a man could be a *prud'homme* even if not nobly born.

a friar: *béguins*. *Béguin* was used for any man living in the world under a religious rule; a tertiary is perhaps a more exact translation than friar.

King Thibault: Thibault II, King of Navarre, who married Saint Louis's daughter Isabelle.

the house of Preaching Friars at Provins: nothing remains of this building.

as an executor should do: executors (*eleemosynarii*) were recognized in French law as early as the Capitularies of Charles the Bald.

VI

Corbeil: Corbeil and its castle were annexed to the Crown at the end of the twelfth century by Louis le Gros. It is about 18 miles from Paris.

upon a Whitsuntide: a charter signed there suggests that this was in 1260.

the Count of Brittany: John I, d. 1285.

the Duke that now is: John II, the first to bear the title of Duke, d. 1305.

I would ask you: a similar question appears in one of Robert de Sorbon's

NOTES

sermons. He severely condemned fine clothes, and bade confessors ask their penitents if they had not dressed up for feast days, and, if they admitted it, to tell them they had grievously sinned. See B. Hauréau, 'Les Propos de Maître Robert Sorbon', in *Mémoires de l'Académie des Inscriptions*, xxxi, pt. 2, p. 133.

minever and green cloth: *de vert et de vair*.

grogram: *camelin*, a camel-hair cloth woven in the East, principally at Tripoli. See Chapter CXVIII.

surcoat: a sleeveless overdress worn by men and women alike.

wise men: *li preudome*.

VII

our ship ran aground: see Chapter CXXII.

garbin: Italian *garbino*, a south-west wind.

before the Body of our Lord: before the reserved Host.

the King that now is: Philippe le Bel.

IX

Bishop William of Paris: Guillaume III (d'Auvergne), born at Aurillac, Bishop of Paris 1228–48.

X

the Count of Montfort: Amauri VI, son of Simon de Montfort, d. 1241.

who do not believe it: the Albigensians.

XI

his Hours: the other biographers of St. Louis, Geoffroi de Beaulieu and Guillaume de Chartres, give a fuller account of the time spent in prayer. At midnight he rose and dressed to be present at matins; he returned to bed half-dressed until awakened for prime. After prime he heard two masses; and in the course of the day tierce, sext, nones, vespers, and compline. At night he said fifty Ave Marias before going to bed.

a friar: Hugues de Digne. See Chapter CXXXII.

XII

my lord of Nesle: Simon, sire de Nesle, who was Regent of France jointly with the Abbot of Saint Denis, during St. Louis's second crusade, in 1269.

the good Count of Soissons: Jean II de Nesle, called 'le Bon et le Bègue', Count of Soissons from 1237 to 1270. He was Joinville's first cousin, through his mother Yolande de Joinville.

we who attended him: Joinville was there in 1258.

why do you not take . . . offer?: Gaston Paris considered that the text here was incomplete.

my lord Peter of Fontaines: a celebrated jurist, Bailli de Vermandois 1253, d. 1289. He wrote a law book called *Li livres de la Reigne*.

my lord Geoffrey of Villette: Bailli de Tours 1261-2, and Ambassador to Venice 1268.

the garden in Paris: the garden of the Palace, now occupied by the Place Dauphine.

linsey-woolsey: *tyreteinne*, a stuff woven of wool on a linen warp.

carpets: some carpets were in the twelfth and thirteenth century imported from Spain, but in the time of Louis IX their manufacture was already established in France. The *Livre des Mestiers* of Étienne Boileau includes the makers of 'tapis sarrazinois' among the free craftsmen.

XIII

on another time: see Chapter CXXXV.

the count of Brittany: Jean I.

XIV

The peace: the treaty signed at Paris in 1258, which ceded to Henry III part of Guienne which his father King John had lost in 1205.

we twain have two sisters to wife: Margaret, wife of St. Louis, and Eleanor, wife of Henry III, were both daughters of Raymond Béranger IV, Count of Provence.

my lord Renaud of Trie: M. de Wailly points out that Joinville's memory here betrayed him; he should have said Mathieu de Trie, and not Renaud. The incident took place in 1266.

the Countess of Boulogne: Mahaut, d. 1258, only child and heiress of Renaut, Count of Dammartin, and Ida, Countess of Boulogne.

the seal: in medieval times the seal had the validity that a signature has now, and a broken seal was then as dubious as a defaced signature is now.

John Sarrasin: the King's chamberlain, whose *Lettre à Nicolas Arrode* gives an interesting account of St. Louis's Crusade.

BOOK II

XV

the black crosses: on St. Mark's Day the churches used to be draped in black and processions used to be made in memory of a plague which

NOTES

devastated Rome in the time of Pope Gregory the Great. The ceremony was known as *Litania Major*.

as he lay dying: see Chapter CXLVI.

XVI

his mother: Blanche of Castille.

the Count of Boulogne: Philippe Hurepel, brother of Louis VIII.

Count Peter of Brittany: Pierre I de Dreux, called Mauclerc, Duke of Brittany 1213–37, took the cross in 1238 and 1248 and died in 1250.

Count Thibault of Champagne: the song-writer, who ruled from 1204 to 1253.

in making peace: in 1234.

XVII

Count Henry Greatheart: *le bons cuens Henris le Larges*. I should perhaps have translated it 'the Liberal'.

Countess Mary: Marie de France, eldest daughter of Louis le Jeune and Eleanor of Aquitaine, and so half-sister both of Philip Augustus and of Richard Cœur de Lion.

Henry: Henry II, the Young, Count of Champagne and Brie, married Isabel, Queen of Jerusalem and Cyprus, as his second wife.

Thibault: Thibault V, Count of Champagne, married Blanche of Navarre.

Acre: Acre was taken on July 13, 1191.

in the book of the Holy Land: *L'Histoire de Eracles empereur* or the *Chronique d'Ernoul*.

the Queen of Jerusalem: Isabelle, heiress of Amauri I, King of Jerusalem, and widow of Conrad, Marquis of Montferrat.

Queen of Cyprus: Alix became Queen of Cyprus by her marriage to Guy de Lusignan in 1208.

My lord Everard of Brienne: Everard, son of André de Brienne, seigneur de Ramerupt, married Philippa, daughter of Henry of Champagne, in 1204.

XVIII

the daughter of Count Peter of Brittany: Yolande, who afterwards married Hugh XI, Count of La Marche and Angoulême.

my lord Geoffrey of La Chapelle: he held the office of 'Panetier de France' and was one of the great officers of the King's Household.

and forthwith sent for the Queen of Cyprus: Joinville relies too much upon his memory of old stories, and confuses the dates. The trouble began in 1230, the proposed marriage was only broken off in 1232, and the Queen of Cyprus only arrived in 1233.

the Duke of Burgundy: Hugh IV, d. 1272.

Count Robert of Dreux: Robert III.

XIX

Simon—Lord of Joinville: father of the writer.

at nightfall: Gaston Paris pointed out that the distance is too great to be ridden in an August night.

the Duke of Lorraine: Matthew II.

the Count of Nevers: Guy V, Count of Forez and Count of Nevers in right of his wife Mahaut, Countess of Nevers. He died on Crusade in 1241.

twenty thousand crowns: *quarante mille livres*. M. Longnon, writing in 1928, estimates this at 4,200,000 francs of modern money. Roughly speaking 4 *livres parisis* were worth 5 *livres tournois*. The livre was divided into 240 *deniers*; 12 *deniers* made 1 *sol*.

the Count of Brienne that now is: Gautier V, Duke of Athens, d. 1312.

the Count of Joigny: Jean II.

the great Count Walter of Brienne: Gautier IV, Count of Brienne and Jaffa, who married Mary, daughter of Alix, Queen of Cyprus. See Chapter CII. He was of the lineage of Joinville through his great-great-aunt, Felicity of Brienne, whose second husband was Geoffrey III of Joinville, the author's great-grandfather.

XX

Artaud of Nogent: he acted as treasurer to Count Henry, and became lord of Nogent about 1158.

the castle of Nogent l'Artaud: on the Marne, below Château-Thierry. The castle has been destroyed.

two hundred and fifty crowns: *cinq cens livres*. M. Longnon estimates this at 52,000 francs of modern money.

XXI

the Count of Poitiers: Alfonse, brother of St. Louis, who became in 1249 Count of Toulouse.

Count John of Dreux: John I, b. 1234, son of Robert III, Count of Dreux.

the Count of La Marche: Hugh X, called 'le Brun', Count of La Marche and Angoulême.

the good old Count Peter of Brittany: see Chapter XVI. Joinville here uses 'bon' in the sense of 'old'.

NOTES

the King of Navarre: Thibault de Champagne, the song-writer.

I carved before him: Joinville was his vassal, and as a young squire of seventeen served him as 'écuyer tranchant'.

the Count of Artois: Robert I, knighted in 1237, who died in the battle of Mansourah. See Chapter XLV.

Count John of Soissons: Jean II de Nesle, 'le Bon et le Bègue', Count of Soissons 1237, took the Cross in 1248 and 1269 and died at Tunis in 1270.

my Lord Imbert of Beaujeu: Imbert de Beaujeu, seigneur de Montpensier et d'Aigueperse, son of Guichard de Beaujeu; he became Constable in 1240 and died in Egypt in 1250.

my lord Enguerrand of Coucy: Enguerrand IV, 'le grand', brother and successor of Raoul II who died at Mansourah, d. 1311.

my lord Archambaud of Bourbon: Archambaud IX; he died in Cyprus.

the great King Henry of England: Henry II.

the white monks: Cistercians.

the Count of Boulogne: Alfonso, nephew of Queen Blanche, who had married Mahaut, Countess of Boulogne, widow of Philip Hurepel. He became King of Portugal in 1248.

Count Hugh of Saint Pol: Hugues de Châtillon, Comte de Saint Pol.

St. Elizabeth of Thuringia: St. Elizabeth of Hungary, daughter of Andrew II, King of Hungary, and wife of Louis IV, Landgrave of Thuringia, d. 1231, canonized 1235.

XXII

to resume possession of his fiefs: Alfonse of Poitiers was suzerain of the Count of La Marche.

the Queen of England: Isabella of Angoulême, widow of King John of England, and mother of Henry III, married Hugh X of La Marche in 1217.

it was not long: in 1242.

XXIII

I had never yet worn coat of mail: this was only worn by knights, and Joinville had not yet been knighted.

five thousand crowns: *dix mille livres de parisis*. M. Longnon estimates this at 1,300,000 francs. The annual rent was afterwards reduced to 5,000 *livres tournois*.

When we were at Poitiers: in 1242.

my lord Geoffrey of Rancon: Rancon, Haute-Vienne, nr. Bellac.

XXIV

Charles Count of Anjou who was afterwards King of Sicily: he conquered Naples from Manfred, took the title of Jerusalem in 1277, lost Sicily in the Sicilian Vespers of 1282, and died in 1285.

Hugh Duke of Burgundy: Hugh IV, b. 1212, Duke of Burgundy in 1218, took the Cross in 1248, and became King of Thessalonica in 1265. He died in 1272.

Count Guy of Flanders now lately dead: he died March 7, 1305.

Hugh count of St. Pol: seigneur de Châtillon, younger son of Walter III of Châtillon and Elizabeth, Countess of St. Pol. He died in Cyprus.

my lord Walter: Gauchier de Châtillon, seigneur de Montjay, son of Gui de Châtillon and Agnes de Donzy. He married Jeanne de Boulogne, daughter of Philip Hurepel.

the Count of Sarrebruck: Jean d'Apremont.

my lord Gobert of Apremont: Apremont, Haute-Saône, near Gray.

all told twenty knights, of whom he had command over nine and I over nine: *dont il estoit li disiesme et je moy disiesme.*

XXV

my first wife: Alix, sister of Henry VI, Count of Grandpré.

the lord of Vaucouleurs: Joinville's mother was Dame de Vaucouleurs, and according to custom the second son bore the title.

five hundred crowns a year in land: *mil livrées de terre*: Longnon estimates it at 100,000 francs.

my mother: Beatrix, daughter of Stephen III, Count of Auxonne, and of Beatrix, Countess of Chalon-sur-Saône. She did not die until 1260.

knights banneret: Du Cange quotes a document which explains what these were: 'Quant un bachelier a grandement servi et suivy la guerre, et que il a assez terre, et qu'il puisse avoir gentilshommes, ses hommes, et pour accompagner sa bannière, il peut licitement lever bannière et non autrement. Car nul homme ne doit porter, ne lever bannière en bataille, s'il n'a du moins cinquante hommes d'armes, tous ses hommes et les archiers and arbalestriers qui y appartiennent.' The three who accompanied Joinville were Hugues de Landricourt, Hugues de Thil-Châtel, Lord of Conflans, and Pierre de Pontmolain.

Count of Sarrebruck in right of his wife: he married Laurette, Countess of Sarrebruck. His name is generally given as Joffroy. He was succeeded by her nephew, Simon de Montbéliard, whose daughter married Joinville's son Ancel.

NOTES

XXVI

for I was not his liegeman: Joinville was a vassal of the Count of Champagne. He became a vassal of the King's before reaching Cyprus. See Chapter XXIX.

the Provost of Paris: the provost was the principal magistrate of the City.

his sergeants of the Châtelet: the Châtelet of Paris had by this time become the seat of the courts of criminal law in Paris.

ye have lost your priesthood: no man who had wilfully shed blood might continue to be a priest.

XXVII

Cheminon: Cheminon, Marne, nr. Vitry-le-François, a Cistercian abbey in the diocese of Châlons.

Clairvaux: a Cistercian house.

my scrip and staff: the Crusade was a pilgrimage, and these were its badges. St. Louis similarly received his scrip and staff, together with the oriflamme, at Saint Denis.

in my shirt: *en langes*, i.e. in a long woollen shirt.

St. Urbain: the monastery here had been founded by Geoffrey III of Joinville in 1168.

my two children: Joinville's eldest daughter and the infant. It is noteworthy that Joinville does not mention his wife. His first marriage, however, was a *mariage de convenance*. He was affianced to Alix de Grandpré when he was only seven years old, and later he wished to break the engagement and marry the daughter of the Count of Bar. This the Count of Champagne, his suzerain, would not permit, and the marriage to Alix de Grandpré duly took place.

Donjeux: Donjeux sur Marne, Haute-Marne, about 10 miles from Joinville.

Roche de Glun: La Roche de Glun, Drôme, near Tain. The *Grandes Chroniques de Saint Denis*, cap. xlii, tell us: 'Le roy ... se parti de Lyon, et vint à un chastel que on nomme la Roche de Glin. Ceux du Chastel furent si oultrecuidiés qu'il robèrent une partie des gens du roy qui aloient devant pour faire garnison à ceux de l'ost. Quant la nouvelle en vint au roy, il commanda que le chastel fust mis par terre et abatu; ceux de dedens furent pris et mis en fers et en liens, le chastel fu tout destruit et gasté.'

XXVIII

the Rock of Marseilles: it was above the port, but is now levelled.

a mountain that is quite round: this has not been identified.

XXIX

when the King was sojourning in Cyprus: between September 1248 and the end of May 1249.

the great King of Tartary: not the great Khan, but his viceroy in Asia Minor, Ilchikhatsi. The Chronicles of St. Denis (1248) give his name as Erchaltay, and Jean Sarrasin as Eteltay.

had wrought: *fist entaillier*; the *Grandes Chroniques de Saint Denis* say 'brodée de riches œuvres' (cap. xlvi).

Friars Preachers: Dominicans. For missionary purposes members of the Order were encouraged to study Oriental languages. Jean Sarrasin, the King's Chamberlain, gives their names as 'frère Andrieus de Saint Jacques et uns siens frère et maistre Jehan Goderiche et uns autres clers de Poissy, et Herbers li sommeliers, et Gerbers de Sens'.

at the moment that the King's brothers were going back to France: see Chapter XCIII.

twelve score florins: *douze vins livres de tournois*. Longnon estimates this at 25,000 francs.

Nicosia: the capital of Cyprus.

XXX

the Empress of Constantinople: Mary, daughter of John of Acre and Brienne, wife of Baldwin II.

Paphos: *Baphe*: near the western extremity of Cyprus.

my lord Everard of Brienne: see Chapter XVII.

surcoat for meals: *seurcot à mangier*. The reading should possibly be *à manges*, with sleeves.

Limassol: *Limeson*.

my lord Philip of Nanteuil: he took the Cross in 1239. He was known as a *trouvère*.

her lord: the Emperor Baldwin II, who then held little more than Constantinople itself.

the Count of Eu: see Chapter CI.

my lord John of Acre: he married Jeanne de Châteaudun, widow of Jean, Comte de Montfort, in 1251. His first wife was Marie de Coucy, widow of Alexander II of Scotland.

XXXI

the Sultan of Iconium: Ezz-eddin. See Vincent de Beauvais, *Speculum historiale*, xxxi, cap. 144, Douai ed. 1624, p. 1281, col. 2.

the King of Armenia: Haiton.

farrā<u>sh</u>: *ferrais*.

NOTES

the King of Tartary: see Chapter XXIX.

the Sultan of Cairo: *li soudans de Babiloinne*: the Sultan was Malik Ṣalāḥ Najmu-d-Dīn 'Ayyūb. 'Babylon' refers to the ancient fortress at Old Cairo which was called in Coptic 'Babilonia-nte-Chemi', Babylon in Egypt, since it had originally been built to receive Babylonian mercenaries. In the Middle Ages, however, it was used to mean the whole city of Cairo, and to avoid confusion I have translated it by *Cairo* throughout the book.

the Sultan of Hama: al-Malik an-Nāṣir Yūsuf, Prince of Aleppo, was in possession of Hama on the Orontes, that belonged to the realm of Egypt.

XXXII

in their ship: the *Lettre de Jean Pierre Sarrasin*, the King's chamberlain, tells us that she was called *La Monnoie*.

the Prince of the Morea: Guillaume de Villehardouin, of the Champenois family.

the Duke of Burgundy: he had spent the winter in the Morea, probably after going to Constantinople to bear aid to the Emperor Baldwin.

XXXIII

my lord John of Beaumont: of a Picard house, one of the King's chamberlains. He had commanded the army sent by the King against the bandit Trencavel in 1240.

my lady of Beyrout: Eschive de Montbéliard, daughter of Gautier de Montbéliard, and widow of Balian d'Ibelin, Lord of Beyrout.

the Count of Montbéliard: Thierry III, Count of Montbéliard, called the Great Baron. He died in 1284.

the ship's boat: *la barge de cantiers*. Jean Sarrasin tells us that before getting into the smaller boat St. Louis heard mass, and that the Legate, when in the smaller boat, held aloft a relic of the True Cross and made the sign of the Cross with it over the men in little boats who were going ashore.

Plonquet: in 1198 Thibault V of Champagne gave as a fief to Raoul *dit Plunquet*, Knight, in recompense for his services, the village of Vendières, near Châtillon. (Père Anselme, *Hist. gén. et chron. de la maison royale de France*, vi, p. 129.)

my lord Hugh of Vaucouleurs: only known from this mention of him.

my lord Villain of Versey: perhaps Verseilles, Haute-Marne.

my lord William of Dammartin: probably Dammartin, Haute-Marne.

in the Morea: they had perhaps accompanied the Duke of Burgundy.

the banner of St. Denis: the oriflamme, or standard of the Abbey of St. Denis. The Kings of France acquired the right of bearing it as

THE HISTORY OF ST. LOUIS

avoués of the abbey when they acquired the Vexin in the time of Louis le Gros, as it was the privilege of the Counts of Vexin to bear it. The oriflamme had been delivered to St. Louis to take on Crusade at a great ceremony at St. Denis on June 12, 1248.

XXXIV

my lord Baldwin of Rheims: only known from this mention of him.

the Count of Jaffa: Jean d'Ibelin, seigneur de Baruth (Beyrout) and Count of Jaffa, son of Balian d'Ibelin and Eschive de Montbéliard. He was the author of the *Assises de Jérusalem.* See Chapter XXXIII.

of the lineage of Joinville: perhaps through the connexion of Joinville with the House of Brienne.

XXXV

the Legate: Odo, Bishop of Tusculum.

carrier pigeons: the historian Djemal-eddin records the arrival in Cairo of a pigeon with the news of the fall of Damietta.

went to encamp before Damietta. the King, the Legate, and other great men were lodged within the town, and the main army outside the walls.

Manifestly ill did the Turks leave Damietta: the Arab historian Makrisi equally condemns the action of Fakhru-d-Din in abandoning Damietta to the Christians.

the Petit Pont: this was covered with shops.

in our fathers' time: Joinville's father had been in the army of John de Brienne, King of Jerusalem, when he took Damietta in 1219. The Franks held it for less than two years.

XXXVI

The Patriarch: Guy, Patriarch of Jerusalem.

my lord John of Valery: Vallery, Yonne, near Sens. He was son of Huon, Sire de Valery.

three thousand crowns: *sis milles livres.*

King John: John of Brienne, King of Jerusalem.

XXXVII

my lord Geoffrey of Sargines: Sergines, Yonne, near Sens. He appears as Seneschal of the Kingdom of Jerusalem in a document of 1277.

my lord Matthew of Marly: Mathieu de Marly, Seigneur de Laye, d. 1249.

my lord Philip of Nanteuil: see Chapter XXX.

my lord Imbert of Beaujeu: see Chapter XXI.

NOTES

the master of the cross-bowmen: Thibaut de Montléart, the first man to hold the official title.

lest the Turks should do it hurt: the Arab historian Makrisi records that 36 Christian prisoners, including 2 knights, were sent to Cairo on July 12, 1249; 37 more on the 17th, 22 on the 19th, and 45, including 3 knights, on the 28th. On Aug. 29, 50 more were dispatched, and on Jan. 14, 1250, 70 more, including 3 lords.

my lord Walter of Autrèche: probably Autrèches, Oise, near Compiègne. He was the son of Guy de Nanteuil, Seigneur d'Autrèche and Châtelain de Bar.

sergeants-at-arms: in later times the sergeants-at-arms were part of the King's guard.

my lord Aubert of Narcy: Narcy, Haute-Marne, near Wassy.

XXXVIII

the Lord of Courtenay: see Chapter XLVIII.

the Count of Poitiers: Vincent of Beauvais states that he stayed in France to aid Queen Blanche in governing the kingdom, and set out from Aigues Mortes on the morrow of St. Bartholomew and arrived at Damietta the Sunday before the feast of St. Simon and St. Jude, Oct. 28.

the yeomen of France: *l'ariere-ban de France.*

The Church of our Lady: Jean Sarrasin tells us that not only was the Mosque converted into a Church but also endowed that it might be served by a College of Canons. The other mosques were given to the Religious Orders, likewise with endowments that many thought to be extravagant.

the rich men: like the Spanish *ricos hombres*, men of great estate.

XXXIX

a stream: on the controversial question of the topography of this part of the narrative, the reader is referred to E. J. Davis, *The Invasion of Egypt . . . by Louis IX of France,* n.d. [1897], p. 32.

Brother Reynold of Vichiers: I have not found any other mention of him.

XL

the river: the Nile.

the feast of St. Remi: October 1. Gaston Paris has pointed out that this is too late, and suggested it was a copyist's error for St. Peter, which would be a more correct date.

pots of white earth: the Arab and Spanish *alcarazas,* in which the water cools by evaporation through the porous jars.

Daraksa: *Rexi*: the channel called 'Ashmūn Thanā.

XLI

chats-châtels: *chats* are covered ways, and *châtels* the wooden towers that protect them.

Jocelyn of Cornaut: possibly Cornant, Yonne, near Sens.

Fakhru-d-Dīn, son of the sheik: *Scecedin le fil au sceic*: Fakhru-d-Dīn, son of the sheik Ṣadru-d-Dīn. Jean Sarrasin gives his name as *Fachardin*.

the Emperor Frederick: Frederick II of Hohenstaufen, emperor of Germany and titular King of Jerusalem.

Sharmisa: *Sormesac*: it is, in fact, on the Damietta channel.

my lord Peter of Avallon: Avallon, Yonne. Elsewhere Joinville calls him cousin. When he was in the Holy Land he married Héloïse, daughter of William of Bures, Lord of Tiberias.

XLII

the feast of St. Sebastian: January 20.

Count Guy of Forez: Guy VI, Count of Forez, son of the Count of Nevers (see Chapter XIX). He died in 1259.

XLIII

a Fowler: *perriere*: Cotgrave gives this equivalent.

my lord Walter of Écurey: Écurey, Meuse, nr. Montmédy.

Greek fire: what used to be called wild-fire. It was a concoction of such substances as sulphur, pitch, charcoal, and tow, with gum and naphtha, lighted and hurled against the enemy's ships or outworks. Its use was known to the ancient Greeks and in an improved form it was a feature of Byzantine warfare.

the swivel crossbow: *l'arbalestre à tour*.

of Albi: *l'Aubigoiz*.

XLIV

five thousand crowns: *dix mille livres*.

XLV

my lord John of Orleans: at this date there was no noble house of Orleans; presumably he was a knight who lived in that city.

'*vivrie*': with the colours of the ground divided by a stepped outline.

my lord Foucauld of Le Merle: probably Le Merle, Ain.

Mansourah: *la Massoure*: about 40 miles from Damietta.

the Lord of Couci: Raoul II.

NOTES

XLVI

my lord Hugh of Trichâtel, Lord of Conflans: I keep the spelling of the manuscript, but it probably represents Thilchastel, nr. Is-sur-Tille, Côte d'Or, though it may also stand for Trie-Château, Oise.

my lord Raoul of Wanou: M. Paris suggests that his fief was Vanault le Châtel, nr. Vitry, Marne.

my lord Everard of Siverey: M. Paris suggests that his fief was Sivri, nr. Epinac, Saône-et-Loire. There are, however, several places named Sivry nearer Joinville's own district: notably Sivry-sur-Ante, near Sainte Ménéhould.

my lord Hugh of Écot: Écot, nr. Chaumont, Haute-Marne.

my lord Frederick of Loupey: probably one of the three places named Louppy in the department of the Meuse.

my lord Renaud of Menoncourt: Menoncourt, territoire de Belfort.

my Lord St. James: St. James of Compostella.

my lord Peter of Auberive: Auberive, nr. Langres, Haute-Marne.

XLVII

the Count of Flanders: Guillaume de Dampierre, who in 1218 had married Margaret, Countess of Flanders, daughter of Baldwin IX, Count of Flanders and Emperor of Constantinople.

XLVIII

the Lord of Courtenay: Courtenay, nr. Montargis, Loiret.

my lord John of Saillenay: M. Paris suggests that his fief was Seignelay, nr. Auxerre, Yonne.

the Count of Soissons: John II de Nesle, 'le Bon'.

my lord Peter of Neuville that was called Caier: Neuville-au-Pont, nr. Vassy, Haute-Marne.

whose cousin german I had married: Joinville's first wife, Alix de Grandpré. Raoul de Nesle, Count of Soissons, was the husband of Joinville's aunt Yolande.

XLIX

William of Boon: Bohon, nr. Carentan, Manche.

John of Gamaches: Gamaches, nr. Abbeville, Somme.

a long quilted footsoldier's coat: *un gamboison d'estoupes*.

L

my lord of Châtillon: Walter of Châtillon, son of Guy I and nephew of Hugh V, Count of Saint-Pol.

THE HISTORY OF ST. LOUIS

Brother Henry of Ronnay: Rosnai l'Hôpital, nr. Bar-sur-Aube, Aube.

the Master of the Temple: Guillaume de Sonnac. See Chapter LIV.

my lord Guy Mauvoisin: second of the name, seigneur de Rosny.

LI

that was uncle to Mahomet: Ali was in fact the cousin of Mahomet and his son-in-law.

the Old Man of the Mountain: the chief of the Ismailian sect of Syria. The province of the 'État des Alaouites' represents what remains of his territory. Masyaf was his fortress at the time of which Joinville writes.

LII

my lord Walter of Châtillon: see Chapter L.

Sir John of Voisey: Voisey, Haute-Marne, nr. Langres.

LIII

a valiant Saracen: Baybars Bunduqdār, whom Joinville, in Chapter LVI, calls *Boudendars*.

the coat of the Count of Artois: Makrisi, the Arab historian, records that 'a great lord, and relation to the King of France, was captured on Jan. 6'.

LIV

my lord Guy of Ibelin and my lord Baldwin his brother: Guy d'Ibelin, Constable of Cyprus, and Baudoin d'Ibelin, Seneschal of Cyprus, the two younger sons of Baudoin d'Ibelin and Eschive de Montbéliard.

a furlong of land: *un journel de terre*.

LV

Walter of La Horgne: La Horgne, Ardennes, near Mézières.

my lord Josserand of Brancion: Brancion, Saône-et-Loire, nr. Mâcon. He calls Joinville nephew, but really they were cousins at some removes through his mother's family of Chalon.

my lord Josserand of Nanton: Nanton, Saône-et-Loire, near Chalon-sur-Saône.

my lord Henry of Cosne: Cosne, Nièvre.

the Count of Chalon: the uncle of Joinville's mother.

nephews: they were related, but not so nearly as this: he was Joinville's uncle's cousin.

the Germans: the church attacked was the Moustier of Mâthons, founded by Geoffroy III of Joinville.

NOTES
LVI

Baḥriyya: *bahariz*: the Mamelukes.

Ḥalqa: the Arab word means 'the ring': either the ring of servant-guards or more probably the slaves with rings in their ears.

the Count of Montfort and the Count of Bar: Count Amaury de Montfort, son of Simon, and Henry II, Count of Bar, were taken prisoner at Gaza in 1239.

Bibars: Baybars Bunduqdār. See Chapter LIII.

the King of Armenia: Haiton. See Chapter XXXI.

LVII

the Sultan that was dead: Malik Ṣalāḥ Najmu-d-Dīn 'Ayyūb. See Chapter XXXI.

a son: Ṭūrān Shāh.

a kingdom: Damascus.

LVIII

eels: *bourbetes*; Cotgrave says 'a small freshwater fish, that altogether lives on, and lyes in, mud'.

the sickness of the host: the illness appears to have been scurvy, of which Joinville describes the typical *petechiae*.

eighty of our galleys: the Arab historian Makrisi records the capture of a large boat on Jan. 12, of a convoy of 52 provision-boats on Feb. 8, and of 32 more on March 16.

forty crowns: *quatre-vins livres*.

LIX

my lord Geoffrey of Mussanbourc: only known from this text.

my lord Hugh of Landricourt: Landrecourt, Meuse, nr. Verdun.

in my chapel: obviously it must have been an oratory by the tent.

LX

my coat: *ma cote*.

the clauses of the treaty: Marino Sanudo states that by this treaty the Sultan agreed to cede to the King Damietta and the land about it, for the Christians who lived in Egypt to inhabit ('Christiani de Cinctura: quia cingulum portabant latum, et vestimentum, per quod recognoscebantur ab aliis, Jacobitis scilicet et aliis Christianis').

LXII

the village: Arab historians state that St. Louis was captured at a place called Minieh.

a burgher woman of Paris: presumably a camp-follower.

my lord Philip of Montfort: Philip, son of Simon III, Earl of Leicester, and later of England. He later became Lord of Tyre.

LXIII

Doulevant: Doulevant-le-Château, Haute-Marne, near Wassy, about 10 or 11 miles from Joinville.

LXIV

a Saracen that was of the Emperor's country: possibly from Sicily, but probably from Syria, where the Emperor was still titular suzerain of what remained of the Latin Kingdom.

the castle of the ship: the officers' quarters on deck.

LXV

my mother was his cousin german: her aunt Beatrice married Frederick Barbarossa.

the Lord of Montfaucon: Ami de Montbéliard. See Chapter LXXX.

LXVII

two hundred and fifty thousand crowns: *cinc cens mile livres*: Longnon estimates this at 52,500,000 francs. The King's personal accounts show a payment of 167,102 livres, 18 sous, 8 deniers tournois; the balance presumably came from the funds allocated to the Crusade.

LXVIII

Count John of Soissons: 'le Bon': see Chapter XXI.

a lodging: Arab historians record that it was built at a place called Farescour.

LXIX

Imams: *evesques*.

Fārisu-d-Dīn 'Uqṭayy: *Faraquataye*.

LXX

Danish axes: axes with highly convex blades.

that well knew the Saracen tongue: the Ibelins had long been established in Syria.

St. Agnes: a virgin, martyred in 304. She was led out to be burnt at the stake, but the faggots would not burn, so the officer in charge of her guard struck off her head.

NOTES
LXXI
my lord Nicholas of Acre: only known from this text.

LXXII
instruments: presumably the drums of the guard.

to make him Sultan of Cairo: no Arab historian confirms this story.

the Queen: St. Louis's wife, Margaret of Provence, whom he married in 1234. She was accompanied by the Countess of Artois, the Countess of Poitiers, and the Countess of Angers.

LXXIII
Ṣabrī: *Sebreci.*

in this book: presumably the Koran.

LXXIV
my lord Philip of Nemours: Philippe de Nemours or de Ville Béon, Chamberlain of France. He followed St. Louis on his second crusade, died with him at Tunis, and was buried at his feet in Saint Denis.

the Marshal of France that they called du Mez: Jean Clément, seigneur du Mez. At this time there was only one Marshal of France.

the Master of the Trinity: Nicolas, general of the Order of Mathurins.

the Count of Flanders: in Chapter LXXXII Joinville speaks of the Count as being still with the King at Acre.

LXXV
that they should lend: the Templars acted as bankers, for which the riches of the Order and their sworn probity well qualified them.

Brother Stephen of Otricourt: Ostricourt, Nord, near Lille.

Brother Reynold of Vichiers: see Chapter XXXIX.

Nicholas of Choisy: evidently a lay client who employed the Templars as his banker.

LXXVI
a full league: *un grant lieue.*

Light up!: to give the signal for departure to the fleet.

ten crowns: *vint livres de parisis*: Longnon estimates this at 2,600 francs of modern money.

LXXVII
Walter of Châtillon: see Chapter XXIV.

my lord John of Monson: only known from this text.

village: Joinville uses the Arabic word *kasel.*

THE HISTORY OF ST. LOUIS

my lord John Fouinon: perhaps a connexion of the Champenois knight Jehan Fuisnons or Foisnons mentioned by Villehardouin.

my lord James of Castel, Bishop of Soissons: M. de Wailly states that Joinville mistook the name, which was Gui de Château Porcien.

Malik an-Nāṣur Dā'ūd: *Nasac*: grandson of Saladin, a pretender to the Sultanate of Cairo. See de Wailly, p. 483.

with King John: with Jean de Brienne, King of Jerusalem, who took Damietta in 1219 and lost it in 1221.

LXXVIII

a son that was called John: Jean Tristan, Count of Nevers, died of plague at Tunis in 1270, three weeks before his father.

the folk of Pisa and Genoa: they came on Crusade rather to provide transport and provisions than to fight.

an hundred and eighty thousand crowns: Longnon estimates this at 37,800,000 modern francs.

LXXIX

Brother Raoul the Friar Preacher: not otherwise known.

Fariṣu-d-Dīn 'Uqṭayy: see Chapter LXIX.

he should bear it in mind: the text is not clear.

at backgammon: *aus tables*.

LXXX

that was called Bartholomew: see Chapter LXV.

Oiselay: Oiselay, Haute-Saône, 5 miles from Gray, Haute-Saône. Remains of the thirteenth-century castle may still be seen.

my lord Peter of Bourbonne: Bourbonne-les-Bains, Haute-Marne, nr. Langres.

two hundred crowns: *quatre cens livres*: Longnon estimates this at 42,000 francs of modern money.

John Caym of Sainte Menehould: Sainte Menehould, Marne.

Brother Reynold of Vichiers: see Chapter LXXV.

as-Ṣāfiriyya: *le Saffran*: a village near Jaffa.

LXXXI

The Bishop of Acre that then was: Gautier, Bishop of Ptolemais, became bishop in 1244 and died in 1253.

St. Michael's: nothing remains of this church.

I awaited naught but death: Joinville was probably the more depressed since his grandfather had died in Acre from sickness in 1190.

Libera me Domine: part of the funeral service.

NOTES

LXXXII

the other men of substance: this was the Grand Conseil, the feudal *curia*, not the *familiares* of Chapter XXXVII.

the Queen my mother: Blanche of Castille.

the Legate: see Chapter XXXV.

my lord of Borlaymont: here Bollaimmont, but in Chapter LXXXIV Boulaincourt. Joinville's aunt, Felicity of Joinville, married Peter, seigneur de Borlaymont.

LXXXIII

my lord Guy Mauvoisin: see Chapter L.

Count John of Jaffa: see Chapter XXXIV. Joinville claimed kinship with him.

my lord John of Beaumont: he and Joinville were not on friendly terms. See Chapters XXXIII and XXXVII.

the lord of Chatenay: Chacenai, nr. Bar-sur-Seine, Aube.

LXXXIV

the Prince of Antioch: Bohemond V.

Poulains: the word was used for a man of mixed Syrian and Frankish parentage. Michel suggests that it may come from the Greek πούλος, son of . . . .

my lord Peter of Avallon: see Chapter XLI.

Tyre: *Sur*. Tyre did not fall into Saracen hands until 1291.

LXXXV

many were there that wept: Monsieur H. F. Delaborde (in *Romania*, xxiii, 1894, p. 148) notes that the letter addressed by the King to his subjects announcing his decision says it had been reached by a majority (*major pars*), and that the continuation of the *Lettre de Jean Sarrasin* describes those in favour of staying as 'presque tous'. He suggests that until it was known that the Emirs had broken the treaty, the King meant to return, and that their default became known between the second and third councils. Joinville may well have misinterpreted the King's kind words to him immediately after the second Council.

LXXXVI

my lord Peter the Chamberlain: not identified.

a thousand crowns until Easter: until Easter 1251. Longnon assesses it at 210,000 modern francs for eight months: this covered the pay of at least fifty men.

my lord Peter of Pontmoulain: perhaps Pont-molin, Seine-et-Marne.

THE HISTORY OF ST. LOUIS

LXXXVII

the Sultan of Damascus: al-Malik an-Nāsir Yūsuf, formerly Sultan of Hama (see Chapter XXXI), who had become Sultan of Damascus on the death of Ṭūrān-<u>sh</u>āh.

Brother Yves le Breton: see Chapter XC.

LXXXVIII

John the Armenian: otherwise unknown.

King Baldwin: Baldwin IV, b. 1160, King of Jerusalem from 1173 till his death in 1185.

LXXXIX

the envoys of the Old Man of the Mountain: see Chapter LI.

the Temple and the Hospital: the Hospitallers' castle of the Krak des Chevaliers and the Templars' of Chastel-Blanc (Safita) were on the marches of the Old Man's territory.

XC

giraffe: orafle.

the amber: solid ambergris was commonly used in jewellery until the beginning of the seventeenth century.

Ali: see Chapter LI.

XCI

my lord John of Valenciennes: Lord of Caiapha in Palestine.

Count Walter of Brienne: Gautier IV (the Great), Count of Jaffa and titular King of Jerusalem, died a prisoner in Egypt in 1244. See Chapter CII.

two hundred knights: Jean Sarrasin states that those freed included the Master of the Hospital and 25 of his knights, 25 Templars, 10 knights of the Teutonic Order, 100 lay knights, and 600 other men and women.

my lady of Sidon: Marguerite de Reynel, dame de Sayette, aunt of Joinville's second wife Alix de Reynel, and niece of Jean de Brienne, King of Jerusalem and Emperor of Constantinople, and Gautier IV de Brienne. Her husband was Balian I of Sidon. The holder of the fief of Sidon had the right of striking his own coins.

XCII

coats and mantles of green: in Chapter VI Joinville mentions that he was in the habit of wearing green.

the heads of Christians: according to the Arab historian Makrisi the heads of those taken with the Count of Bar in 1239 and with the Count of Montfort at Gaza in 1244 were exposed stuck on lances on the walls of the citadel at Cairo.

NOTES

Caesarea: *Cesaire*.

my lord Raoul of Soissons: Sire de Cœuvres, married Alix of Champagne, Regent of Cyprus, *c.* 1240, d. 1269.

the envoys . . . from the Tartars: see Chapter XXIX.

XCIII

as I have told you: see Chapter XXIX.

two Friars Preachers: one was the Dominican André de Longjumeau.

the port of Antioch: the port of Antioch at the mouth of the Orontes is over 20 miles from the city.

Gog and Magog: see Ezekiel xxxviii–xxxix and Rev. xx. According to Josephus they were the Armenians.

Prester John: the legendary name of a King of Central Asia, a Nestorian Christian, dethroned by Ghengiz-Khan, the founder of the Tartar Empire early in the thirteenth century.

the Emperor of Persia: the Khwarizmī King. He and his son, Jalālu-d-Dīn Mankōbirti, were both conquered by Genghiz-Khan.

a wise man: presumably Genghiz-Khan.

XCIV

one of the princes: the story is to be found in the *Bonum Universale de Apibus* of Thomas of Cantimpré, II, liv, no. 14.

a Queen kneeling: evidently the Blessed Virgin.

George: St. George, patron saint of the Greeks, to whom this legend is probably due.

this Emperor: Mahomet, King of the Khwarizmī, who, having been defeated by Genghiz-Khan, made his way into Syria, and defeated the Christians there in 1244.

XCV

the law of the Greek Church: Nestorian Christians.

Khwarizmī: *Coremin*.

XCVI

my lord Alenard of Senaingan: Mademoiselle Jeanne Vielliard suggests that this may be Waldemar, Duke of South Jutland, son of Abel, King of Norway, d. 1257.

lions: probably panthers, which are still found in the hills of Syria; I have seen one recently killed in Tripoli.

XCVII

my lord Philip of Toucy: Joinville confuses him with his father and calls him *Nargoes de Toci*. Philippe de Toucy, son of Narjot de Toucy

THE HISTORY OF ST. LOUIS

and the daughter of Agnes, sister of Philip Augustus, by her second husband, a Greek named Branas. Her first husband was Andronicus, Emperor of Constantinople.

the Emperor of Constantinople: the Frankish Emperor Baldwin II.

Comans: a tribe of the Huns established in Moldavia.

Vataces: John Ducas Vataces, Greek Emperor of Nicaea 1222–55. He was the rival of the Frankish Emperors of Constantinople.

XCVIII

no more of his moneys: in April 1252, at Jaffa, the King endowed Joinville with 200 livres annually for himself and his heirs.

the feast of St. Remi: Oct. 1.

my own ten: the nine knights over whom Joinville was banneret, and himself.

according to the custom of the country: in France it was the custom to sit on one side of the table only, as at a College high table.

XCIX

a gazelle: *gazel*.

sitting on their mantles: presumably upon the floor. Jacques de Vitry, *Historia Hierosolymitana*, cap. lxv, refers to this punishment: 'to eat scanty meals upon the ground, without napery'.

on pilgrimage: that is, the Crusaders, since a Crusade was a pilgrimage under arms.

the Glutton: *le Goulu*.

Brother Hugh of Jouy: he succeeded Brother Reynold of Vichiers as Marshal when the latter became Commander.

writing that is called credential: *en escrit que on apeloit monte-joy*.

the Count of Alençon: Peter, the fifth son of Saint Louis, born at Châtel Pèlerin.

Châtel Pèlerin: a castle of the Templars, still existing in a ruined state at Athlit, near Haifa.

the Queen: Margaret of Provence, wife of Saint Louis.

C

the Count of Jaffa: see Chapter XXXV.

an elephant: two years later St. Louis sent it as a present to the King of England.

CI

the Count of Eu: John, son of Alphonse de Brienne and of Marie de Lusignan, Comtesse d'Eu.

NOTES

my lord Arnoul of Guines: Arnoul, younger son of Arnoul II, Count of Guines.

the prince of Antioch: Bohemond VI, prince of Antioch and Count of Tripoli, son of Bohemond V, d. 1251, and of Lucia, daughter of Count Paul of Rome. Joinville claimed kinship with him.

Tripoli: in Syria, between Beyrout and Laṭakiyya.

'*gules*': the arms are generally given as gules, a bend chequy argent and azure.

CII

the Count of Brienne: Walter the Great, Count of Brienne and Jaffa. He was a kinsman of Joinville's.

his wife: Mary, sister of Henry I, King of Cyprus. See Chapter XIX.

the Emperor of Persia: the successor of Jalālu-d-dīn as commander of the remnant of the Khwarizmī army.

Bārbaqan: *Barbaquan*.

Tiberias: *Tabarié*, captured by the Franks in 1099, captured by Saladin in 1187, was again in Christian hands from 1240 to 1247, and after 1247 was a fief of Galilee.

my lord Odo of Montbéliard: he married Eschive, daughter of Raoul and granddaughter of Guillaume de Bures, Prince of Tiberias.

Châtel Pèlerin: see Chapter XCIX.

Acre: Baldwin I captured Acre in 1104 and it remained the most important Frankish military base in Palestine (except for the two years after 1187, when Saladin captured it) until it fell in 1291.

Safad: *le Saffar*: a hill-town north of the Lake of Tiberias where Fulk of Anjou built a castle in 1140. Saladin captured it in 1188, but it was again Frankish in 1240. Beibars finally captured it in 1266.

the Sultan of Cairo: see Chapter XCI.

the Patriarch: the Patriarch of Jerusalem.

the Sultan of Homs: Malik-Mansour.

Bishop of Ramleh: not far from Lydda, and a see of the Latin Kingdom. The fine Romanesque Cathedral still survives.

CIV

the Order of St. Lazarus: this order of knights under vows was especially devoted to the care of sick pilgrims.

twelve miles: *trois grans lieues*.

THE HISTORY OF ST. LOUIS

CV

the barons of the country: that is, those holding fiefs in the kingdom of Jerusalem.

CVI

the lord of 'Arṣūf: Jean III d'Ibelin, seigneur d'Arṣūf, a castle on the coast to the south of Acre, on the site of the ancient Antipatris.

fifty thousand besants: Longnon estimates this at 2,533,000 modern francs.

the sands of Acre: the sands at the mouth of the river between Haifa and Acre.

my lord John the Great: a knight of Genoa in Italy.

CVII

Sidon: the city was captured by Baldwin in 1111 and was the seat of the second of the four great baronies of the Latin Kingdom.

my lord Simon of Montléart: *Symons de Monceliart*: this seems to be an error for Thibaut de Montléart, who was at this time Master of the Crossbowmen.

the Castle of Sidon: the Château de la Mer, built by the Crusaders during the winter of 1227-8. The picturesque ruins still survive on an island just off the quay at Sidon.

a hillock where there had once been an old castle: probably Latrun, in the middle ages Toron des Chevaliers.

CVIII

the great King Philip: Philip Augustus, in 1191.

the Duke of Burgundy: Hugh III, died at Tyre 1193.

the Duke that is newly dead: Hugh IV, d. 1272. The reference is of great importance as giving the date of the first recension of Joinville's book; see G. Paris, in *Hist. lit. de la France*, xxxii, p. 429. De Wailly, however, considered that it referred to a Hugh who died in 1306.

another Sultan: probably the Sultan of Homs.

King Richard: cf. Chapter XVII. The incident is apocryphal.

CIX

Count John of Chalon: Jean, Comte de Chalon et d'Auxerre, had by his first wife, Mahaut, daughter of Hugh III, Duke of Burgundy, a son named Hugh.

to fortify Jaffa: the town was divided into the Castle quarter and the *Bourg-neuf*: it was the latter that St. Louis fortified. Nothing remains of the walls he built.

fifteen thousand crowns: *trente mille livres*. Longnon estimates this at 3,150,000 modern francs.

NOTES

CX

'Arṣūf: the ruins of the Castle are on the coast about 11 miles north of Jaffa.

Naplous: *Naples*: it fell to the Saracens in 1161.

Passe-Poulain: this spot has not been identified.

Giles the Black: see Chapter V.

CXI

Sur: Tyre had been a Frankish centre since it was taken by the Venetians in 1124. It did not fall to the Saracens until 1291.

Bāniyās: *Belinas*: the fortress had been taken by the Franks in 1130, lost in 1132, regained in 1139, lost in 1164, and never regained.

A fountain which is called Jor: possibly derived from the *Chronique d'Ernoul*, but the derivation was widely current.

CXII

Ṣubayba: the fortress of Bāniyās still bears the name.

the Germans: the knights of the Teutonic Order.

my lord John of Bussey: probably Bussy, Haute-Marne, about a mile from Joinville.

my lord Hugh of Écot: see Chapter XLVI.

the town ditch: *la longaingne*.

my lord John of Valenciennes: see Chapter XCI.

my lord Oliver of Termes: son of Raymond, seigneur de Termes, a fief in Languedoc.

of Languedoc: *de la corte laingue*.

CXIII

to fortify the city: the city of Sidon, where the Château de Saint Louis and the curtain walls still stand. (1936: they are menaced with destruction in the interest of archaeological excavation.)

the Count of Eu: see Chapter XXX.

a little engine: *une petite bible*.

CXIV

the city of Bagdad: the rumour was untrue: Bagdad did not fall to the Tartars until 1258.

CXV

a little church: possibly the Christian church now called Sayyidatu-l-Manṭara.

THE HISTORY OF ST. LOUIS

the pax: the substitution of a pax of metal, ivory, or wood, to be offered by the celebrant or his assistant to each person present, for the kiss of peace interchanged between them, took place in the twelfth century.

CXVI

the Great Comnenus: Comnenus, Lord of Trebizond.

bows of horn: composite bows built up of horn, wood, and sinews, with the horn as the only visible part of the structure.

whereof the nocks were set by a screw within the bow: *dont les coches entroient à vis dedans les ars.* Dr. Henry Balfour informs me that the Oriental composite bows usually have the nock-bearing piece wedged into the end of the bow, like the splice of a cricket-bat.

when one thought them outside . . . well made: *quant on les sachoit hors, si trouvoit l'on que il estoient dehors mout bien tranchant et mout bien fait.* The passage seems to be corrupt: *dehors* should, perhaps, read *dedans.* Dr. Henry Balfour suggests that it may refer to the reflexed ($\pi\alpha\lambda\iota\nu\tau o\nu o\varsigma$) curvature of the bow in its unstrung state, that in extreme instances is so exaggerated that the nocks are turned inwards, but when the bow is strung the reverse position turns them outward, away from the archer. He further suggests that 'tranchant' may refer to the lateral thinning of the nock-bearing ends of the bow, which are usually flattened laterally.

the Emperor: Baldwin II.

my lady Blanche: Blanche, born at Jaffa 1252, married Ferdinand de la Cerda, son of Alfonso X of Castile.

CXVIII

Tortosa: now Tartūs: between Tripoli and Laṭakiyya. It was the most important Christian shrine in Syria, its shrine of the Virgin being earlier than 387. It was the seat of a Frankish bishopric after 1123; its fine late Romanesque church still stands. Kalaun finally took the city in 1291.

grogram: *camelins*, a kind of camel-hair cloth manufactured in Syria.

the Grey Friars: Franciscans.

Tripoli: the city was taken in 1109 and remained in Frankish hands for 180 years. It was a fief of the Kingdom of Antioch, and the seat of the princes of Antioch when that city became too dangerous.

the prince: Bohemond VI. See Chapter CI.

a stone: fossil fish are still found in the neighbourhood.

CXIX

his mother: Blanche of Castille died in November 1252. Joinville may have been mistaken as to the moment when the news reached his

NOTES

master; according to the *Grandes Chroniques*, it was soon after the birth of Blanche at Jaffa.

my lady Mary of Vertus: Vertus, Marne, near Châlons-sur-Marne.

Pontoise: Pontoise, Seine-et-Oise. It became a royal residence under Louis le Gros.

CXX

is fulfilled in part: the Saracens under El Ashraf Khalīl took Acre in 1291 and massacred its inhabitants.

CXXI

seven leagues: Sidon is 25 miles distant from Tyre by the present road.

CXXII

the island of Cyprus: see Chapters II and VII.

the mountain of the Cross: Stavrovouni or Santa Croce, 2260 ft.

the ship's castle: see Chapter LXIV.

Brother Raymond: not otherwise known.

my lord John of Monson: see Chapter LXXVI.

the Body of Our Lord: the reserved Host.

CXXIII

full four and twenty feet: *quatre taises*.

the Count of Joigny: see Chapter II.

my lord Gervase of Escraines: probably Escrennes, Loiret, near Pithiviers.

the King's Master Cook: the 'Grand Queux de France' is found as early as 1060 as one of the great officers of the Household. The office was suppressed in 1490.

the Archdeacon of Nicosia: Raoul Grosparmi: he became Bishop of Évreux in 1259, and Cardinal Bishop of Albano in 1261.

Oliver of Termes: see Chapter CXII.

CXXIV

the King's chamber: evidently a superstructure upon the deck.

St. Nicholas of Varengéville: Saint Nicolas du Port, near Nancy. An inventory of its goods drawn up in 1584 includes 'un navire avec des chaînes d'argent, pesant dix-neuf marcs'.

the King's sister: Blanche, daughter of Philippe le Hardi, married in 1300 Rudolf, son of Albert, Emperor of Germany.

CXXV

the four master winds: the winds blowing from the four cardinal points. See Chapter VII.

the saint: Chapter VII gives St. Anselm.

CXXVI

Lampedusa: *la Lempiouse*.

Nicholas of Soisy: probably Soisy, Seine-et-Marne, near Provins. He is possibly identical with the Nicolas of Choisy of Chapter LXXV.

CXXVII

Pantelleria: *Pantennelée*.

the King of Sicily: Conrad II, grandson of the Emperor Frederick II.

in the ship's boat: which was towed behind the ship.

CXXVIII

all naked: the custom of wearing nightgowns had not yet come into fashion.

in the ship's boat: see Chapter CXXVII.

Master Geoffrey: not otherwise known.

my lord Gervase: Gervase d'Escraines: see Chapter CXXIII.

CXXIX

my lord Dragonet: not otherwise known.

Vauvert: a Carthusian monastery near Paris.

Joinville: the author built (or rebuilt) the chapel of his castle at Joinville, Haute-Marne.

Blécourt: a village adjacent to Joinville.

CXXX

the Count of Provence: Charles I, the brother of St. Louis.

Aigues Mortes: Aiguesmortes, Gard, on the coast near Nîmes. It was from here that Saint Louis sailed on his last crusade.

my lady of Bourbon: Yolande de Châtillon, Countess of Nevers, Auxerre, and Tonnerre, had accompanied her husband Archambaud IX of Bourbon oversea, but he had died in Cyprus in 1248.

CXXXI

the Abbot of Cluny: Guillaume de Pontoise, Abbot of Cluny and afterwards Bishop of Olena in the Morea.

NOTES

CXXXII

a Grey Friar: a Franciscan. See Chapter XI.

Brother Hugh: Hugues de Digne.

CXXXIII

your grandfather: Philip Augustus.

your father: Louis VIII.

CXXXIV

the body of Magdalene: this (or part of it) was a relic venerated at Saint Maximin.

a high vault of rock: La Sainte Baume.

the Dauphine of Viennois: Beatrix de Savoie, daughter of Peter, Comte de Savoie, and of Agnes de Faucigny. Her mother-in-law was Joinville's sister Marie.

the Count of Chalon: Hugh, son of Jean de Chalon (see Chapter CIX) had married Alix, heiress of the county of Burgundy. Joinville's father's second wife was Beatrix de Chalon.

Count John of Brittany and his wife: he had married Blanche, daughter of Thibault IV, Count of Champagne (the song-writer) and King of Navarre, by his second wife Agnes of Beaujeu. She claimed to be his heir, rather than Thibaut V, his son by his third wife, Marguerite of Bourbon.

King Thibault: Thibault V married Isabel of France.

CXXXV

grogram or watchet cloth: *de camelin ou de pers*. Joinville here follows fairly closely the *Grandes Chroniques de Saint Denis*, cap. xlii, which, however, speaks of the year 1248. See also Guillaume de Saint Pathus, *Vie de Saint Louis*, ed. H. F. Delaborde, 1899, p. 111.

wild goat or hares' legs: *gamites, ou de jambes de lievres*.

of glass: the use of glass was commoner in the middle ages than is always realized. Its manufacture is described in the *Schedula diversarum Artium* of Theophilus. In the thirteenth century glass-factories are recorded at Vendôme, La Roche sur Yon, Moustiers (Deux-Sèvres), and Quiquengrogne. (Havard, *Dictionnaire de l'ameublement*, s.v. Verrerie.) 'Voirre' was already in use to signify a vessel shaped like a glass, and in fact such a vessel seems to be in question here, for the inventory of Charles V records as a relic 'une tres petite couppe d'or plaine, en façon d'un voirre, qui fut Mons. Saint Loys, où il mesuroit la porcion de l'eaue qu'il buvoit en son vin, pesant ung marc demye once d'or'.

all the prelates: see Chapter XIII.

the Count of Brittany: John I.

CXXXVI

when we had come back: the trouble began in 1258.

the monks of Saint Urbain: Saint Urbain, Haute-Marne. The Abbey of St. Urbain was not quite five miles from Joinville and was surrounded by Joinville's lands. This case about it came before the Parlement in 1261. Louis IX's judgement was reversed in 1308, when Philippe le Bel appropriated the wardship.

Bishop Peter of Châlons: Pierre de Hans, a connexion of Joinville's first wife.

my lord John of Mimery: not otherwise known.

Abbot Geoffrey: he is called Chaplain to the Pope in a charter of 1263.

Countess Margaret of Flanders: Margaret, daughter of Baldwin, Count of Flanders.

the Archbishop of Rheims: Jean de Courtenay.

St. Remi of Rheims: the most ancient religious foundation in Rheims, of which the wardship was in dispute between the King and the Archbishop.

the relics that are here: that is, in the Sainte-Chapelle at Paris.

Compiègne: for the abbey of Saint Corneille de Compiègne.

that he is excommunicate: *que vous estes escommeniés*: the King is reported as speaking to Joinville.

against him who is my liegeman: i.e. Joinville. The whole speech appears to be addressed to the Abbot.

CXXXVII

the King of England: Henry III.

the Count of Chalon: see Chapter CXXXIV. He was the brother of Joinville's mother.

the abbey of Luxeuil: an ancient abbey in the department of Haute-Saône.

Count Thibault of Bar: Thibault II, d. 1296.

Count Henry of Luxembourg: Henri IV, d. 1288.

my lord Peter the Chamberlain: see Chapter LXXIV.

CXXXVIII

I would be branded: Joinville took this story from Geoffroy de Beaulieu, *Vie de Saint Louis*, chapter xxxiii.

NOTES

CXXXIX

to wash the feet of the poor: a ceremony still carried out by the Bishops of the Catholic Church on Maundy Thursday. It was one of the customs enjoined by the Benedictine Rule.

what the King of England doth: Henry III.

Royaumont: Royaumont, Seine-et-Oise, a Cistercian house in the diocese of Beauvais, founded in 1228 by St. Louis, in accordance with the will of his father Louis VIII. Its ruins still exist.

the Abbey of St. Anthony: Saint Antoine des Champs, which gave its name to the present Rue Saint Antoine near the Bastille. It became Cistercian in 1204.

the Abbey of the Lily: *l'abbaïe dou Liz*: a Cistercian abbey near Melun (Seine-et-Marne) founded by Blanche of Castille about 1230.

the Abbey of Maubuisson: near Pontoise. Queen Blanche, its foundress, was buried there. Its ruins may still be seen.

Saint-Cloud: on the Seine just outside Paris.

As any benefice: this passage also is taken from Geoffroy de Beaulieu, chapter xx, or from the *Grandes Chroniques* (Bibl. Nat. MS. fonds français 2615, f. 235).

CXL

This is the only chapter in the book to have a sub-title in the manuscript.

a general ordinance: ordinances to this effect were passed in December 1254 and December 1256. Joinville probably takes his account of them from the *Life of St. Louis* written by Guillaume de Nangis; but a closely similar version also occurs in the *Grandes Chroniques de Saint Denis*.

judges, castellans, provosts, mayors: *baillif, viconte, prevost, maieur*.

officers or rangers: *serjant ou forestier*. The King's domains in France proper were divided into nine great *bailliages*—Paris, Senlis, Vermandois, Amiens, Sens, Orléans, Bourges, Mâcon, and Tours; in Normandy they were administered as *vicomtés*. The provosts were officials under the *baillis*, who farmed the King's lands; the *maieurs* were stewards of his courts. The foresters and serjeants were officers of a lower grade.

a shilling: *dix sous*.

in all these things: I follow M. de Wailly's suggestion and insert this paragraph here instead of in Chapter CXLI, where it appears—obviously misplaced—in the manuscript.

CXLI

the Provostship: see Chapter XXVI. The present account is taken from a version of the *Chroniques de Saint Denis* (cap. lxxiii).

265

THE HISTORY OF ST. LOUIS

Stephen Boileau: he accompanied St. Louis on the Crusade, and was a prisoner with him. He became Provost of Paris about 1258, and died about 1269. He compiled the well-known *Livre des Métiers*.

CXLII

This chapter is taken from the *Vie de Saint Louis* by Geoffroy de Beaulieu, or from the *Grandes Chroniques*, cap. lxxx.

Royaumont: see Chapter CXXXIX.

the Abbey of St. Matthew of Rouen: nothing remains of this foundation.

Longchamps: or Saint-Cloud. See Chapter CXXXIX.

the Abbey of the Lily: see Chapter CXXXIX.

Vauvert: see Chapter CXXIX.

the House of the Daughters of God: a house for fallen women in the suburbs of Paris.

CXLIII

This chapter is taken from Geoffroy de Beaulieu, or from the *Grandes Chroniques*.

the Brothers of the Carmel: the Rule of the Carmelite Order dates from 1210. St. Louis visited Mount Carmel in 1254 and brought six French hermits thence to Charenton.

the Brethren of St. Augustine: probably a community of Augustinian canons.

the Brethren of the Sacks: or of the Penitence of Jesus Christ. St. Louis established them in the parish of Saint André des Arts. The Order did not last long.

the Order of White Mantles: 'les serfs de la Vierge Marie' were founded at Marseilles and came to Paris in 1258.

the Council of Lyons: in 1274.

the Brethren of the Holy Cross: an unrecorded order that cannot have lasted long.

CXLIV

Rheims serge: a coarse stuff of little value.

at the church of the Magdalene: built in the thirteenth century, at the corner of the Rue de la Ville l'Évêque and of the present Boulevard Malesherbes.

the King's chapel: the Sainte-Chapelle, which King Louis built between 1246 and 1248 to enshrine his relic of the Crown of Thorns.

and his three sons: the eldest, Philip, who succeeded him; Jean Tristan, Count of Nevers; and Peter, Count of Alençon.

NOTES

the house of the Count of Auxerre: near the Tour de Nesle, the site of the present Mint, in the present rue de Nevers.

the Grey Friars: established in 1230 where the Faculty of Medicine is now.

CXLV

the precepts: these are taken from a version of the *Chroniques de Saint Denis*, cap. cxv, which accounts for the otherwise meaningless statement that they are in French. On the text see P. Viollet in *Bibliothèque de l'École des Chartes*, 6th series, v, 1869, p. 134.

and if any man have an action against thee: the manuscript of Joinville runs 'Et se aucuns a action encontre toy, ne le croi pas jeusques à tant que tu en saches la verité'. This, however, does not seem to represent the thought of Saint Louis, who, according to the *Grandes Chroniques* (MS. fonds français 2615, f. 246), said, 'se aucuns a afaire ou querelle contre toi, soies tousjours pour lui encontre toi, jusques à tant que l'en sache la vérité'.

CXLVI

This chapter is based on a version of the *Grandes Chroniques*.

my Lord St. James: St. James of Compostella, the patron of those that fight against the Infidel.

'Esto, Domine': the *Grandes Chroniques* give this more fully: 'Esto, Domine, plebis tue sanctificator et custos.'

my Lord St. Denis: the *Grandes Chroniques* give this more fully. Viollet cites from MS. Bibliothèque Nationale fonds français 2615: 'il ne cessoit d'appeler l'aide des sains a qui il avoit dévocion, mesmement de Saint Denis de France qui est especial patrons as rois de France et disoit souvent une oroison que est chantée le jour de la Saint Denis, c'est assavoir: Tribue nobis, Domine, quesumus, prospera mundi despicere et nulla ejus adversa formidare'.

my lord of Alençon: the son of St. Louis, born at Châtel-Pèlerin in Palestine.

a bed spread with ashes: following the monastic use for the dying.

and his bones were kept: this passage is taken from the *Grandes Chroniques* or a version of them.

CXLVII

the Pope: Martin IV.

the Bishop of Rouen: Guillaume II de Flavacourt.

Brother John of Samoys: he became Bishop of Lisieux in 1299.

the Pope: Boniface VIII.

the Archbishop of Rheims: Pierre Barbet.

my lord Henry of Villers: Archbishop of Lyons from 1296 to 1301.

the King and his brethren: Philippe le Bel, Charles, Comte de Valois, and Louis, Comte d'Évreux.

CXLVIII

Chevillon: Chevillon, Haute-Marne, a few miles from Joinville.

the chapel of St. Lawrence: the chapel was burnt in 1544.

CXLIX

a book written in French: a version of the *Chroniques de Saint Denis* (which is related to Geoffroy de Beaulieu's *Life of Saint Louis*). M. P. Viollet found the closest approximation in Bibliothèque Nationale fonds français 2615. See *Bibliothèque de l'École des Chartes*, Paris, xxxv, 1874, p. 18.

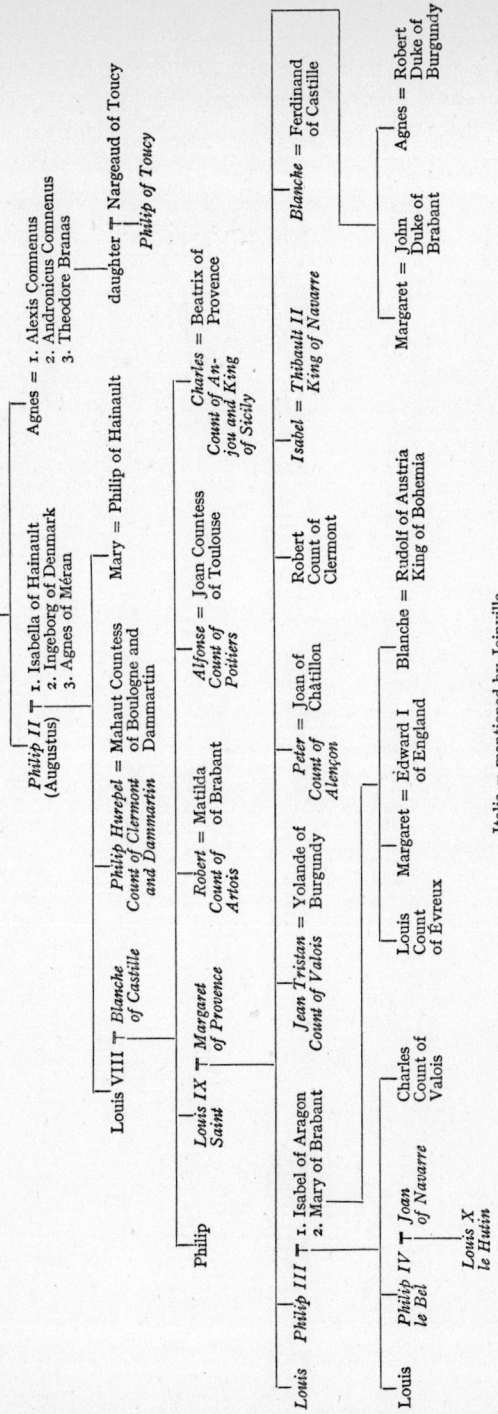

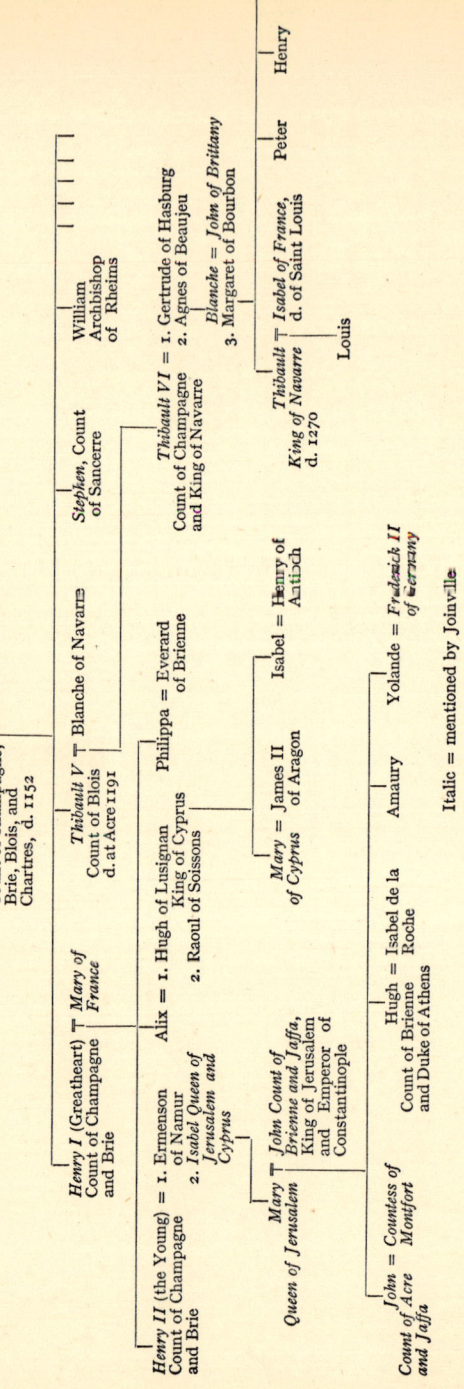

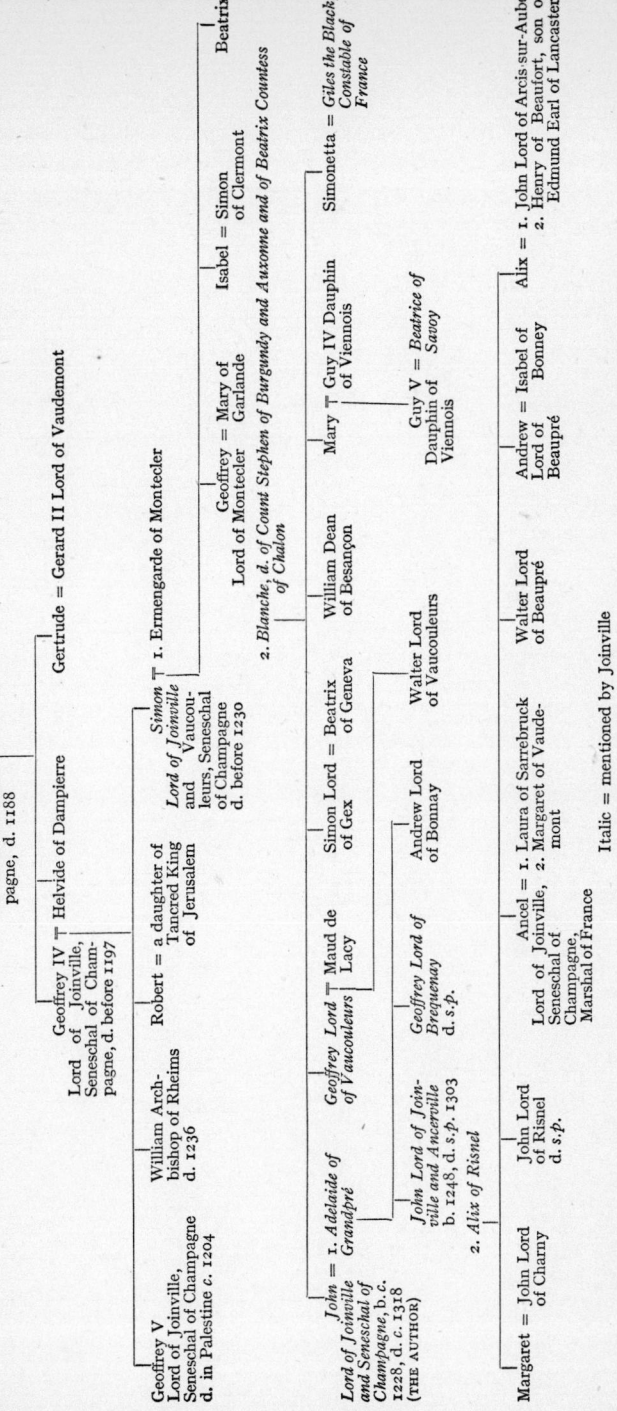

INDEX OF PERSONS AND PLACES

Acre, xiv, xviii, xx, 3, 23, 40, 41, 44, 107, 120 et seqq., 160, 166–8, 171, 186, 187, 237, 239, 251, 252, 257, 258, 261
— Bishop of, 124, 252
— John of, 42, 242
— Nicholas of, 107, 108
Aigueperse, *see* Beaujeu
Aigues Mortes, 198, 262
Aix en Provence, 202
Alaouites, 248
Albi, 61
Alençon, Peter, Count of, 1, 156, 227, 233, 256, 266, 267
Aleppo, Sultan of, 59
Alexandria, 54, 57
Ancerville, John of, xv, xvii, 33
Angers, Countess of, 251
Angoulême, *see* La Marche
Anjou, Charles, Count of, 33, 59, 60, 62, 63, 67, 80, 88, 90, 112, 113, 121, 125, 127, 132, 240
Anselm, St., 11
Antioch, 158, 255
— port of, 142
— Bohemond V, Prince of, 129, 253
— — VI, Prince of, 158, 257
— Princess of, 158
Apremont, Gobert of, 33, 82
Arles, 36, 37
Armenia, Haiton, King of, 42, 85, 242
'Arṣūf, 171, 259
— John III of Ibelin, Lord of, 165–7, 258
Artois, Robert, Count of, 29, 33, 54, 59, 64, 65, 69, 73, 78, 87, 121, 132
Assassins, 136–9, 179
Auberive, Peter of, 67, 247
Augustine, Brethren of St., 220, 266

Autrèche, Walter of, xxiv, 51, 52, 245
Auxerre, Bishop Guy of, 18, 204
— Count of, 223
Auxonne, 36, 37
— Stephen III, Count of, xiv, 240
Avallon, Peter of, 58, 129, 246

Babylon, *see* Cairo
Bagdad, 177, 259
— Caliph of, 177, 178
Bāniyās, 172–6, 259
Bar, Henry II, Count of, xv, 85, 86, 104, 141, 157, 249, 254
— Thibault II, Count of, 208, 264
Barberino, Francesco da, xvii
Bartholomew, a child, 98, 122
Baud, Pierre de, xxvii
Baybars Bunduqdār, 78, 85, 248
Beaucaire, 202
Beaujeu, Guichard of, 239
— Imbert of, Constable of France, 29, 51, 63, 69, 70, 73, 102, 106, 131, 234, 239
Beaulieu, Geoffrey of, xxi, 235
Beaumont, xviii
— John of, xxiv, 51, 128, 243, 253
— William of, 128, 175
Beauvais, Vincent of, 245
Bedouins, 74, 75, 76, 79, 95, 138
Beyrout, Eschive of Montbéliard, Lady of, 45, 243
Blécourt, 37, 198
Blois, Thibault, Count of, 28
Bohon, 247
Boileau, Stephen, 236, 265
Boon, William of, 72, 247
Borlaymont, Peter of, 126, 129, 253
Boulogne, Alfonse, Count of, 30
— Philip Hurepel, Count of, 22, 237, 239, 240

T   273

INDEX OF PERSONS AND PLACES

Boulogne, Ida, Countess of, 236
— Mahaut, Countess of, 20, 236, 239
— Jeanne of, 240
Bourbon, Archambaud IX of, 29, 239, 262
— Yolande of, 198, 262
Bourbonne, Peter of, 122, 123, 252
Branas, 256
Brancion, Henry of, 82
— Josserand of, 82, 83, 248
Brienne, Alfonse of, 256
— Andrew of, 237
— Everard of, 24, 41, 237
— Felicity of, 238, 253
— John of, King of Jerusalem, xiv, 50, 118, 242, 244, 252, 254
— Walter IV, Count of, 'the Great', 27, 140, 146, 159 63, 238, 254, 257
— Walter V, Count of, 27, 238
Brittany, John I, Count of, 19, 236
— John II, Count of, 9, 202, 203, 205, 235
— Peter, Count of, 23-5, 29, 54, 70, 71, 74, 102, 106, 113
— Yolande of, 24, 237
Bures, Héloïse of, 246
— William of, Lord of Tiberias, 246, 257
Burgundy, Count of, 202, 208
— Hugh III, Duke of, 168, 169, 258
— Hugh IV, Duke of, xv, 25, 26, 33, 44, 64, 68, 70, 79, 82, 88, 168, 238, 240, 258
— Mahaut of, 258
Bussey, John of, 175, 259

Caesarea, 40, 141, 149 et seqq., 187, 209, 255
— Philippi, see Bāniyās
Caiapha, see Valenciennes, John of
Caier, see Neuville, Peter of
Cairo, 54, 141, 162, 243

Cairo, Malik el-Ashraf Mūsā, Sultan of, 160, 162
— Malik Salāḥ Najmu-d-dīn 'Ayyub, Sultan of, 43, 48, 56, 59, 86, 242, 249
— Turān Shāh, Sultan of, 102-5, 108, 109, 111, 120, 132, 139, 249
Cange, Charles du Fresne, Seigneur du, xxviii, 232
Capperonnier, xxviii
Carmel, Brethren of the, 220, 266
Carthage, see Tunis
Castel, James of, Bishop of Soissons, 117
Castille, Alfonso X of, 260
— Blanche of, xxvi, 22, 23, 30, 33, 125, 130, 183-5, 260
Caym, John, 123, 124, 252
Cerda, Ferdinand de la, 260
Chalon sur Saône, Hugh, Count of, 202, 248, 263
— — John, Count of, 83, 169, 202, 208, 258
— — Beatrix, Countess of, xiv, 240
Châlons-sur-Marne, Peter, Bishop of, 205, 206, 264
Champagne, Blanche of, 202, 263
— Henry Greatheart, Count of, 23, 27, 28, 237
— Henry the Young, Count of, 23, 24, 237
— Mary, Countess of, 23, 237
— Philippa of, wife of Everard of Brienne, 237
— Thibault IV, Count of, 'the Great', xvi, 26, 27
— Thibault V, Count of, xvi, 23, 202, 237, 243, 263
— Thibault VI, Count of, see Navarre, Thibault, King of
Chaource, 27
Chapelle, Geoffrey of La, 25
Charenton, 220
Chartres, Bishop of, 206
— William of, 235

INDEX OF PERSONS AND PLACES

Château Porcien, Guy of, Bishop of Soissons, 252
Châtel-Blanc, 254
Châtel-Pèlerin, 156, 160, 256
Châtel-Thierry, 24, 25
Chatenay, lord of, 128, 253
Châtillon, Guy I of, 240, 247
— Walter III of, 73, 77, 80, 88, 116, 117, 240, 247
— Yolande of, 98, 262
— *and see* Autrèche
Cheminon, Abbot of, xxvi, 36, 37, 241
Chevillon, 230, 268
Choisy, Nicholas of, 114
Clairvaux, 37
Clari, Robert of, xx
Cluny, Abbot of, xxii, 15, 199, 262
Comans, 150, 151, 256
Comnenus of Trebizond, 180
Compiègne, 206, 219
Conflans, *see* Trichâtel
Constantinople, 41
— Andronicus, Emperor of, 149, 256
— Baldwin II, Emperor of, 41, 150, 180, 242, 243, 256, 260
— John of Brienne, Emperor of, 254
— Mary, Empress of, 41, 42, 242
Corbeil, xv, 9, 22, 234
Cornaut, Jocelyn of, xxv, 57, 90, 246
Cosne, Henry of, 82, 248
Coucy, Enguerrand IV of, 29, 239
— Mary of, 242
— Raoul II of, 65, 239, 246
Courtenay, Peter of, 52, 61, 70, 123, 247
Cyprus, 3, 6, 11, 39, 40, 41, 53, 126, 187, 190, 191, 194
— Alix, Queen of, 24 et seqq., 237, 238
— Isabel, Queen of, 24, 237

Damascus, 133, 134, 167, 249
— Sultan of, *see* al-Malik an-Nāṣir Yūsuf
Damietta, xiv, xxvi, 2, 44 et seqq., 87, 88, 90, 91, 93, 94, 101 et seqq., 117
Dammartin, Renaud, Count of, 20, 236
— William of, 46, 243
Daraksa, 57–9, 79, 245
Denis, St., 227, 267
Digne, Brother Hugh of, xxvi, 16, 200, 201
Doulevant, 95, 250
Dragonet, 197
Dreux, John, Count of, 29, 238
— Robert III, Count of, 25, 238
Donjeux, 241
Donzy, Agnes of, 240

Écot, Hugh of, 66, 67, 175, 247
Écurey, Walter of, 60, 246
England, Henry II, King of, 29
— Henry III, King of, 19, 31, 207, 208, 210, 236
— Isabella of Angoulême, Queen of, 31, 239
— John, King of, 19, 236
— Richard, Cœur de Lion, King of, 23, 168, 169
Épernay, 26
Escraines, Gervase of, 190, 197, 208, 261
Eu, John, Count of, 41, 158, 173, 174, 177, 181, 256
Évreux, Louis, Count of, 268

Fakhru-d-Dīn, 58, 59, 78, 244, 246
Farescour, 250
Fārisu-d-Dīn 'Uqtayy, 105, 120, 250
Faucigny, Agnes of, 263
Flanders, Baldwin IX, Count of, 247, 264
— Guy, Count of, 33, 240

INDEX OF PERSONS AND PLACES

Flanders, Margaret, Countess of, 205, 247
— William of Dampierre, Count of, xv, 33, 69, 81, 82, 87, 105, 106, 112, 125–7, 247
Fontainebleau, 5, 233
Fontaine l'Archevêque, La, 37
Fontaines, Peter of, 17, 18, 236
Forez, Guy VI of, 60, 246
Fouinon, John, 117, 252
France, Blanche of, daughter of St. Louis, 180, 260
— Isabel of, wife of Thibault II of Navarre, 184, 202, 203, 211, 234
— Louis VIII, King of, 201, 263
— Louis IX, King of, Saint, *passim*
— Louis X, King of (King of Navarre and Count of Champagne), xvii, 1, 4, 230, 232
— Louis of, eldest son of St. Louis, 5, 233
— Mary of, wife of Count Henry of Champagne, 23, 237
— Philip Augustus, King of, 23, 149, 168, 170, 201, 225, 256, 259
— Philip 'le Hardi', King of, 6, 7, 223, 227, 233
— Philip 'le Bel', King of, xvii, xviii, 10, 235, 266, 268
— *and see* Castille, Blanche of; Navarre, Jeanne of; Provence, Margaret of; and Alençon, Anjou, Artois, Évreux, Nevers, Poitiers, and Valois, Counts of
Frederick Barbarossa, Emperor, 250
Frederick II, Emperor, 59, 95, 97, 132, 133, 136, 246

Gamaches, John of, 72, 247
Gaza, 156, 157, 160, 163, 164, 249
Geneviève, St., 21
Genoese, 119, 120, 252
Geoffrey, the Queen's clerk, 196, 197
George, St., 146

Giles the Black, Constable of France, 8, 131, 172, 173, 190, 191, 197
Gilles le Brun, *see* Giles the Black
Goderiche, Brother John, 242
Gog and Magog, 143, 255
Grandpré, Alix of, xxvi, 241, 247
— Henry VI, Count of, xiv
Guillemin, a chamberlain, 122, 124, 125
Guines, Arnoul of, 158, 257

Hagenau, 192
Hama, 58
— Sultan of, *see* al-Malik an-Nāṣir Yūsuf
Holy Cross, Brethren of the, 220, 266
Homs, Malik Mansūr, Sultan of, 160–2
Horgne, La, Walter of, 82, 248
Hospital, Order of the, xiv, 73, 101, 136, 153, 163, 171, 173, 254
Hungary, St. Elizabeth of, *see* Thuringia
— King of, 136
Hyères, 16, 198, 199, 201

Ibelin, Baldwin of, 80, 100, 102, 105, 106, 248
— Guy of, 80, 100, 102, 106, 248
— *and see* 'Arṣūf, Beyrout, and Jaffa
Iconium, 'Izz-ed-dīn, Sultan of, 42, 242
Isle, 26

Jaffa, 156, 157, 159, 160, 162, 170, 180, 187, 258
— John of Ibelin, Count of, xxv, 47, 127, 156
— Walter IV of Brienne, Count of, *see* Brienne
James, St., 67, 131, 227, 267
Jerusalem, 40, 168, 169
— Baldwin IV, King of, 134, 254

INDEX OF PERSONS AND PLACES

Jerusalem, Charles, King of, *see* Anjou, Count of
— John, King of, *see* Brienne, John of
— Isabel, Queen of, 24, 237
— Guy V, Patriarch of, 49, 108, 109, 160, 186, 244
John, Brother, of the Order of the Trinity, 105
— the Armenian, 134, 135
— the Great, a knight of Genoa, 166, 167
Joigny, John II, Count of, 4, 27, 190, 238
Joinville, xiv, xviii, 34, 36, 37, 198, 202, 210, 230, 262
— Ancel of, 240
— Beatrix of, xiv, xvi, xxvi, 34, 96, 97, 130
— Felicity of, *see* Brienne
— Geoffrey III of, Seneschal of Champagne, xiv, 238, 241, 248
— Geoffrey 'le Jeune' of, Seneschal of Champagne, xiv
— Geoffrey 'Trouillard', Seneschal of Champagne, xiv
— Jean of, Seneschal of Champagne, *passim*
— Mary of, 263
— Simon of, Seneschal of Champagne, xiv, xxi, 13, 21, 26
— Simonette of, 234
— Yolande of, 236, 247
Jordan, River, 173
Jouy, Brother Hugh of, Marshal of the Temple, 154–6, 256
Jully, 26

Krak des Chevaliers, xiv, 254

Lagny, 27
Laignes, 27
Lampedusa, 194, 262
Lancaster, Henry, Earl of, xvi
Landricourt, Hugh of, 88, 240, 249
Latrun, 258
Lawrence, T. E., xiii, xxvii
Lazarus, St., Master of the Order of, 163, 164, 257
Legate, Papal, *see* Tusculum, Odo of
Ligny, 208
Lily, Abbey of the, 211, 219, 265
Limassol, 41, 44, 242
Longchamps, 219
Longjumeau, Brother Andrew of, of the Order of Friars Preachers, 255
Lorraine, Matthew II, Duke of, 26, 238
Loupey, Frederick of, 66, 67, 247
Lusignan, 30, 31
— Mary of, Countess of Eu, 256
Luxembourg, Count Henry of, 208
Luxeuil, 208
Lyons, 37
— Henry of Villers, Archbishop of, 229

Makrisi, 244, 245, 248, 249, 254
al-Malik an-Nāṣir Yūsuf, Sultan of Hama and Damascus, 43, 118, 133, 139, 140, 154–7, 163, 164, 168, 243, 252
Mansourah, xxv, xxvi, 2, 65 et seqq., 98, 117, 246
Marcel, a man-at-arms, 92
Marche, La, Hugh the Black, Count of, 29–33, 238
Marly, Matthew of, 51, 244
Marseilles, xv, 17, 35, 38, 201
Masyaf, 248
Mâthons, 248
Mathurins, *see* Trinity, Order of the
Maubuisson, 211, 219, 265
Maurupt, Dean of, 39, 53
Mauvoisin, Guy II, Lord of Rosny, xxv, 74, 81, 126, 127, 248
Mello, William of, 18

277

INDEX OF PERSONS AND PLACES

Melun, 203
Menoncourt, Renaud of, 66, 247
Merle, Le, Foucauld of, 65, 246
Metz, 34
Mez, Le, Jean Clément of, Marshal of France, 112, 113, 251
Mimery, John of, 205
Minieh, 249
Monson, John of, 116, 188
Montbéliard, Ami of, Lord of Montfaucon, 98, 122
— Odo of, 160, 257
— Simon of, 240
— Thierry III, Count of, 47
— and see Beyrout
Montfaucon, see Montbéliard, Ami of
Montfort, Amauri VI, Count of, 15, 85, 86, 104, 141, 157, 235, 249, 254
— Philip, Count of, 92, 100, 116, 173, 250
— Jeanne of Châteaudun, Countess of, 42, 242
Montjay, see Châtillon
Montléart, Simon of, 167, 258
— Thibault of, 245, 258
Montlhéry, 14, 22
Montmartre, 20
Montpensier, see Beaujeu
Morea, the, William of Villehardouin, Prince of, 44, 243
Mussanbourc, Geoffrey of, 88

Nangis, William of, xxvii
Nanteuil, Philip of, 41, 51, 242
— and see Autrèche
Nanton, Josserand of, 82, 248
Naplous, 171, 259
Narcy, Aubert of, 52, 245
Navarre, Isabel, Queen of, wife of Thibault III of Navarre, see France, Isabel of
— Jeanne of, wife of Philip 'le Bel', King of France, xx, xxvi, 1, 4, 232

Navarre, Margaret, Queen of, wife of Thibault I of Navarre and VI of Champagne, 203
— Thibault I, King of, and VI, Count of Champagne, xv, xxvi, 23, 24, 239
— Thibault II, King of, xxiv, 9, 10, 23, 29, 202, 203, 208, 222
— Louis, King of, see France, Louis X, King of
Nemours, Philip of, 112, 115, 129, 251
— Walter of, 121
Nesle, Simon of, 17, 235
Neuville, Peter of, 71, 247
Nevers, Guy IV of Forez, Count of, 27, 238
— John Tristan, Count of, 119, 252, 266
Nicosia, 40, 242
— Raoul Grosparmi, Archdeacon of, 190, 261
Nile, River, 55, 56 et passim
Nogent, Artaud of, xxiii, 28, 238
Nogent l'Artaud, 28, 238
Norway, 149
— Abel, King of, 255

Oiselay, 122, 252
Old Man of the Mountain, 135–9
Orleans, xv, 209
— John of, 64, 246
Otricourt, Brother Stephen of, Commander of the Temple, 113, 114

Pantelleria, 194, 262
Paphos, 41, 190, 242
Paris, xv, xvii, 18, 33, 35, 48, 135, 209, 211, 218–22, 241
— William of Auvergne, Bishop of, 13, 235
Passe-Poulain, 171
Persia, Bārbaqān, Emperor of, 159, 160–2
— Mahomet, Emperor of, 143, 146

278

INDEX OF PERSONS AND PLACES

Peter the Chamberlain, 131, 173, 190, 197, 208
Pisans, 119, 120, 252
Plonquet, 45, 243
Poissy, xvii
Poitiers, xxv
— Alfonse, Count of, 29–33, 53, 59, 60, 69, 82, 90, 112, 113, 116, 118, 121, 125, 127, 132, 238, 245
— Countess of, 116, 251
Ponce the groom, 201
Pontmoulain, Peter of, 132, 240, 253
Pontoise, 184, 211, 219, 261
— William of, Abbot of Cluny, 199, 262
Portugal, King of, see Boulogne, Alfonse, Count of
Prester John, 143–6, 148, 255
Provence, Charles, Count of, 198, 262
— Eleanor of, 236
— Margaret of, wife of St. Louis, xv, xxvi, 41, 101, 102, 110, 118, 119, 156, 180–3, 186, 187, 191, 192, 194–9, 236, 251
— Raymond Béranger, Count of, 236
Provins, xxiv, 9, 118, 124, 203

Ramleh, 164, 257
— Bishop of, 161
Rancon, Geoffrey of, 32, 239
Raoul, Brother, of the Order of Friars Preachers, 120
Raymond, Brother, of the Temple, 188, 189
Reynel, Alix of, xvi, xvii, 140
— Margaret of, see Sidon
— Walter of, 140
Rheims, xv, 209
— Baldwin of, 46
— John of Courtenay, Archbishop of, 205, 206, 229, 264
— Peter Barbet, Archbishop of, 267

Rieux, Pierre-Antoine de, xxvii
Roche de Glun, 37, 241
Rochelle, La, 14
Ronnay, Henry of, Provost of the Hospital, 73, 248
Rosny, see Mauvoisin
Rouen, 219
— William II of Flavacourt, Bishop of, 228, 267
Royaumont, 211, 219, 265

Ṣabri, a Saracen, 111, 251
Sacks, Brethren of the, 220, 266
Sadru-d-Dīn, 246
Ṣafad, 160, 257
as-Ṣāfariyya, 123, 252
Safīta, 254
Saillenay, John of, 70, 247
St. Antoine, Abbey of, 211, 265
St. Cloud, 211, 265
St. Denis, 228
Sainte Baume, La, 263
Saintes, 31, 32
St. Jacques, Brother Andrew of, 242
St. Pathus, William of, xxii
St. Pol, Hugh, Count of, 30, 33, 240, 247
— Elizabeth, Countess of, 240
St. Urbain, 37, 205, 206, 207, 241, 264
— Abbot Adam of, 37
— Abbot Geoffrey of, 205–7, 264
— Abbot William of, 188
Saladin, 98, 134
Samoys, Brother John of, 228
Sancerre, Stephen, Count of, 27
Salimbene, Fra, 233
Sanudo, Marino, 249
Sargines, Geoffrey of, 51, 90, 92, 110, 112, 131, 173, 244
Sarrasin, John Peter, xxii, 20, 236, 242–6, 254
Sarrebruck, John, Count of, 33, 35, 36, 240
— Laurette, Countess of, 240

279

INDEX OF PERSONS AND PLACES

Saumur, xv, 29, 30
Savoy, Peter, Count of, 263
Sayette, *see* Sidon
Seignelay, 247
Senaingan, Alenard of, 149, 255
Sens, Gerbert of, 242
Sergines, *see* Sargines
Sézanne, 26
Sharmisa, 58, 246
Sicily, King of, *see* Anjou, Count of
— Conrad II, King of, 194, 195
Sidon, 167, 168, 170 et seqq., 187, 258, 259
— Balian I of, 254
— Margaret, Lady of, 140, 254
Siverey, Everard of, 66, 67, 247
Soissons, 202
— Bishop of, 117, 252
— John II, Count of, xxvi, 17, 29, 71, 72, 102, 106, 112, 236, 239, 247
— Raoul, Count of, 142, 247, 255
Soisy, Nicholas of, 194, 262
Sonnac, William of, Master of the Temple, 74, 80, 81, 248
Sorbon, Robert of, xxi, xxiii, 8-10, 234
South Jutland, Waldemar, Duke of, 255
Şubayba, 174-6, 259
Sur, *see* Tyre

Taillebourg, 31
Tanis, 57
Tartars, Genghiz Khan, King of, 148, 242
— Ilchikhatsi, King of, 39, 40, 42, 177, 178, 242
Temple, Order of the, 55, 58, 64, 65, 80, 81, 101, 113, 114, 123, 136, 155, 163, 171, 173, 188, 189, 251, 254
— — Master of the, 74, 80, 81, 123, 172, 174, 248, 256
Termes, Oliver of, 4, 175, 176, 191, 259

Thessalonica, King of, *see* Burgundy, Hugh IV, Duke of
Thilchastel, 247
Thuringia, St. Elizabeth of, 30
Tiberias, 160, 257
— *and see* Bures
Toron des Chevaliers, 258
Tortosa, 181, 182, 260
Toucy, Narjot of, 255
— Philip of, 149, 255
Toulouse, Count of, *see* Poitiers, Count of
Trebizond, 180
Trencavel, 243
Trichâtel, Hugh of, Lord of Conflans, 66, 240, 247
Trie, Matthew of, 236
— Renaud of, 20, 236
Trinity, Order of the, 105
— — Master of the, 112-15
Tripoli, 158, 182, 235, 255, 257, 260
Troyes, xiv, xxi, 25, 26, 28
Tunis, xvii, 2, 21, 223, 251, 252
— King of, 194, 195
Tusculum, Odo of, Papal Legate, 48, 53, 97, 125-8, 151, 165, 170, 172, 179, 182, 185, 186, 243, 244
Tyre, 172, 173, 179, 186, 259
— *and see* Montfort

Val, Le, Lord of, 58
Val Secret, 25, 26
Valenciennes, John of, 140, 141, 175
Valery, Everard of, 88
— Huon of, 244
— John of, 49, 68, 69, 73, 88, 100, 244
Valois, Charles, Count of, 268
Varengéville, 191, 192, 261
Vataces, John Ducas, Emperor of Nicaea, 150, 180, 256
Vaucouleurs, lord of, 34, 240
— Hugh of, 46
Vauvert, 198, 219, 262

INDEX OF PERSONS AND PLACES

Vendières, 243
Vernon, 211, 219
Versey, Vilain of, 46, 243
Vertus, 26
— Mary of, 183, 261
Vichiers, Brother Renaud of, Marshal of the Temple, 55, 113, 114; Master, 123, 256
Viennois, Beatrix of Savoy, Dauphine of, 202, 263
Ville Béon, *see* Nemours
Villehardouin, Geoffrey of, xviii, xx, xxii, 252
— Mabel of, xx
— *and see* Morea, Prince of

Villers, Henry, Archbishop of Lyons, 229
Villette, Geoffrey of, 18, 236
Vincennes, 17
Vitry, James of, 256
Voisey, John of, 77, 78, 89, 97

Wailly, Natalis de, xxviii
Wanou, Raoul of, 66, 67, 96, 247
White Mantles, Order of the, 220, 266
William, a priest, 221

Yves le Breton, Brother, of the Order of Friars Preachers, 133, 138, 139

PRINTED IN
GREAT BRITAIN
AT THE
UNIVERSITY PRESS
OXFORD
BY
JOHN JOHNSON
PRINTER
TO THE
UNIVERSITY